HURRICANE

A CAPT. MARK SMITH NOVEL

HURRICANE
A Capt. Mark Smith Novel
Copyright © 2019 Dan Stratman.
All rights reserved.

ISBN 978-1-7325992-2-2
eBook ISBN 978-1-7325992-3-9

No part of this book may be used or reproduced or transmitted in any manner whatsoever without written permission from the author, except in the case of brief quotations in a review.

HURRICANE is a work of fiction. Names, characters, businesses, organizations, places, events, and incidents either are the product of the author's imagination or are used fictitiously. Any resemblance to actual persons, living or dead, events, or locales is entirely coincidental.

Printed in the USA.

Cover Design and Interior Format

HURRICANE

A CAPT. MARK SMITH NOVEL

DAN STRATMAN

DEDICATION

To Cyndi. My wife, my best friend, my lifeboat.

FORWARD

Thank you very much for buying my book, *HURRICANE*. In order to get the greatest amount of enjoyment from reading it I recommend reading the previous book in the series, *MAYDAY*, first. Knowing everything that led up to the story in *HURRICANE* will make the experience even better.

Dan Stratman

ACKNOWLEDGMENTS

Thank you first and foremost to my beautiful wife, Cyndi. Thanks for being my sounding board, first round editor, and constantly challenging me to be the best writer I am capable of being. I love you more than you will ever know.

Thank you to Phil Heffley for all the time you took reviewing and editing the manuscript. Your advice and input was invaluable.

Thanks to Drs. Mark and Luellen Malley for not only helping me understand the medical aspects of cancer but also for your dedication to helping women live healthier lives.

A double thank you to Luellen for your insightful editing.

Merci to Blair Lacy for all your help with a language I know nothing about.

For letting me crawl around your Gulfstream jet and ask tons of questions, I thank Hal Cosgrove.

Thanks to members of my Advance Reader Team, including Chris St. Germain.

Words can't describe how indebted I am to my editor, Jason Whited. Your advice and guidance are irreplaceable in helping my writing shine.

And last but certainly not least, I want to thank my readers. I'm eternally grateful for not only buying my books but also for telling so many people how much you enjoy them. Good word of mouth is the best form of praise there is for an author and is greatly appreciated.

Sincerely,
Dan Stratman

CHAPTER 1

"VESSEL *LYNDA RAY*, THIS IS the National Weather Service. The tropical depression east of Bermuda we told you about yesterday has tripled in strength overnight and switched to a northeasterly track. A Category 3 hurricane is barreling directly toward you!"

The stunned officers and crew on the bridge turned and looked to their captain for reassurance.

"Roger" was his only response to the unnerving weather warning. He placed the radio handset back in the cradle, paused for a moment, then stroked his thinning white beard. Captain Oliveira grabbed binoculars off the console and walked with a slight limp slowly across the faded, cracked linoleum. He slid open the rust-stained door leading out to the left-bridge wing and drew in a deep breath of salty sea air. High atop the superstructure, Oliveira had a commanding view of his domain.

Swells rocked the 510-foot-long container ship in a rhythmic dance all too familiar to old sea dogs. Dressed in the traditional black double-breasted uniform jacket with polished gold buttons, he stood in the doorway, unfazed by the constant rocking motion.

The skipper brought the binoculars up to his weathered eyes and peered south across the undulating Atlantic Ocean. On the southern horizon, the cottony white clouds that littered the sky had been forced aside by roiling gray and black storm clouds bristling with lightning.

Captain Oliveira turned back, his Portuguese temper on

full display. "Mr. Whitaker, you had the watch last night. Why wasn't I woken and informed about this?"

As Whitaker was about to respond, a dark brown rat darted out from under a nearby console and scampered out the open door to freedom. Being from a younger generation less respectful of tradition, Whitaker wore an open collared white shirt and black pants. He hoped to project an image of being fashion forward by wearing an Italian leather satchel, slung across his torso, everywhere he went. The tall, gangly first officer nervously ran his fingers through his oily black hair. "Well, I…" he stuttered.

"You checked the weather at the beginning of your shift as required, did you not?"

The crew focused their collective gaze on Whitaker.

"Yes, of course," he muttered as he stared down at his shoes.

"Then the radio call should have been entered in the ships log, correct?" Oliveira walked over to the large vinyl-covered captain's chair in the middle of the bridge and pulled out the logbook from its side storage pocket.

"Captain, I assure you I did check the weather with the company last night. I may have…I may have inadvertently neglected to enter it in the log. But sir, more importantly, we have a hurricane approaching. I recommend we increase our speed to full ahead for New York immediately."

Oliveira replaced the log in its pouch. "The company's com log in New York will have the answer to my question, Mr. Whitaker." He hefted his portly frame into his chair and took command. "Navigator, I want the exact distance back to the Azores and to New York City. Communications Officer, there is to be no more use of our radios by our two chatty passengers. Crew use only."

Oliveira picked up a handset attached to the arm of his chair. "Engine room, this is the captain. Prepare the engine to run at 110 percent for the foreseeable future. You have one hour." He replaced the handset then looked each man in the eyes. "This weather information is not to leave the bridge. Am I understood?" Everyone nodded fearfully at the prospect of incurring the captain's wrath. "Oh, and Mr. Whitaker…"

The crew on the bridge stopped what they were doing and looked back over their shoulder at the captain.

"If any harm comes to my men or ship because of your oversight, I'll see you are brought up on charges of dereliction the instant we dock."

CHAPTER 2

MARK SMITH AND NOELLE PARKER navigated the confusing maze of dimly lit, narrow passageways deep in the bowels of the ship. Every surface was constructed from one-inch-thick reinforced steel. Runs of conduit and asbestos-covered piping snaked along the top of the bulkheads throughout the ship. Most everything in sight was painted the same faded puke-green color—the majority of it chipped and peeling. The second most common color was rust. Not the paint color but the inevitable reddish-brown flaky coating of iron oxide that happens when steel cohabitates too long with moisture and salt.

Mark and Noelle failed miserably trying to walk a straight line. The rough seas caused them to weave and stagger down the passageways like proverbial drunken sailors. Despite his athletic build and strong muscles from daily runs, Mark had difficulty getting his sea legs. He widened his stance and took small, deliberate steps in an attempt to keep his balance. Walking on the ship reminded him of scurrying across the gyrating fun house catwalk at Coney Island as a kid—the big differences being he didn't feel like vomiting back then and the rocking motion only lasted as long as it took to run across it.

Noelle fared no better. She was relegated to gripping the handrail with her left hand as she walked. Her right forearm was encased in a fresh white cast. An unseen wave slammed into the side of the ship, breaking her grip and sending Noelle careening into the right wall. She reached out with her right arm to soften the impact. Although the reset bones were protected by a cast, pain radiated up her arm. Her knees buckled.

Mark grabbed Noelle around her slender waist and drew her to him. Even the unpleasant surroundings—and the years that had passed since embracing his ex-wife—couldn't diminish the thrill Mark got when holding her close. Noelle's captivating crystal-blue eyes had enthralled Mark since the day they first met. And she knew it. She possessed a type of effortless beauty women half her age yearned for.

Ruefully, Noelle turned and looked at him. "Maybe we should have flown." Two days of constantly bobbing up and down had her rethinking their decision not to fly back home from the Azores.

"You know why we didn't. It's a little late now." Mark brushed her fiery red hair back from Noelle's eyes. "Two more days on this tub, and we'll be home. Mary will be waiting for us when we dock. You'll be fine. You just need to tough it out."

Noelle had a mischievous grin on her pretty face as she flashed a mock salute. "Yes, sir, Captain, sir."

Mark shook his head and opened the door for her.

A dozen crewmen sipped coffee and finished off the last of their breakfast in the cramped mess hall. Despite the hard work, grimy surroundings, and long stretches away from their families, the promise of three meals a day and a meager wage was a vast improvement from their previous lives. Crewmen earned three times as much money plying the high seas as they would at most jobs on land back home in their impoverished countries. The men wore bright orange hard hats and coveralls—the theory being they would be easier to spot if washed overboard.

Between puffs on unfiltered cigarettes and mouths full of food, conversations in broken English were loud and lively.

Mark and Noelle walked in and sat down at an empty

table. It was securely bolted to the deck and covered in a common disco era color, harvest gold. Pungent smells of body odor and grease assaulted their nostrils.

Upon seeing the strangers, conversation among the crew grew hushed and reverted to indecipherable foreign languages.

Noelle smiled politely at the man sitting closest to her. With bloodshot brown eyes, he looked her up and down then flashed a big smile her way. His grin clearly indicated he hadn't gotten the memo about that new high-tech dental instrument called the toothbrush.

A short, round olive-skinned man wearing a soiled apron walked up and plopped two plates down in front of Mark and Noelle. Grease splattered onto the table and Mark's new shirt. The man uttered something in Italian and walked off in a huff.

"Just what my stomach needs, undercooked eggs swimming in grease." Mark pushed his plate away and dabbed a paper napkin at his shirt.

Noelle looked down at her plate, frowned, and pushed it away as well. "Do you think the cook is offended because we haven't been eating his food?"

"I have no idea, but the next time he throws my food down in front of me like that he's going to be wearing it."

Men at the other tables leaned closer to each other and talked quietly, occasionally stealing quick glances at the two.

After twenty-five years as a flight attendant, Noelle had mastered the art of reading body language. She bent forward and whispered, "I think they're talking about us."

"Ya think?"

Noelle ignored his sarcasm. "Surely, I can't be the first woman to hitch a ride on a container ship?"

"Gentlemen, may I?" Mark reached over and grabbed a folded newspaper sitting on the edge of the table next to him. He opened the two-day-old edition of the *Diário dos*

Açores and flopped the front page down in front of Noelle.

Under the bold headline written in Portuguese was a color picture of Mark and Noelle. Mark stood next to her hospital bed with a forced smile on his face. The photographer had asked Mark to give a big thumbs-up because, of course, that's what all pilots did after surviving a harrowing flight.

Noelle scrunched up her face at seeing the picture. "Hmmm…that's not going to work. Now that you're famous, that smile of yours is going to need some adjusting." She delighted in teasing him. "If you need any pointers, I'd be happy to help."

"Thanks. I'll remember that when *Cosmo* calls." He pointed at the paper. "Any idea what it says?"

"My Portuguese is a little rusty, but I think it says, 'Heroic pilot saves his passengers and highjacked plane with an incredible dead-stick landing at Lajes Field. Pilot says he never could have pulled off this amazing feat without the help of his able Purser, and beautiful ex-wife, Noelle Parker.' Yep, I'm pretty sure that what it says."

"Rusty is right."

"I might not have gotten the translation *exactly* right, but that's what it should say." She reached across the table and held Mark's hand. "You're a hero. What you pulled off was nothing short of a miracle. How many times have you heard of everyone on board surviving something like that? Once? Maybe twice?" Tears welled up in Noelle's eyes. "You saved my life."

Mark pulled his hand away. "I'm not a hero. I was just doing my job. Any other pilot would have done the same thing. Besides, it's not like I had a choice. What was I supposed to do when everything went to hell, eject and parachute to safety?"

"You might not want to hear this, but your life, our lives, have changed forever because of what happened. Crash-landing the Tech-Liner in the Azores will have been front page news on every newspaper in the world by now. In the eyes of the public you're a hero." She had visions of stardom. "I'll bet when we get back to New York City they are going to throw a tickertape parade down Broadway for you. Think of all the opportunities, Mark. Talk show interviews. A book deal. We could get invited to sit with the commissioner at the Super Bowl." Her excitement continued to grow. "I wouldn't be surprised if they eventually made a movie about it. I hope they cast my character with—"

"Slow down, slow down. Before you go all Hollywood on me, take a breath." Mark angled forward and looked at Noelle with his intense seafoam-green eyes. "I don't want to be famous. I don't want a parade. And I don't want a movie. I just want to go back home, retire in peace, and be left alone."

"No Super Bowl tickets? Please, I know you better than that."

"Maybe one Super Bowl—two at the most. Then that's it." Mark looked down at his eggs floating in grease. "Let's head back to the cabin before my stomach jumps ship." He tossed his napkin onto his plate and walked away. The napkin sank down into the pool of grease until it vanished from sight.

CHAPTER 3

Each collision with a wave caused the massive ship to shudder and creak as if in pain. As they approached their cabin at the end of the passageway, Mark turned back and looked down the long corridor. Either his eyes were playing tricks on him after two rough days at sea, or the corridor—constructed with marine grade steel—was flexing and twisting.

He unlocked the door and held it open for Noelle. Their cabin was so small that if it had been a jail cell the ACLU would have had a credible lawsuit for cruel and unusual punishment.

Mark walked over and stared out the small porthole, mere feet above the waterline. "I'm not so sure I'm cut out to be a sailor. I'm seriously rethinking the promise I made to you. I mean I don't even know how to swim."

Noelle wheeled him around. "Oh no you don't. I'm not letting you off the hook that easily. Before they put me in the ambulance you said you were going to give up flying, marry me, and buy a boat. We were going to sail off into the sunset together. I would be the captain, and you would be my copilot. Remember?"

"One, it's first officer on a boat, not copilot."

Noelle shook her head at his Type A personality need to be accurate.

"And two, I had just crash-landed an airliner that was run out of fuel by a suicidal geek who hacked into the plane's computers. I think I'm allowed to have second thoughts."

"Don't you remember how you said you wanted to start a new chapter in your life?" She pointed back and forth between them. "With us? Well, today is page one."

Mark looked down at his left hand. The pale circle on his ring finger had long ago disappeared. He looked longingly into Noelle's blue eyes. She wasn't just the only woman he had ever truly loved; she was his lifeboat. Without her, his life had been miserable. Without her in his future, he felt destined to a life alone, eventually falling back into old habits—even going back to the bottle. He wanted to believe in a future with the two of them together but doubt silently whispered in his ear. Mark asked, "You really think people like us can change? What makes you think we'll be able to get along this time?"

Noelle pressed her body up against Mark and wrapped her arms around his broad shoulders. She playfully fondled his salt-and-pepper hair. "It'll be different this time; you'll see. We were young and naïve back then. And yes, I can be a little hardheaded at times. But we're older and wiser now. We both know what we're getting into. Have faith in us. I do." She gave him a peck on the cheek then grinned. "Besides, I can't wait until you have to call me captain."

Mark tried unsuccessfully to hold back a smile. He took a breath, let out a long sigh, then leaned forward and pressed his lips to Noelle's.

She closed her eyes and parted her lips.

Mark softly stroked Noelle's long red hair then lowered his hand down to the small of her back and pressed her body tight against him. Their kiss grew more passionate with every passing second.

Every part of her body tingled. Noelle silently recalled the past when lovemaking with Mark was a regular and wonderful occurrence. It had been a long time since she'd been with a man. Too long. Mark's embrace awakened an unfulfilled hunger in Noelle. She took his free hand and slowly guided it up to her breasts.

Suddenly, the PA speaker in the hall came alive. "Attention. This is the captain speaking. Everyone on board report to the bridge immediately. Everyone to the bridge. That's an order."

CHAPTER 4

MARK OPENED HIS EYES AND pulled back. "You've got to be kidding me."

"You think he meant us, too?" Noelle asked, hoping to be wrong.

"He said everybody."

She clung to Mark. "Should we be worried?"

"We'd better go find out what's happening." Mark gave her a quick kiss on the lips then parted Noelle's arms. He opened the door to the cabin and waited.

Noelle straightened her hair, smoothed out her blouse, and stepped out into the passageway. The two walked to the stairwell and quickly ascended eight flights of stairs behind the crew.

The bridge was perched on top of the superstructure at the back of the ship. Thirty years of harsh life at sea had taken its toll on the rundown space. Communications equipment and navigation instruments two generations out of date occupied four large metal-sided consoles evenly spaced along the width of the bridge.

Surrounding the ship were enormous waves topped with rolling, foaming whitecaps. Howling wind sprayed the foam off the top of the crests like they were being blown off an overfilled latte. The landless horizon rose and fell in a slow stomach-churning rhythm.

Anxious crewmen silently filed onto the bridge, trailed by Mark and Noelle. When they looked forward from the bridge, the view was dominated by a thousand multicolored shipping containers stacked together like forty-foot-long Legos. A deck crane rose up out of the center of the stacks. Its boom projected aft across the tops of the containers, the end secured to a mount on the roof of the bridge. Communication antennas and a radar dome sprouted up from the roof as well.

Perched in his chair, Captain Oliveira looked out at his crew. Their demeanor troubled him. "As you men know, this is the last voyage for the *Lynda Ray*. After unloading in New York, she will be sent off to the scrapyard." Oliveira's face tightened. "An undignified ending for such a loyal, hardworking gal. I'm proud to serve as her final skipper. Men, the last two days I've been observing you. I must say, I am very impressed. You are doing a satisfactory job."

A second career as a motivational speaker was probably not in the cards for Oliveira.

"I have some unsettling news. Through an unfortunate oversight"—he looked directly at Whitaker—"we are in the path of a very strong storm approaching from the south."

Noelle gulped and clutched Mark's hand.

"I've just contacted Seawind Shipping's operations control center. They've assured me the safest course of action is to proceed full speed ahead to New York rather than turn back. I want everyone to complete the heavy-weather checklist for your stations. Secure everything that is not bolted to the deck. All the lashings on the containers are to be tightened down."

Grumbling from the crew was cut off when their union shop steward stepped forward. "How could this happen? Were the officers not aware of the weather before now?"

"I assure you we are doing—"

With the crew outnumbering the officers four to one, the union rep felt emboldened to cut off the captain. "This strong weather…it is a Category 3 hurricane, is it not?" News traveled fast on a small ship.

Hurricane

Silence flooded the bridge. All eyes fixated on the captain. Oliveira stood up and marched over to the taller union man. He stood toe-to-toe with him. It felt like the captain was going to sentence the man to walk the plank. Oliveira gritted his teeth and growled, "Begin preparing the ship *immediately*. Am I clear, mister?"

The rep took a step back and glared at Oliveira. "Aye, aye...*Captain*."

The cook began ranting in Italian to the man next to him. His hand gestures spoke even louder. He ended his tirade by lifting his right hand and shaking the back of it at Mark.

"What the hell is he saying?" Whitaker asked.

The crewman whom the cook had spoken to was visibly shaken. "It's nothing. Don't pay no attention to him. He's a superstitious old fool."

"I asked you what he said," Whitaker demanded.

With his limited fluency in English, the man did his best to interpret. "He says to me," the crewman sheepishly pointed in Mark's direction, "he says this man has brought us bad luck. He should have never been allowed on our ship. He says this man is cursed."

Panic erupted among the crew. The bridge sounded like the Tower of Babel as the frightened men reacted in different languages to the ominous accusation.

"Enough!" Captain Oliveira slammed his fist down on a console.

The crew fell silent, fear visible in their eyes.

"I won't stand for anyone on my crew talking like that. You are all experienced sailors. I expect you to act like it! Communications Officer, no one is to use the radios for nonessential calls. I want updates every hour on the speed and track of the hurricane."

"Aye, Captain."

Captain Oliveira turned to Mark and Noelle. "I don't want you two getting in the way of the crew while they prepare my ship. Go below. You are restricted to your cabin until further notice."

They had no choice but to nod silently in agreement.

"Engineer, cancel the limits. Can you give me 110 percent RPM yet? I want to see eighteen knots out of her, Mr. Schmidt."

Chief Engineer Schmidt scoffed. "Captain, this tin can is thirty years old. She could barely do eighteen knots brand new. In heavy seas like these, she'd be lucky to stay in one piece at anything over twelve knots."

"Eighteen knots, Mr. Schmidt. You have my order."

The cook blessed himself with the sign of the cross and muttered, "*Moriremo tutti.*"

"Now what is he saying?" Whitaker barked.

"He says"—the interpreter made the sign of the cross as well—"he says we are all going to die."

CHAPTER 5

WAVES—SOUNDING LIKE BEATS ON A tribal war drum—pounded against the glass porthole in their cabin. The most destructive weapon Mother Nature had in her arsenal had the ship directly in its sights, and there was nothing anyone could do about it. Disoriented by the magnitude of the unstoppable peril Mark and Noelle faced, minutes passed before either of them could put together a coherent sentence.

"What should we…shouldn't we put on our…oh God, I can't even think straight." Noelle grabbed Mark's arm. Her eyes spoke volumes. Her chin quivered as she whimpered, "I'm scared."

Mark stood motionless as he stared blankly at the growing threat outside the porthole.

"Mark? Did you hear me?"

Mark turned to face Noelle. "What if he's right?"

"What are you talking about?"

"What if I am cursed?"

Noelle took Mark's hand. "Come on, you're not going to believe some frightened old man, are you?"

Mark shook his head. "I don't believe in that superstition crap but look at the evidence. I've brought nothing but bad luck to everyone close to me since I was a kid."

"What evidence?"

"For starters, my mom."

"What about her?"

"My dad told me…he said she left because of me. He

said she couldn't handle me anymore."

Fury replaced the fear in Noelle's eyes. "That son of a bitch. Mark, your dad was a spiteful, violent drunk. That's why your mom left. It wasn't because of you. She loved you. She just couldn't take it anymore. It was either leave or eventually die at the hands of your father. Don't you see that now? He's wrong, and he can rot in hell as far as I'm concerned."

"What about you and Mary? Look at all the pain I've caused you two. Why you put up with me all those years I'll never know."

Noelle took Mark's other hand. A tear rolled down her cheek. "Because I loved you, that's why."

Mark continued. "Why is it when we're together bad things always happen? How do you explain the fact that the first time we fly together since our divorce I end up crash-landing on some tiny little island in the middle of the ocean?"

Noelle looked down at the white cast on her arm. She let go of Mark's hands.

"And now, I talk you into sailing back home, and we end up trapped on a ship thousands of miles from land with a damned hurricane headed right for us."

Noelle turned her back to Mark, walked over to the bed, and sat down.

"If I'm not cursed, then those are a hell of a lot of coincidences for one lifetime. Are you sure remarrying me is smart?"

Noelle sat silently on the edge of the bed, avoiding eye contact with Mark.

A huge wave slammed into the side of the ship, causing Mark to tumble into the wall. A thin stream of seawater trickled down the wall beneath the porthole.

◆

"Commo, an update."

The communications officer snapped to attention. "Aye, sir. The outer wall is forty miles south of our current position. Diameter of the hurricane is 150 miles. It's moving due north at twenty-five knots. Wind speeds have increased to 128 knots."

Oliveira paced slowly across the floor. "Our speed?"

"Ten knots, sir."

"The bastard is stalking us," he muttered. Oliveira stopped pacing, picked up the handset attached to the captain's chair, and squeezed the transmit button. "Engineer, increase power to 115 percent." He hung up before Schmidt could protest his order. Sitting tall, Captain Oliveira took his rightful position at the helm. Ensnared in a no-win situation, the captain took the ultimate gamble. "Mr. Whitaker, hard to port. Bring us around to a heading of one-eight-zero degrees."

The color drained from Whitaker's face. "Captain?"

"South, Mr. Whitaker. Now."

"Sir, I must protest. You are making a dreadful mistake. The company has assured us the best course of action is to continue toward New York. I agree completely."

"*You* agree?!" Anger overwhelmed Oliveira at the insolence of a lowly first officer questioning his order. "This is my ship, Mr. Whitaker. I'll operate her however I see fit. Now bring us around to one-eight-zero degrees!"

Whitaker mumbled profanities under his breath then grudgingly did as ordered. The heavily laden ship listed to the right as it slowly began a turn to port. Two miles of ocean were needed to complete the turn. The *Lynda Ray* was now face to face with an angry black wall of storm clouds.

Despite being cowed into silence, it was obvious the crew on the bridge thought the captain had lost his mind. Oliveira sensed this and clarified his seemingly suicidal decision. "Men, at this speed, outrunning the hurricane is impossible. Continuing west would only prolong the time our ship would have to endure the storm. Combining its speed with ours will minimize the time needed to punch through to the eye of the hurricane. Once we are in it, we'll reverse course, follow the eye, and hope the storm weakens as it passes over colder water. Mr. Whitaker, full speed ahead."

CHAPTER 6

THE *LYNDA RAY* BREACHED THE outer wall of the hurricane an hour later. The thirty-thousand-ton vessel corkscrewed through the ocean as if trapped on a demonic roller coaster. It groaned and screeched with each assault from the merciless waves. Torrential rain overwhelmed the wipers as they frantically tried to clear the bridge windows.

The captain went to each console on the bridge and carefully examined the information presented on the aging equipment. He hoped for a clue to use in his battle with the sea. When he looked at the inclinometer, Oliveira froze. The instrument registered roll readings over forty degrees both port and starboard. The lashings holding down the stacks of shipping containers were never designed to withstand that amount of roll. Oliveira looked up just as the forward stack of shipping containers broke free.

The trickle of seawater running down the cabin wall beneath the porthole had turned into a steady stream.

The relentless pitching and rolling of the world around her became too much for Noelle. She dashed over to the cabin sink just in time. What little food that remained in her queasy stomach splattered against the sides of the bowl.

Mark paced back and forth in the tiny cabin like a caged tiger. "I can't stand not knowing what's going on up there."

Noelle muttered in agreement from the bowl of the sink.

Rendered helpless in their tiny cabin, Mark decided to provide some measure of comfort and reassurance to his ex-wife. He rubbed her back and searched for the words to tell Noelle that everything would be okay. When nothing materialized in his brain, Mark did what little he could—he held back her wavy red locks as Noelle pressed her face farther into the bowl.

When her vomiting stopped, Mark said, "I should go up to the bridge. Maybe I can help. I'll be back in a few minutes."

Noelle turned her ashen face toward Mark. "You heard the captain; he told us to stay in our cabin until further notice."

"Since when do you do what you're told by a *captain*?" Mark had her there.

Noelle staggered to a standing position. "You're not leaving me down here by myself. If you're going, I'm going."

Mark opened his mouth to argue but realized the futility of trying to change the mind of his beautiful but hardheaded ex-wife.

He opened the door, allowing Noelle to exit first. Just as Mark stepped into the doorway, the porthole shattered. Hundreds of gallons of seawater shot into the ship like it came from a fire hose. The force of the impact on Mark's back slammed him face-first into the opposite wall. He slid down the wall into a pool of rapidly rising water. Dazed but conscious, he grabbed for the handrail and tried to pull himself up. When he looked back toward the cabin, a blast of water hit him in the face. Mark turned away and coughed, violently gasping for air.

Noelle hooked her good arm under Mark's back and helped him to his feet. "Come on, we gotta go! Move it!"

The two sloshed down the passageway toward the stairs.

"Wait!" Mark turned and ran back.

Noelle reached out to stop him. "Mark, no!"

He went to a break in the corridor and slammed shut a

watertight door, isolating the flooding to that end of the passageway.

Mark and Noelle bounded up the steps two at a time. When reaching the top of the superstructure, they burst through the door to the bridge. What they saw stopped them in their tracks. Mark had flown through some violent weather during his career, but the ferocity of the Atlantic Ocean surrounding them sent a chill down his spine.

CHAPTER 7

Hill-size waves attacked the *LYNDA Ray* from every direction. Intact shipping containers that had fallen overboard bobbed up and down in the water like gigantic steel corks. Contents from containers that had broken open littered the ocean like a trash dump after a tornado. Pieces of furniture, boxes containing cheap electronics, and a cornucopia of various fruits encircled the ship. Stacks of containers that remained on board sagged precariously over the side like branches of a willow tree.

"Commo, get US Maritime Emergency on the radio. Tell them our position, direction, and speed," Oliveira commanded.

An alarm bell sounded on the bridge.

"Captain, look." First Officer Whitaker pointed to a board displaying a profile view of the ship and each deck. Red warning lights for decks one and two flashed, indicating they were flooding.

Captain Oliveira picked up the PA microphone. "All crew, we are taking on water on levels one and two. Evacuate the engine room. Proceed immediately to level three. Seal off all doors on level three." He waved furiously at the crewmen on the bridge. "Go! Go help!"

They bolted through the door at the back of the bridge and down the stairs. Only Whitaker remained. In total, sixteen crewmen rushed down to the third level, trying to save their ship.

Oliveira turned and saw Mark and Noelle frozen in place,

mouths agape. Pointing to Noelle, he ordered, "You, take the helm. Keep the ship facing into the oncoming waves."

She rushed over and gripped the wheel like a terrified student driver.

"Smith, I want you on the radios."

Mark stepped up to the communications console. He studied the nautical radios and quickly started matching them in his mind with their aviation counterparts.

The deck crane had been hit and damaged by the metal shipping containers when they broke free from the stack. The end of its boom had been ripped away from the securing mount on the roof of the bridge by the impact. Now the boom swung freely side to side each time the ship rolled.

A monster wave crashed up and over the bow of the ship. The spray from it engulfed the struggling vessel, dropping the forward visibility from the bridge to zero. When the windows finally cleared, what came into view was terrifying. The ship was perched over the edge of a massive trough. The front of the ship projected out so far out into the air that the bow bulb was exposed meters above the waterline.

"Hang on!" Mark screamed.

The *Lynda Ray* pitched down like it had been shoved off a cliff. Everyone on the bridge was slammed forward into the metal consoles. The ship hurdled down the sloping ocean, gaining speed as it went.

That's when Oliveira saw it. "Oh my God!"

A rogue wave taller than the superstructure had taken direct aim at them. Before the ship could lift its nose, the bow plunged into the wall of water. Millions of gallons of water crashed down on the *Lynda Ray*. More of the heavy containers snapped off their mounts as easily as sand being blown out of a hand. The bow didn't rise back up. The front of the ship was now completely swamped under twenty feet of water.

"Captain, more decks are flooded!" Whitaker screamed.

Every red light on the panel for decks one, two, three, four, and five were lit up.

Oliveira braced himself against the downward tilt of the ship and grabbed the intercom microphone. "Crew, report your status immediately."

Seconds that felt like minutes passed. No one responded. "This is the captain; report in." Still no response. Oliveira yelled into the microphone. "This is Captain Oliveira! I order you to report your status immediately!"

Out of the sixteen crewmen, most with wives and young children, none answered the call.

Mark looked knowingly at Noelle and shook his head.

The captain slumped against his chair and weakly repeated, "I *order* you to report."

Mark gently pried the microphone out of Oliveira's hand. He clipped it back into its cradle then helped the defeated man into the captain's chair. Mark walked back over to the communications panel and picked up the mic. He depressed the button on the side and coolly announced, "Mayday. Mayday. This is the vessel *Lynda Ray*. We are abandoning ship. I say again, we are abandoning ship. Our present position is latitude—"

Before Mark could get the words out, the damaged crane boom swept back across the roof of the bridge. It crashed into the radar dome and radio antennas, ripping them off their mounts and tossing them out to sea.

CHAPTER 8

"TO HELL WITH THIS." WHITAKER dashed out of the bridge and down the stairs on the exterior of the superstructure. He headed for the only lifeboat.

"Get back to your station, you mutinous dog!" Oliveira roared.

Noelle tugged on Oliveira's arm. "Captain, it's time to go."

He ignored her and slumped back in his chair, head bowed in resignation.

"Captain, we have to get to the lifeboat."

He lifted his head and looked into her crystal-blue eyes. "I won't abandon my ship. My men might still be alive."

A million more gallons of seawater flooded into the forward part of the ship and its lower decks. Red lights for deck six lit up. The *Lynda Ray* began sinking nose first.

◆

One twenty-person freefall lifeboat sat ready on the stern. Its launch rails pointed down at the sea at a forty-five-degree angle. The fully enclosed bright orange fiberglass boat was the only way off the doomed ship.

Whitaker quickly prepared it for his escape. He climbed on the roof and detached the davit crane cables from the top of the lifeboat. The wind, stinging rain, and wet surface made his preparations even more dangerous than they already were. After climbing down, he pulled the safety pin inserted into the holdback release mechanism and disconnected the battery charger cable. Whitaker looked up toward the bridge. No one was coming his way. He pulled open the door on the back of the lifeboat, went in, then latched it shut behind him.

"I'm afraid your men are gone, Captain. There's nothing more you can do for them." Noelle hooked her hand under Oliveira's arm and tried to lift him out of the chair.

He was having none of it. He sat back even deeper in the chair. A rueful expression formed on Oliveira's face. "Did you know my father was a famous Portuguese seaman? And his father before him, and his father before him."

"Sir?"

"I never really had any say about it. I was going to have a career at sea whether I wanted to or not. Family tradition and all." Oliveira shook his head. "I will have forever brought dishonor and shame on my family's name because of this."

"No, Captain, that's not true. You did everything you could. It's not your fault."

His expression hardened. "Madame, it's always the captain's fault."

Mark knew exactly what he meant. "Noelle, I've got this. I'll talk to him. Go to the lifeboat and tell that son of a bitch he's not leaving without us."

Noelle didn't budge.

"Please?"

She nodded silently and looked back at Oliveira. Noelle leaned down and planted a soft kiss on his cheek. A tear ran down her face as she left the bridge and headed for the lifeboat.

Oliveira got out of his chair, straightened his uniform jacket, and took control of the wheel at the helm of the doomed ship. A meaningless gesture to everyone but himself. He turned and said, "Captain Smith, you more than anyone know why I must do this. The only honorable option I have is to go down with my ship. Please, go be with your wife."

"You're right, Captain Oliveira, I do know." Mark walked up beside Oliveira and placed his hands on the wheel as well. "That's why I'm staying."

◆

Noelle pounded on the lifeboat door with her fists. "Whitaker open the door! They're on the way! Open the damned door!" The inboard diesel motor fired up. She shielded her eyes with her hands and pressed her face up to the window in the door.

Whitaker was sitting in the driver's seat at the helmsman station, preparing the boat for launch.

Noelle banged harder.

Whitaker turned and saw her through the window. He looked briefly at Noelle then turned back and continued his preparations.

She desperately searched the area for any way to stop the launch. Noelle spied the release mechanism safety pin and picked it up. She banged the pin against the glass. Whitaker turned to see Noelle waving the safety pin back and forth then duck out of view.

Whitaker rushed to the back of the lifeboat and flung open the door. Noelle had reinserted the safety pin.

"Take that out! We have to leave, now!"

Noelle stood between Whitaker and the pin. "You're not going anywhere until my husband and Captain Oliveira get here. Got it?!"

"You don't understand. If I don't launch the lifeboat now, it won't slide down the rails."

The front of the ship had sunk farther under the water. The normal downward angle of the slide rails, relative to the horizon, were cut in half by the low pitch angle of the ship.

"At ten degrees or less, there won't be enough speed built up when the lifeboat leaves the rails to avoid hitting the stern. We have to go!" Whitaker ran back to the helm and looked at the instrument showing the pitch of the lifeboat. "Twenty degrees!" he yelled back to Noelle.

"It's a boat. If the ship sinks, it will float and we will be on our way, right?"

Apparently, Noelle had never seen the movie *Titanic*.

"No. We'd be pulled under by the suction," he explained. Looking at the gauge, he yelled, "Eighteen degrees!"

"Absolutely not! You are leaving the ship. That's an order, Smith."

Mark ignored Oliveira and looked straight ahead.

"Look, I appreciate why you want to stay, but I can't let you. Don't be an ass, Smith. You have the rest of your life ahead of you. You have a beautiful ex-wife who, if you had any brains, you'd remarry the minute you got to land. I'm an old man. My wife passed away years ago. We had no kids. This is all I've got. Now I don't even have this," he said, sweeping his hand across the evacuated bridge.

Mark stood resolutely at the helm.

"Dammit, Smith, abandon ship. That's an order!"

He turned toward the captain. "Sir, I'm not leaving you here to die alone. Either we both go, or neither of us go."

Oliveira's stubborn pride finally broke. "Okay, you win, Smith." He gestured toward the door. "To the lifeboat. Lead the way."

Mark knew a con when he heard one. "No, sir, you lead the way. I'll follow."

Oliveira flashed a wily grin.

The men walked out onto the bridge wing and were met with howling winds and horizontal rain. The wind-driven raindrops stung like needles piercing their exposed flesh. They clambered down the metal stairs, holding on for dear life.

"Sixteen degrees! I'm not waiting." Whitaker stepped out of the boat and forced Noelle aside. He pulled the safety pin and threw it in the ocean.

Noelle grabbed Whitaker and spun him around. "Look!"

Mark and Oliveira were negotiating the steep steps down the side of the superstructure, careful not to be swept away by the hurricane.

"Hurry!" she yelled at the top of her lungs. Her words were carried away with the wind.

Whitaker had retaken the driver's seat. "Fourteen degrees!"

Noelle sprinted over to the stairway and helped Oliveira to the lifeboat.

Mark ran ahead and opened the door. He looked down at the raging sea, then inside the tiny fiberglass lifeboat. The angry waves had tossed the container ship around as easily as a feather in a gale. Getting in the lifeboat meant signing up for a far worse ride, for far longer.

"Twelve degrees!" Whitaker yelled.

He took a deep breath, buried his fear of the water deep down in his consciousness, and stepped aboard. Mark grabbed a seat and tightly strapped in.

Noelle gestured for Oliveira to get in the lifeboat as they approached the door.

"Madame, at least allow me the dignity of being the last person to leave my ship."

"Of course." Noelle nodded and climbed aboard. As she finished strapping in, Oliveira stepped over to his right and stomped down on the foot pedal, activating the secondary release mechanism holding the lifeboat back.

The lifeboat jerked forward, slowly picking up speed as it lumbered down the rails. Noelle screamed and reached out in a futile attempt to stop what Oliveira, and gravity, had put in motion. The last image Mark and Noelle ever saw of Oliveira was a proud, dedicated sailor standing at attention, saluting the Portuguese flag.

CHAPTER 9

WHEN THE BOAT CLEARED THE launch rails, Mark and Noelle momentarily became weightless, only to be slammed back into their seats a second later when the bow of the lifeboat plunged under the ocean. Just as quickly, it sprang back up. The impact with the water slammed the back door shut. Whitaker engaged the propeller and pulled away from the *Lynda Ray* at an exasperatingly slow top speed of six knots.

Mark jumped up and looked out the window on the door. The superstructure was the only thing visible, and it was disappearing quickly. The stern of the ship rose completely up out of the water and pointed skyward. Geysers of air shot upward as the ship slowly met its fate. Once it sank out of sight, a gigantic whirlpool began spinning counterclockwise where the ship had been.

The lifeboat stopped moving forward. It was now being pulled backward against its will.

"Full power, full power!" Mark screamed.

There was nothing more Whitaker could do. The throttle was already pushed as far forward as physically possible.

Suction from the whirlpool clawed at the tiny lifeboat. Even with its blunt back end digging in against the water, the boat's rearward speed accelerated. The boat spun sideways as it got trapped in the jaws of the whirlpool.

Mark jumped back in his seat and strapped in. He reached across the aisle and grabbed Noelle's hand. He held it tightly and whispered, "I love you."

She squeezed his hand and closed her eyes.

The lifeboat swirled around in ever tightening circles as if caught in a massive blender. Shipping containers and their cargo vanished down into the center of the whirlpool. As the lifeboat edged closer to the center of the vortex, the G forces increased. Mark and Noelle forced their heads back against the headrest in an attempt to stay upright.

Mark closed his eyes and was transported back in his mind to centrifuge training in the Air Force. Student pilots had to successfully withstand a crushing nine times the force of gravity while sitting in a simulated cockpit at the end of a spinning arm in order to graduate. He survived the test, but shortly after getting out of the contraption Mark got a chance to see his lunch for the second time that day.

His eyes popped open. The lateral Gs felt as if they were subsiding. The spinning motion was slowing down. The orange lifeboat started moving forward again. Eventually, the funnel-shaped whirlpool filled in and went back to being part of the next hurricane-tossed wave.

Mark yelled to Whitaker, "Let's get the hell out of here!"

"Perfect." Mary Smith stepped back to admire the festive decorations hung with care in her mother's drab apartment. Crepe paper streamers corkscrewed out in every direction from the light fixture hanging over the kitchen table. WELCOME HOME was spelled out in colorful cardboard letters strung together over the doorway.

April Parker put her arm around her cousin's shoulder. "Not bad. I always said you had a flair for decorating."

The striking twentysomethings both had lean, athletic bodies. Mary's long blonde hair was tied back in a ponytail, while April wore her red hair in a stylish rounded bob. Even when clad in yoga pants and baggy sweatshirts, they attracted plenty of attention from the opposite sex.

April glanced over at the refrigerator. A front-page article cut out from the *New York Times* was mounted to the door with magnets shaped like states. Mark's headshot, unfortunately sourced from his driver's license photo, filled the page under the banner: Capt. Hero!

"How are you holding up?" April asked.

"I'm…fine," Mary tentatively replied.

April wrapped her arms around her younger cousin. "Don't BS me, Mary. I know you better than that. I can't imagine what it's been like for you. The thought of possibly losing both your parents in a plane crash. I cried my eyes out when I saw the pictures of Uncle Mark and Aunt Noelle on the screen. And then finding out they made it out alive from a TV newscast of all places. Is there anything I can do?"

"Having you stay with me these past few days has meant the world to me." Mary's eyes lit up. "You're coming to the dock to greet them when they arrive, aren't you?"

"Of course. I wouldn't dare miss it." April scrunched up her face. "That doofus boyfriend of yours isn't coming, is he?"

"No. And he's not a doofus."

"I'm sorry, I'm not trying to be mean. Just looking out for you; that's all. You could do so much better."

Mary's eyes misted up. "Randy broke up with me."

April suppressed a smile.

"He didn't think I was smart to postpone my last semester of medical school so I could be with my folks. I told him that after what they went through, they are going to need my support."

April beamed with pride. "You are going to make a great doctor, Mary."

"Thanks; tell Randy that. He told me he thought we needed a breather." Her shoulders slumped.

"All heart, isn't he? More like he saw the odds of his future meal ticket not paying off and decided to jump ship.

That's what I think. Trust me; you are better off without him."

"You really think so?" Mary knew in her heart April was right, but getting dumped by her first serious boyfriend still stung.

"Absolutely." April put her arm around her younger cousin. "Tell you what. Tonight, we are going to put on our tightest outfits and go out dancing. You'll forget all about Randy and all the crazy things that have happened to your parents. Hot guys will be lined up around the block to dance with us."

"Thanks, Cuz." Mary hugged April.

Mary's iPhone vibrated on the kitchen table. Seawind Shipping popped up on the caller ID. She went over and picked it up, tapping the green answer icon. "Mom? Dad? Is that you?"

An ominous silence was followed by a male voice. "Is this Mary Smith?"

"Yes. Who's this?"

"Ms. Smith, my name is John Baxter. I'm general counsel for Seawind Shipping."

"Has there been a change in the arrival time?"

"Uh…sort of, but that's not why I'm calling. Ms. Smith, I need to verify whom I'm talking to. Could you please tell me your middle initial?"

"What?" Mary looked over at her cousin with concern.

"Your middle initial, please."

"It's K. Tell me what the hell is going on."

"There's been a serious problem. I need to speak to you in person. We've sent a car around to your apartment. It should be arriving any minute."

CHAPTER 10

NIGHT FELL OVER THE STORMY Atlantic Ocean. The merciless sea pounded on the puttering lifeboat like it had a vendetta against it.

Out of nowhere, a tremendous jolt sent the lifeboat lurching sideways. Whitaker was catapulted out of the driver's seat and slammed headfirst into a steel pole in the center of the aisle. His body crumpled to the floor.

"What the hell?" Mark jumped up and looked out the side window at the helmsman station. A wayward shipping container had surfed down the front of a wave and broadsided the lifeboat. Seawater started seeping in through a crack in the fiberglass. The dented container silently floated away after the nautical hit-and-run, looking to claim its next victim.

Mark and Noelle carefully lifted Whitaker off the floor and into a seat. Noelle grabbed the two halves of his seat belt, inserted the metal tip into the buckle, and adjusted the strap so it was low and tight across his lap. The strap of his leather satchel had gotten wrapped around Whitaker's neck during his tumble to the floor. Noelle carefully unwound the strap and set the satchel aside.

Whitaker moaned and wailed in pain. He pressed his palm against his left temple. Bright red blood oozed out between his fingers and down the back of his hand.

Noelle gently peeled his hand back. A deep crack in his skull was visible. "Hand me the first aid kit," she ordered.

Mark grabbed the kit from the wall and handed it to her.

It was well stocked with a variety of medical supplies.

She ripped open a package of gauze and pressed the pad gently against Whitaker's skull. Noelle secured the pad by wrapping loop after loop from a roll of gauze around his head. She ignored the warm blood staining her hands as she tended to his wound. Luckily for everyone, Whitaker quickly passed out from the intense pain.

Mark jumped up into the driver's seat and did his best to keep the lifeboat pointed south.

Hour after hour, the lifeboat was tormented by the nautical equivalent of being strapped to an angry Brahma bull with no way off. Each jolt caused Whitaker to writhe in pain. Water slowly seeped into the boat.

"Any idea where we're at?" Noelle yelled over the cacophony of the storm.

Mark squinted out the window. Nothing but rain and darkness, masking endless rolling waves, were visible. He scanned the basic instrument panel. "Not a clue!" he yelled. "Hopefully, someone heard my mayday call and will be looking for us. If we're lucky, we might still be near where the *Lynda Ray* went down. Or the wind and waves could have blown us hundreds of miles by now. No way to tell."

Mark and Noelle clung tightly to the hope that search-and-rescue efforts had begun. And that the rescuers would stumble across a sixteen-foot lifeboat, in the dark, adrift in the forty-one million-square-mile Atlantic Ocean—during a hurricane.

CHAPTER 11

MARK WAS ASLEEP AT THE helm when the view out the front window started to brighten. The rain eased up. The pitching and rolling slowly subsided. He opened his eyes just as the lifeboat pierced through a curtain of clouds and entered the eye of the hurricane.

The faint glow of the rising sun peeked above the horizon. An eerie tranquility enveloped them. For the first time since getting on the lifeboat, the water was calm. The contrast between the raging ocean they'd just spent the last twenty hours getting thrown about in and the placid blue water couldn't have been starker.

Mark spun the boat around to a northerly heading, locked the wheel in place, and opened storage lockers under the floorboard, searching for something to eat. He pulled out a flare gun and spare flares. Next came a sea anchor and a whistle. Finally, he found what he was looking for. Mark pulled out a large bag stuffed with emergency rations and twenty plastic liter bottles of water. He handed a bottle to Noelle and tore into the rations. They both began ravenously downing the bland, vacuum-packed food.

"Wait." Mark grabbed Noelle's wrist. "Let's slow down. If we eat too fast—"

His warning came too late. Noelle dashed for the door at the back of the lifeboat. She knelt down on the back step outside the door and threw up everything she just ate. When finished, she scooped up a handful of seawater and rinsed off her mouth.

After that lovely learning experience, they each took smaller, constrained nibbles of food and sips of water until they had their fill.

Whitaker opened his eyes and started to come around.

Noelle went to his side with a bottle of water. She raised the bottle to his lips but he pushed it away.

Between low moans he mumbled, "I'm sorry. I'm so sorry."

She tried to comfort him. "Please, try to remain still." Noelle lifted the gauze pad to take a look. Hair matted down by dark, coagulated blood was all she could see.

He became more and more agitated. "I did this. I'm to blame."

"Try not to talk." Noelle lightly patted Whitaker's arm.

Mark spoke up. "He does have a point. If he'd checked the weather at the beginning of his shift, we could have turned around and had an eight-hour head start back to the Azores. None of this would have happened."

Whitaker's head slumped. Tears formed in his eyes. "I did."

"Shhh…please don't talk. Save your strength."

"Wait a minute, Noelle." Mark glared at Whitaker. "You did what? What are you trying to say?"

Whitaker avoided Mark's glare. "I did check the weather. I knew about the hurricane."

Mark's jaw dropped. Fury bubbled up inside him. "You knew a hurricane was coming right at us, and you did nothing?"

"I thought we could outrun it. We'd get kicked around for a while, then everything would be okay. I never planned this."

Mark's eyes narrowed as he cocked his head. "Planned? What do you mean planned?"

Whitaker started bawling.

Mark grabbed the front of his shirt and screamed, "What did you do?!"

Whitaker looked up at Mark with bloodshot eyes. "They promised me they'd give me my captain's rating."

"They, who?"

"The company. When I called for the weather update, they said not to worry, that everything would be fine. They promised me if our ship got in ahead of schedule I'd be rewarded by getting my captain's bars early."

"That's why you did this?"

Whitaker glared at Mark. "Yes. Do you know what it's like to work for slave wages for years under these old, grouchy tyrants? Captains constantly barking orders at you and looking down on you? I couldn't take it anymore. As the captain, *I* would be giving the orders. My pay would triple. I could finally afford the lifestyle I deserve."

Mark didn't bother stating the obvious about his own lean years as a copilot and the many unpleasant experiences flying with difficult captains. He couldn't contain his fury any longer. "How could you do that?! We trusted you with our lives. You had a duty to protect your ship. What about your crew? Their kids are going to grow up without fathers because of what you did. How could you believe that bullshit your company was feeding you?"

Unmoved by Mark's anger, the tears flowing down Whitaker's face slowed. "I didn't. Not really. I knew the real reason they wanted us to get in early."

"Why?" Noelle asked.

"If our shipment got in early, Seawind Shipping stood to make an early delivery bonus. We were ahead of schedule, and they wanted to keep it that way. After we offloaded, that rust bucket was going to be sold off for scrap, anyway. No harm done if it got roughed up a little in the storm."

"No harm done? All your crewmates drowned. The *Lynda Ray* sank," Noelle soberly reminded him.

"Please, the company is even better off now that she's sunk."

"How?" Noelle asked, confused.

"Most of the crew are from wretched Third World countries. A gigantic company like Seawind knows their families can't afford to hire lawyers. The families will be easily bought off by dangling the paltry amount of money prescribed by maritime law in front of their faces."

"What about the ship?" Mark asked.

"Insurance. The cargo in those containers is insured. If it's lost at sea, the shippers don't lose a dime. And the company will make a hell of a lot more than a bonus and a few pennies of scrap money by filing a claim for the loss of the ship. A lot more."

"And of course, don't forget, you'd get your captain's bars if we made it." Mark released Whitaker's shirt. "You disgust me." He climbed back into the driver's seat and glared out at the calm sea.

CHAPTER 12

WHITAKER HAD FALLEN BACK TO sleep. The lifeboat puttered north at a blazing six knots trying to maximize the time spent in the calm eye.

Mark slouched back in the driver's seat and stared aimlessly out the window, scratching the stubble on his cheeks. Seawater was now a foot deep inside the boat.

Mark bolted upright in his seat. "Crap, we've got company."

Two fins projected above the water as the predators slowly circled the lifeboat.

Noelle came to the window as Mark pointed toward the sharks. "They must have been attracted by the vomit."

"How big do you think they are?" she asked.

"From the size of their fins, I'd guess big." Mark opened the emergency escape hatch in the ceiling above the helmsman station and stood on the seat to get a better look at their new friends. The water was clear enough to estimate the size of the sharks based on the dark shadow beneath each fin. "Jesus…" He ducked back in to the lifeboat.

"Well?"

Mark climbed down and went to the back door. He pushed down on the latches to ensure it was tightly closed.

"Mark, how big are they? Tell me."

"I waited until they swam next to us so I could have something to compare them to." He shook his head side to side. "Each shark is longer than this lifeboat."

"Oh my God." Noelle's head sank. Her spirits were

at their lowest since the lifeboat launched. She came up beside Mark and clutched his arm. "Are we going to make it out of this?" Her voice choked with fear. "No bull."

He looked into her crystal-blue eyes—eyes desperate for reassurance. Mark decided not to say what he was thinking. So, he lied. "After what we've been through, we definitely don't have all our nine lives left. But yes, we are going to make it. Trust me."

"I do." A smile slowly formed on Noelle's face. She thought about her response for a second then chuckled.

"What?" Mark asked.

"Look how things turned out the last time I said 'I do' to you. Not so good."

Mark laughed and shrugged. "That's what you get for marrying a pilot."

"Great, *now* you tell me."

"I'm not trying to be morbid, but if this is *it* for me, I wouldn't want to be with anyone else." He leaned down and kissed Noelle.

She plopped down in a seat across from the helmsman station and smiled. "Yeah, me too. But don't let that go to your head, flyboy. I bet dozens of men would have jumped at the chance to get stuck on a tiny lifeboat with me during a hurricane."

"At least a dozen," Mark jokingly replied.

"You want to hear something weird?"

"Shoot."

"I was sure we wouldn't make it. I thought the plane would run out of gas and we would die in the ocean. The weird thing was I wasn't worried about me dying so much as my daughters living the rest of their lives without a mother, like I have."

Mark narrowed his eyes. "Daughters?"

Noelle quickly caught herself. "My mind is fried." She rubbed her tired eyes. "I haven't slept for two days. I meant Mary." She continued. "After my mother died from breast cancer, I felt so alone. I had no one to talk to on the phone for hours about nothing. No one to go shopping with. No one to cry over guy problems with." Tears filled Noelle's blue eyes. "I miss my mom so much. I couldn't bear the idea of Mary going through the same thing."

"She won't. I promise you; we'll both be seeing her very soon."

Whitaker stirred in his seat and let out a weak cough. Then a second one. Then silence.

Noelle went over to him and checked his pulse. She lifted her fingers from his carotid artery then pressed down again. Twenty seconds passed. Noelle looked up at Mark and slowly shook her head.

Despite everything Whitaker had done, Mark felt it was his duty to contact the first officer's next-of-kin if they made it back. As was tradition in the military, regardless of their true feelings about the person, the last ones to be with a fallen serviceman would recount favorable memories of them when visiting loved ones to deliver the dreadful news. The rationale behind this custom was to give those left behind some semblance of closure and peace.

"I'm going to contact Whitaker's family when we get back. Let them know how he…how he was…hell, I don't know. I'll make up something. Do you know what his first name was?"

Noelle looked down at the dried blood on her hands and shrugged. "I never heard anyone call him anything other than Whitaker." She rubbed her hands on her pant legs, trying to erase the stains. "Check his satchel. Is there a name tag on it? Hopefully, there's an address."

Mark retrieved the satchel. Blood dotted the fine leather. "No tag. Maybe there's something inside that will help." He unlatched the flap and dumped the contents onto a seat. Four large bricks of cocaine wrapped in tin foil fell out in a cloud of white dust. Nothing else was in the bag.

Noelle's mouth dropped open.

Mark shook his head. "Whitaker, you friggin' idiot."

"No wonder he never let that satchel leave his side."

"Noelle, we have a big problem," Mark warned.

She looked at him with the innocence of someone who still believed that 'right' always wins out in the end. "We don't have a problem, Whitaker has a problem. I mean had a problem."

Mark looked her in the eyes. "If this stuff is found in our lifeboat, you and I will be suspected of being drug mules."

"But those aren't ours. We didn't have anything to do with them."

"You're not hearing me. Think about it. We booked last-minute tickets on the ship rather than flying back home. By coincidence or fate, we three were the only survivors from the ship. Whitaker then had an 'accident' and died. Conveniently for us, there are no witnesses. Lo and behold, there just happens to be four bricks of cocaine probably worth a million dollars in our lifeboat that we claim we've never seen before. How are we going to explain all that?"

"This nightmare just keeps getting worse." Noelle dropped her face into her hands.

"I'm sure as hell not going to bet my freedom that the DEA is in an understanding mood when we tell them we have no idea how cocaine ended up on the same lifeboat as we did. I'm positive my name is still in their database after that stupid, stupid mistake I made years ago."

Noelle instantly recalled how close Mark had come to life in prison before evidence surfaced proving his poorly chosen "friend" was the guilty party, fully exonerating him. "Oh God, I can't believe this is happening. If we get rescued, instead of going home we could be put in jail." By then she was sobbing.

"Okay, okay, calm down. I've got a plan. We are tossing this shit in the ocean right now. We will never, ever speak about this to anyone. Understood?"

"Understood," Noelle said as her sobbing subsided.
"Help me dump it."

Mark opened the door. They each grabbed two bricks and tossed them in the ocean. Mark retrieved the satchel and threw it overboard as well. Mark and Noelle slumped down into their seats, relieved to have defused that bomb.

Something suddenly occurred to Mark. He turned to Noelle. "We have to rinse off our hands. There can't be any trace of coke on us."

"Good idea," she responded.

Mark looked out the door for signs of the sharks. Not seeing any, he assumed they were safe to venture outside. They went out and knelt down on the back step of the boat, swishing their hands back and forth in the water, trying to cleanse them.

Noelle was grateful for the opportunity to finally rinse Whitaker's blood from her hands.

The predators lurking nearby were grateful as well. The swishing noise sounded like a dinner bell to the ravenous sharks. They turned and bolted directly toward the sound at full speed.

Noelle inspected her hands. A few red stains remained after the saltwater rinse. She dunked her hands back into the ocean and swished them even more vigorously.

The sharks arced upward toward the surface, beginning their attack.

Determined to wash away all reminders of Whitaker's untimely death, she rubbed her hands together under the water. If only it was that easy to wash away the memories of the gruesome event as well. When satisfied her hands were free of any blood, she stood up.

Ever the gentleman, Mark opened the door, stepped back, and let Noelle enter first.

The two leisurely stepped back inside and locked the door—never realizing they came within two seconds of being torn to pieces.

Years later, when the foil deteriorated enough to let seawater seep into the bricks of cocaine, the sea life in that part of the Atlantic were going to have one hell of a party.

CHAPTER 13

THE SKY BEGAN TO DARKEN. Thunder rumbled in the distance. Wind-tossed waves and heavy rain returned. The backside of the eye wall bared down on the tiny lifeboat, ready to swallow it up back into the raging hurricane.

Mark perked up in his seat. "Did you hear that?"

"Hear what?"

Mark opened the emergency escape hatch in the roof and poked his head up. He shielded his eyes from the rain and scanned the horizon. Nothing but ocean and angry clouds surrounded them. Mark reached down and shut off the engine. He closed his eyes and concentrated on the sounds in the air. The chirping of seagulls braving the storm was all he heard.

Mark jumped down from the helm and grabbed the flare gun, along with two flares. He flung the door open and scanned the water for fins before venturing out on the back step. Mark loaded a flare and shot it skyward. Silently, he waited in the rain, listening.

Nothing.

After a minute, he fired off another one. He yelled back inside, "Bring me all the flares!"

Noelle scooped up the remaining signal flares and brought them to him. "What is it, Mark? What did you hear?"

He put his finger to his lips. "Listen."

Standing on the back step, the two held each other

tightly and listened for any sounds of imminent rescue.

Impatiently, Mark fired off another flare. Then two more. Before Noelle could stop him, he fired the final flare. They strained to hear any unusual sounds. Seagulls were all they heard.

Dejected, Noelle walked back inside and slumped down in her seat.

Mark soon followed. "Dammit. I could have sworn I heard something." He looked over at Noelle. "Happen to have any extra flares in your purse?"

Soaking wet, Noelle wasn't the least bit amused at Mark's inopportune attempt at humor. "My purse went down with the ship."

"Figures. Just our luck."

Noelle tipped her head back against the headrest, closed her eyes, and let out a long sigh. Suddenly, she sat up straight. "Mark, did you hear that?"

"Very funny. I'm in no mood."

"I'm serious." She jumped up and bounded out onto the back step. A distinctive rapid-fire thumping sound gradually got louder. Noelle searched the sky for the source. Suddenly, an orange-and-white Coast Guard MH-65D Dolphin helicopter, coming from behind her, roared past, mere feet above the lifeboat. The rotor wash rocked the tiny boat side to side, almost dumping Noelle into the ocean to become a light snack for the sharks.

Mark sprang out of the boat just in time to see the helicopter fly off, seemingly oblivious to their presence. "Back here, dammit! Look back!" he yelled.

The two jumped up and down, flailing their arms and screaming. Their only hope of being rescued before the hurricane enveloped them again flew away.

Tears mixed with raindrops streamed down Noelle's face as she shouted, "No! Come back! No…"

Mark wrapped his strong arms around Noelle as she sobbed.

Suddenly, the helicopter banked sharply left and came around in a long swooping turn until it was pointed directly at them. Its nose tipped up as the craft slowed to a crawl, gaining altitude until it hovered directly over the lifeboat. The stinging rain, wind, and sea spray whipped up by the rotors forced Mark and Noelle to retreat into the boat. Within moments, a Coast Guard rescue swimmer, clipped to a cable, lowered down into view.

CHAPTER 14

WHITAKER'S LIFELESS BODY LAY AT their feet on the floor. Mark and Noelle stared silently ahead, strapped in the rear bench seat of the Dolphin helicopter.

Mark turned to Noelle and lifted up the ear cup on her headset. He leaned in close. "I'm not buying a boat."

Those were the last words ever spoken on that topic.

Thirty minutes later, the aircraft swung around and matched its speed with the Coast Guard cutter *Hamilton*. It inched forward from fifty feet astern the ship until the tips of the rotors were within feet of the steel midsection. The landing pad convulsed up and down under the helicopter as the cutter crashed through the waves. Just as the pilot was about to land, spray tossed up in the air from a wave blanketed the windshield.

The copilot screamed, "Abort! Abort!"

The pilot yanked up on the collective. The helicopter shot up and backward to escape the dangerous situation. He moved safely away from the *Hamilton* to calm his nerves and reset for another try.

A warning tone sounded in the pilot's headset. Looking down, he saw a red LOW FUEL warning light flashing on the instrument panel. Thousands of miles out to sea with time running out, the pilot ignored it and concentrated on getting the helicopter and its passengers aboard the ship in one piece. On the second attempt, he hovered over the pad, trying to time the undulating waves. The pilot reduced power and committed to landing just as the pad unexpectedly rose up and rolled to the right. The MH-65D slammed down hard on the left side of the aft deck—two feet from the edge. The shaken pilot quickly put the blades in zero pitch to keep the helicopter from inadvertently getting airborne again.

Crewmen wearing colored vests and goggles rushed up to the craft and chocked the wheels. Still recovering from the lingering effects of shock brought on by the harrowing last few days, Mark and Noelle sat motionless, unsure what to do. The crewmen reached up, unbuckled their seat belts, and helped the couple down onto the deck.

A medic yelled over the roar of the engines, "Sir! Ma'am! Follow me! I'm taking you to sick bay!"

They hunched down and strode quickly across the helipad until they were past the reach of the guillotine-like rotors.

Entering the sick bay, Mark and Noelle were met by a team of medical personnel.

A tall, thin man with tufts of gray hair dotting his temples stepped forward. "Welcome aboard, folks. I'm Dr. Sullivan. Everything's going to be okay. You're safe now." The physician motioned to the exam table. "Please take a seat so I can have a look at you."

After trying to hold it together day after day while facing imminent death, the emotional dam finally let loose. Noelle broke down crying, covering her face with her hands.

Mark rushed to her side. "It's okay, Noelle. We're safe. It's over." He wrapped his arms around his ex-wife and held her trembling body.

The medical team understood. The doctor handed her a box of tissues, backed away, and let them take the first step toward emotional healing.

After a few minutes Noelle calmed down. Dr. Sullivan motioned for them to sit on the exam table. He turned to Noelle and pointed to the cast on her right arm. "What have we got here? When did this happen?"

Dabbing the last of the tears from her eyes, she said, "What? Oh, that. My arm is fine. It's been a rough week, Doc. If you don't mind, I'd rather not go into it right now."

"Of course, I understand," he responded, not wanting to upset Noelle. Besides, intel sources had already briefed him on everything his patients had been through. The doctor did a quick check of their vitals, poked and prodded, then scribbled some notes on a chart. "To be honest, you both seem to be in fairly good shape. A little dehydrated maybe, but I can't find anything obviously wrong. Do you have any pain or discomfort?"

Mark and Noelle looked at each other, shrugged, then said simultaneously, "No."

"Well then, why don't we get you two to the showers and into a fresh set of clothes."

The medical personnel in the room were discretely pinching their noses and nodding. A medic gestured toward the door. He escorted them out of the exam room and down the narrow passageway.

As Mark and Noelle approached the head, they saw a handler and a drug-sniffing German shepherd headed their way. Before the dog could get a whiff of them, the two popped into the room and closed the door behind them.

An hour later, Mark and Noelle emerged smelling like new. Icons of fashion they weren't. The best option the supply chief could come up with on short notice was ill-fitting dark blue operational dress uniforms and black combat boots.

Noelle had cut off the right shirt sleeve at the elbow to accommodate her cast. Considering she had worked as a fashion model in Paris after high school, Noelle was surprisingly lighthearted about her current outfit. "What do you think, Mark?" She twirled around for him. "I think I'll start a new collection. I'll call it *Baggy, Bland, and Blue.*"

"I'm sure the fashion world will fall all over themselves raving about it."

Noelle strutted down the passageway doing the model walk.

Mark was thankful to see his ex-wife smiling again.

They were brought to the spacious, spotless mess hall. The room had an overpowering smell of clean. A fresh, steaming buffet lay before them.

Dr. Sullivan was waiting for them. "Please, eat whatever you'd like, but take it easy at first. Let your stomachs get used to real food again." He tried a little bit of levity. "Of course, we have some MREs on board if you'd prefer."

"MREs?" Noelle questioned.

Mark waved off the question. "No, this will be just fine. Thanks, Doc."

"Do me a favor. When you two get back home, I'd like you to go see your regular physician and get a complete checkup." He paused for a second, not sure how to put his next piece of medical advice. "Sometimes, people underestimate the emotional damage that going through frightening events can do to them. The medical profession uses the acronym PTSD to label it." After two tours in Afghanistan treating severe battle wounds, Sullivan spoke from experience. The doctor discretely handed Mark a card. "I've written down the name and number of a colleague of mine. She is very experienced helping people who've gone through trauma. I think you would benefit greatly from speaking with her."

Mark looked warily at the card. "You mean a shrink?"

"Yes, something like that."

He thrust the card back at the doctor. "We're fine."

The doctor nodded reluctantly and took the card. "As you wish." He looked over at Noelle and shrugged in resignation. "Once you guys have finished eating, the captain would like to see you. But please, take your time."

Noelle went over to the doctor and gave him a big hug.

"Thank you for rescuing us."

Although not part of the helicopter crew, he knew what she meant. "You're welcome. Now, eat."

She tucked the card the doctor had slipped her into her back pocket.

CHAPTER 15

"COME IN, COME IN. WELCOME aboard the *Hamilton*. I'm Art Mancuso, the skipper." He was dressed in a crisply pressed white uniform and ball cap. If the Coast Guard hadn't recognized it already, Mancuso's rugged good looks and welcoming smile made him a perfect specimen for recruiting commercials.

Mark and Noelle accepted the invitation onto the bridge of the 418-foot Legend-class cutter. It bristled with modern communications, navigation, and surveillance equipment. The *Hamilton* was more than capable of protecting itself from anyone foolish enough to threaten it. The unblinking eye of a radar-controlled Phalanx close-in weapon system sat ready to spit out 4500 armor-piercing rounds per minute at any aggressor. Four M2 .50-caliber machine guns were strategically located around the ship also.

Noelle vigorously shook the captain's hand. "Thank you so much for saving our lives."

"Just doing my job, ma'am. Sorry we couldn't get to you any sooner but, you know, the hurricane and all."

"Any sooner?" Mark questioned.

"We picked up your distress signal from the COSPAS-SARSAT satellite network the moment your lifeboat hit the ocean. Its emergency beacon is water activated. I sent up two ScanEagle drones to search for you, but we lost both of them. I couldn't risk endangering my ship by entering the hurricane, so we had no choice but wait for it to move north to eventually come get you." Mancuso beamed as he pointed to his navigator. "That was until this sharp sailor over here noticed something strange. During a routine check he noticed that your signal appeared to correlate exactly with the position of the eye. I launched the helicopter before the rescue window closed up, and here you are." His pride in his crew was evident. "Now we're trying to locate the *Lynda Ray*."

Mark looked down and shook his head. "You won't find it. I watched it go down. There are no survivors."

Mancuso pursed his lips and nodded. "Sorry. I'm sure that wasn't an easy thing to witness."

"Will the bodies be recovered and returned to their families?" Mark asked hopefully.

Mancuso dodged his question. "Trust me, the Coast Guard will start an all-out search for the vessel as soon as the weather calms down. We will convene an investigation board immediately after finishing the search to determine what happened."

"And the crew?" Mark asked again.

Mancuso paused, unsure how to phrase his answer to Mark's question. "We'll do our best sir, but the water in this part of the ocean is fifteen thousand feet deep. Because of the extreme pressure at that depth, most likely there won't be anything left to recover."

Mark silently nodded, knowing the captain was right.

"Why don't we get you two home. Where do you want to go?"

"New York City. Our daughter is waiting for us," Noelle said. Then she asked, "Any chance I could call her and let her know we're okay?"

"Of course." He turned to the communications officer on the bridge. "Commo, set up the call." The captain turned back to Mark. "We've got more searches to conduct, so I'll get you close and then one of the helicopters will fly you the rest of the way. Any place in particular you want to be dropped off?"

Mark thought for a moment then looked up at the captain. "JFK airport."

"Why JFK?"

"Let's just call it closure."

CHAPTER 16

MARY SMITH WAITED ANXIOUSLY INSIDE the general aviation terminal building at John F. Kennedy International Airport, holding a handmade cardboard sign. Standing next to her were the only family she had. April Parker, holding her own sign, and Mary's aunt and uncle nervously searched the sky to the east for the helicopter's arrival.

Noelle's best friend, Charlotte, burst through the door. "Danged New York traffic. Did I miss it? Are they here yet?" Her big hair, Southern drawl, and outsize personality were more than matched by her big heart. She walked up to Mary and smothered her in a bear hug. "Oh, darlin', it's so good to see you again. How you doing? You holdin' up okay?"

Her hug felt more like a Southern version of a straitjacket than a greeting. Mary looked up. "I'm better now that I know they're safe. I can't wait for them to get here."

Charlotte guided Mary back by the shoulders until at arm's length then pointed toward Mary's relatives. "Who is this handsome bunch?"

Noelle's brother extended his hand. "Hi, Charlotte. I'm Tommy Parker, and this is my wife, Stephanie." His resemblance to his sister was obvious, even down to his red hair—curly in his case.

Charlotte ignored his hand and engulfed both of them in a hug. She released the stunned couple and looked over at April. "And you must be April. Your aunt has told me all about you. It's so nice to finally meet you. Thanks for lookin' after Mary these last few days."

April smiled and put her arm around Mary's shoulder. "Hey, that's what big cousins are for. I'm glad I could be there for her. Besides, someone has to help her with her awful taste in boys."

Charlotte's protective side and Georgia roots came out. "Girls, you need someone to knock some sense into some young dumb yokel, you just give ol' Auntie Charlotte a call. I'll straighten 'em right out."

Mary and April had no doubt she was serious.

"I'm not so sure there are any *yokels* in New York City," Mary said.

"Honey, as long as we're talking about males, there's always bound to be a few yokels."

Everyone but Tommy chuckled at the Southern truism.

"Charlotte, Mary says you were on the plane, too," April remarked.

"Yep, hell of a ride, that one. Enough that I've decided to hang up my flight attendant wings and find a real job." She made a big display of rubbing a fake neck injury. "Mary, you tell that dad of yours to land a little softer next time."

"Be nice, Auntie Charlotte." Mary's face contorted as she drew in a breath and hesitantly added, "You know they're getting back together, right?"

Charlotte crossed her beefy arms across her chest. "Yep."

"I know how you feel about him, but please give my dad a chance. I've decided I'm going to put the past behind me, and I'd really appreciate it if you did, too. We have a chance to be a family again. I don't want anything to mess that up."

"Okay. I'll do it for you, darlin'."

"They're here!" April shrieked, as she ran to the window.

The Coast Guard helicopter approached low over the field toward the general aviation ramp on the west end of the airport, far away from the aluminum traffic jam at the passenger terminals.

Noelle saw the welcoming committee in the window first. From her seat in the helicopter, she waved her right arm at them. Her cast was covered in signatures from the crew of the *Hamilton*.

The craft touched down on the ramp and put its rotors in zero pitch.

Mark and Noelle couldn't unbuckle and hop out fast enough

Mary raced across the ramp and into the arms of her parents. Tears gushed down everyone's faces as they embraced for a full three minutes. Mary examined Noelle's cast and asked a dozen clinical questions about the break. The screaming engines and whirlwind created by the helicopter went unnoticed as it lifted off and flew back out to sea. Arm in arm, the three entered the building.

"Charlotte! I didn't know you were going to be here." Noelle rushed up to her friend and melted into a hug.

Mark walked up to her and nodded hesitantly. "Charlotte."

"Mark" was Charlotte's frosty response.

"Come here, Sis." Tommy and Stephanie joined in the hug-fest. Tommy reached out and enthusiastically shook Mark's hand. "Welcome back. Thanks for getting my little sister back in one piece." He looked at their outfits and tilted his head. "They make you guys join the Navy in order to get a ride back?"

"It's Coast Guard, actually." Interservice rivalry quickly reared up its competitive head. "I'd rather swim home than be rescued by a bunch of Navy squids."

Sibling rivalry also poked up its head. "So, Mark, how did you survive all that time trapped in a tiny lifeboat alone with her?" No matter how old they got, brothers seemed to never outgrow the need to tease their sisters.

"Tommy!" Noelle smacked her older brother across the arm with her cast.

Mark winked at his ex-wife. "It wasn't that bad. Fortunately, I have the patience of a saint, so I was able to put up with her."

He broke away from the group as they fired off question after question at Noelle about the events of the last week. Mark wandered over to the window and surveyed the beehive of aerial activity typical of a large airport. What looked like chaos felt very comfortable to him after forty-five years as a pilot. Despite all the insanity that plagued the airlines, the missed Christmases, and the permanent scar 9/11 had left on the industry, he felt an unexpected pang in his heart at the thought of no longer being part of it. Flying was the only job he'd ever had as an adult. It was a childhood dream come true. There was no better feeling for Mark than escaping the demands of life by soaring above the clouds, defying gravity. Realizing this important chapter in his life was over forever, he shielded his face from view and dabbed at his eyes. A minute later, Mark turned around and quietly said, "It's time to go."

As they approached the front door, Mark saw a large cluster of reporters and cameramen eagerly waiting on the sidewalk outside the building. He looked around, searching for another exit.

Noelle hooked her arm through Mark's and steered him back toward the door. "Come on, let's go. Time to meet your adoring public. Remember, smile and try to appear humble. People want to see Sully, not Captain Ahab."

Tommy took Mark and Noelle aside as they approached the front door. "Guys, I need to warn you about something. There won't be any cheering crowds out there. Things have changed in the last week."

When Mark stepped outside, the mob of reporters surrounded him like hungry cannibals. Microphones were thrust in his face from every direction. Bright lights mounted on top of TV cameras blinded him. Rabid reporters screamed questions from every direction.

"Captain Smith, is it true your plane ran out of gas?

How could you let that happen?"

"I understand you are a recovering alcoholic. Did you have anything to drink before or during the flight?"

Stunned and disoriented, Mark shielded his eyes from the glare and looked around for Noelle. She was behind him, straining to reach out for his hand.

Suddenly, Noelle was knocked to the ground by the mob. Her eyes pleaded for Mark to rescue her.

He screamed at the crowd to step aside so they wouldn't trample Noelle, but the reporters only pressed in tighter. Mark launched a right cross into the jaw of the nearest reporter between himself and Noelle. The punch sent the man tumbling to the sidewalk. Cameras clicked and whirred. The crowd finally opened up enough for him to get through. Mark scooped up Noelle and plowed through the mob toward Tommy's car. Once everyone was safely inside, Tommy nudged the car forward. The gang of reporters that encircled the car parted without injury, although none of its passengers would have shed a tear if a few had ended up with some bumps and bruises.

CHAPTER 17

Mary made her parents close their eyes before she opened the apartment door. She led them by the hand into the middle of the room, then said, "Welcome home, Mom and Dad."

They opened their eyes with great anticipation. Although it was the same cramped two-bedroom walk-up in Queens, after what they'd been through the past week it was a sight for sore eyes. Noelle hugged Mary then reached out and drew April into the fold as well. "You did a beautiful job with the decorations. Thank you, girls."

Mark walked over and awkwardly added his arms around the group embrace.

"Why don't we leave these three alone so they can get settled in and find some descent clothes!" Tommy said as he led his family to the door. "Call us if you need anything. Seriously." Tommy gave Noelle one last hug. "Love ya, Sis."

Charlotte nearly squeezed the air out of Noelle with her goodbye hug. "I'll call you tomorrow, honey." She walked hesitantly over to Mark. Charlotte was uncharacteristically tongue-tied. "Uh, Mark…I owe you…I just wanted to say…Hell, what I'm tryin' to say is thanks for not letting me die back there in the Azores." She opened her arms wide and wrapped Mark in a hug. Quietly enough so Noelle couldn't hear, she added, "If you break Noelle's heart again, I will break both your legs." Charlotte walked out and closed the door behind her.

"You're moving in, right Dad?" The excitement in

Mary's voice confirmed the irreplaceable role fathers—even less-than-perfect ones—have in a daughter's life. She looked expectantly at Noelle. "Mom?"

"Yes, sweetie, your dad is moving in with us."

"Cool!" Mary bounded away to her bedroom, already planning in her mind how the furniture in the apartment needed to be rearranged to accommodate a third person. Once she had that figured out, dress options and decoration colors for her parents wedding would be next on her list.

The sound of jangling keys outside the apartment was quickly followed by the door swinging open. Ralph Simpson, the building superintendent, poked his bald head in. Simpson looked the part: 250 pounds, hairy back, and clad in a dull white wife-beater T-shirt.

Feigning surprise, he said, "Hey, Ms. Parker, I didn't know you were back. I thought I heard some commotion up here. Here's your newspaper." He waved that day's edition, hoping to divert attention from his snooping. "Boy, that was some week you just had. Mary told me all about it."

"Hello, Mr. Simpson." Noelle scolded him. "Didn't we talk about you calling first before coming by?"

Simpson somehow took that comment as an invitation to come in. "Sorry, Ms. Parker, I don't mean to intrude. I like to know everything that's going on in my building. Just looking out for my two best tenants; that's all."

Noelle did appreciate knowing Simpson kept an eye out for her and Mary—this was New York City, after all. She gently chided him. "Okay, but don't let it happen again."

Mark came out from the kitchen, munching on potato chips. Simpson looked him up and down. "Who's this character, Ms. Parker?"

Noelle put her arm around Mark. "Mr. Simpson, this is Mark Smith. He's my…we were…"

"I'm Noelle's ex-husband." Mark wiped the grease off on his pant leg and reached out to shake Simpson's hand.

He reluctantly accepted Mark's greeting, clamping down hard to send him a message. "Ex, huh? You're not going to be any trouble, are you?"

Noelle stepped between them. "Okay, you two, be nice." They released their grasps.

"Mark is moving in with us. We're getting remarried."

Simpson cocked his head and cast a suspicious eye toward Noelle. "Is that right?"

She pointed to the faded newspaper article stuck to the refrigerator door. "I figured it was the least I could do for him since Mark saved my life with his flying," Noelle joked.

Simpson looked at the picture, over to Mark, then back to the newspaper article. "You're *that* Mark Smith?"

He just shrugged.

Simpson's hostile demeanor did a 180. "Why hell, I'd be honored to have you move into my building. That was some piece of flying you did there, Smith. I don't care what those friggin' idiots in the press are saying today."

Confused, Noelle and Mark looked at each other.

Simpson tried to nonchalantly tuck the newspaper under his arm.

Noelle furrowed her brow then reached out to Simpson. "May I have my paper?"

Simpson handed it over. She opened it to the front page. The love affair headline writers have with alliteration was on full display. In bold black letters, the headline read, "Avoidable Agony in the Azores" A picture of the Alpha Airlines badly mangled Tech-Liner, with its wing tip embedded in the hangar door, followed the headline.

CHAPTER 18

Next Day

NOELLE HOVERED BEHIND MARK, HER hands resting on his wide shoulders. "Go ahead, push it," she urged.

Mark looked up and saw her encouraging smile. He turned back to the laptop screen and tapped the enter key, followed by a long sigh. "Well, that's it. We're both officially retired from Alpha Airlines."

Noelle pantomimed opening a book and announced, "Chapter one in the steamy romance novel *A Flame Rekindled* begins." She pulled out Mark's chair and sat in his lap. Snuggled up against him, she continued "reading" the imaginary book. "Mark and Noelle started their new life together with the wedding of the century. Royalty from around the world clamored to get invited to—"

Mark put his hands under Noelle's and closed the "book." "We should be fine with my pension from Alpha, but sorry, a royal wedding is not within our budget."

Noelle pouted. "Can't I just invite the queen?"

Mark chuckled and shook his head side to side.

"Okay, but you're not cheaping out again like last time with a justice of the peace and one night in Atlantic City. I'm not letting you off the hook that easily."

"I'll make a deal with you. You and Mary can plan something a little better than that—on one condition."

Noelle looked at Mark suspiciously. "What?"

"Leave me out of it."

"Deal." Noelle quickly grabbed Mark's hand and shook it to make it official. She put a hand to her mouth and yelled toward Mary's bedroom, "Mary, your dad said we can plan the wedding of the century!"

Mark chuckled. Hoping to change the subject before things got out of hand, he said, "Before the two of you bankrupt me with this wedding, I need your help moving out of my place. Let's do it this afternoon."

"Gladly. I'm surprised you haven't come down with bubonic plague after living in that dump."

"It's not *that* bad. Besides, lots of airline crew live in crash pads."

In the graveyard humor typical among airmen, he was referring to the name given to apartments shared by a large number of itinerant pilots. A common arrangement in the airline industry, total strangers from any number of airlines would rent out a slot (not a specific room, or even a bed) in a crash pad from one enterprising crewmember who leased the apartment. After flying in to their base the night before an early morning trip, they would sleep in whatever bunk bed was open. Because everyone worked different schedules, up to a dozen people could share the same apartment and rarely see each other. Such was the glamourous life of an airline pilot.

Mark continued, "I don't commute here to my base in New York like the rest of my roommates, but I figured why waste money on a place of my own when I'm gone two to three weeks a month flying?" He paused for a moment. His expression saddened. "I wonder how long it's going to take until I stop talking about flying for the airlines in the present tense."

◆

Mark, Noelle, and Mary pulled up to the curb in front of a brownstone with a faded red door. Mark's crash pad was located in the Kew Gardens neighborhood in the borough of Queens. The rundown neighborhood borrowed its name from the lush botanical gardens in London. But no one would ever get the two places confused with each other. Located between LaGuardia and JFK airports, Kew Gardens was a haven for crash pads. Airline employees jokingly refer to the neighborhood as Crew Gardens.

Mark unlocked the door and steered Noelle and Mary in. The two locked arms and cautiously stepped into the room. An unpleasant odor permeated the air. The sparse apartment was furnished with a ratty old couch that looked like it came from a nearby garage sale—after failing to sell. A small kitchen table with two chairs occupied most of the floor space in the tiny kitchen. A sign taped to the refrigerator door read, "Clean up after yourself. Your mommy doesn't live here!" The movie *Top Gun* looped continuously on the TV.

Andy Wilson, official lessee of the apartment, walked out of the bathroom clad in sweatpants and a T-shirt. He was vigorously brushing his teeth and scrolling through his phone screen. Andy looked up. "Mark! How's it going, man. Good to see you." The handsome, blond-haired thirty-year-old Jet Blue copilot ducked back into the bathroom, spit out the toothpaste, and emerged wiping his mouth with the back of his hand. "That was one hell of a landing you made there in the Azores. Glad to see you're still in one piece." It didn't take long for Andy to notice Mark's daughter. He wiped his hand on his pant leg and extended it. "You must be Mary. Hi, I'm Andy."

Mary declined to accept his hand. She looked confused. "Yes, yes I am. How do you know my name?"

"Your dad talks about you all the time. Duke med school, right?" He turned on the charm. "I have to say, you're even more beautiful than the picture your dad showed me on his phone."

Knowing a flirtatious pilot when she heard one, Noelle's

protective instincts kicked in. She glared at Andy and inserted herself between the two. Then she asked, "So, this is *your* crash pad?"

Andy was no fool when it came to getting on the good side of a girl's mother. "Yes, this is my place. You must be Mary's mother. It's obvious where she gets her stunning good looks from."

Noelle rolled her eyes.

Mary had the opposite reaction.

Mark jumped in. "Okay, Romeo, now that we've all met each other, I came by to tell you I'm moving out."

The agreement to rent a slot in a crash pad is never more lasting or formal than a handshake. Crewmembers regularly rotate in and out, and there is always someone else waiting to take an empty spot.

"That's cool. Are you getting your own place?" Andy asked.

"I'm moving back in with my family. Noelle and I are getting remarried. I officially retired today, so we're here to get my stuff."

"Hey, man, great news. I'm glad for you. Got any big plans for your retirement after you get hitched?"

Mark shrugged. "Hell if I know. But I'll tell you this, I won't be doing anything that involves boats."

Andy laughed. "I don't blame you. You'll figure something out." He shook Mark's hand and gave him a big bro hug. "We sure are going to miss your smiling face around here," he said facetiously.

"Yeah, I'm sure you will," Mark snickered.

Andy suddenly remembered something. "Wait! Before you clear out your stuff, I've got something for you." He disappeared into a bedroom then emerged a few seconds later holding an envelope. "Your roommates and I wanted to do something to cheer you up after the rough week you've had. We chipped in and got you a little something." He opened the envelope, pulled out a fake certificate, and read it aloud. "To Capt. Mark Smith. In recognition for one of the worst landings in the history of aviation, your prize is an all-expenses-paid cruise on the next rowboat leaving for the Azores." Andy beamed with pride at his idea of a practical joke. He handed the certificate to Mark.

"All right, smart ass, I'll make you do the rowing if you're not careful." Mark chided Andy but inside he was grateful for the gesture. "Why don't you make yourself useful and help us load my stuff in the car?"

Andy snapped to attention and saluted. "Yes, sir, Captain Smith, sir."

It only took fifteen minutes to load all of Mark's worldly possessions. Mary was last to leave the crash pad. Andy gladly got the door for her. Before walking out she turned to Andy with a puzzled expression. "No offense to your lovely establishment, but why would my dad live in a dump like this?"

Andy stuck his head out of the door and looked down the hallway to make sure Mark was out of earshot. "I hope I'm not speaking out of school here, but it's all he can afford."

"All he can afford? He's a senior airline captain."

"Between paying New York's sky-high taxes, alimony to your mom, and, well…you know…you, he told me by the end of the month he is flat broke."

"What do you mean, *me*?"

"All he ever talks about is how proud he is that his daughter is going to be a doctor. Top of her class at Duke med school and all that. Your dad chose to live in this *dump* so he could pay your way through medical school and let you graduate without a dime of student debt. I thought you knew."

CHAPTER 19

THE MEDIA LAID IN WAIT in front of Noelle's apartment building. Local TV station vans topped with satellite dishes and telescoping antennas were double-parked along the street. Reporters and cameramen milled around on the sidewalk, waiting to ambush their prey. Curious onlookers from the neighborhood milled around the area.

A familiar thumping sound came from the sky. Overhead, a Bell 407 helicopter, owned by Channel Two, slowly circled the chaotic scene. A high-definition, gyro-stabilized camera hung under the chin of the helicopter. Regardless of where the craft was in the sky, the camera stayed pointed directly at the front door of the building. With its incredible zoom capability, the camera could spot differences between identical twins.

Mark spotted the media circus as he rounded the corner. He sped up, hoping to get past without being noticed. A sharp-eyed reporter leaning against a van saw them headed his way. Risking life and limb for his profession, he jumped out in front of Mark's car. For a second, he considered stomping on the gas pedal. Not wanting to pay to fix the dent the reporter would make, Mark screeched to a stop instead. The mob of reporters surrounded his car.

Mark and his family got out and tried to make their way through the thicket of microphones and cameras thrust in their faces, trying to reach the apartment building front door. It was as if the reporters were making a goal-line stand to win a football game. They blocked every attempt Mark made to get through them. He looked around for a way out of the scrum when suddenly the mob parted. Ralph Simpson, the building super, was throwing elbows and lowering his shoulder into the reporters.

"Follow me!" he yelled. Simpson took on the role of lead blocker, clearing a path to the door. Although badly shaken, they made it inside the foyer in one piece. "Sorry you had to go through that, Ms. Parker," Simpson said. "They showed up an hour ago. Don't worry, though; ain't none of them getting past this old Marine."

"Thanks, Mr. Simpson. You're always looking out for Mary and me. We really appreciate it."

Awkwardly, Mark was not included in the conversation.

Mark peered down on the mob of reporters from the apartment window then looked over at Noelle. She was busy consoling their daughter.

Simpson hovered nearby in case reinforcements were needed. He tried to reassure his tenants by saying, "Those jackals can camp out in front of my building until hell freezes over before I let them bother you again."

Mary spoke up with some well-meaning advice. "Dad, maybe if you go out and answer their questions, they will leave us alone."

Oh, the innocence of youth, Mark thought.

Like sharks that smelled blood, the reporters would never leave him or his family alone until they got what they wanted. Mark knew this. He looked back out the window then grudgingly announced, "I'll go talk to them. Might as well get this over with."

"Are you sure?" Noelle asked.

Mark just nodded.

"Then we are going with you."

"No, I won't allow you two to go through that again."

"Allow?" Noelle was not accustomed to having any man tell her what she was *allowed* to do. "If you're going out there, we're going out there. We are going to stand by your side to show them we support you. That's just what family does."

Mark sighed. "I don't suppose I can talk you out of it?" he asked, already knowing the answer.

Mary laughed out loud. "Dad, you *have* been gone for a long time." She couldn't help voicing her opinion. "Mom? Changing her mind? She doesn't have red hair for nothing," she teased.

Noelle shot Mary *the look*. "Hold on a minute, young lady. I seem to remember plenty of times when you stomped off and slammed your bedroom door, vowing never speak to me again because you didn't get *your* way."

As his ex-wife and daughter traded playful barbs, Mark couldn't help but crack a smile. He missed the normal ups and downs that all families go through. Even the bickering. Like Noelle said, that's just what family did.

Simpson stepped out of the front door of the building, closing it behind him. Reporters and cameramen rushed up the stairs. He raised his hand to stop their advance. "If any of you so much as set one foot on my stoop, I'll have you arrested for trespassing."

"Who the hell are you?" one of the reporters yelled.

"I'm Simpson, the building super. You got a problem with that, asshole?"

The reporter slinked away with his tail between his legs.

"Captain Smith has decided to answer some questions now. But let me set you clowns straight first. Out of respect for the privacy of his family, only he will be answering questions." Simpson enjoyed being the law in these parts.

Mark, Noelle, and Mary waited inside the foyer, safely beyond the reach of the reporters. Noelle cautioned Mark,

"Please control your temper this time. The reporters are just trying to do their jobs. I don't need to be bailing you out of jail tonight."

Mark's mind flashed back to his childhood and being led by the hand by his mother down to the police station. More than once she had to bail out his dad. Mark winced at the memory of his dad's temper. His volatile personality had gotten him fired from every job he ever had. By far, his worst memory was what his dad had done to his mom after she finally stood up for herself and threatened to leave him sitting in jail the next time he got arrested.

Despite inheriting a quick temper, Mark had never broken the vow he made to himself that night. He vowed to never touch his family in anger—and he never had.

Simpson pulled the door open. The three walked out on the stoop and into the blinding lights of the news cameras. The microphone-wielding reporters were made up of the usual cast of characters: blonde Barbie Doll clones who were sleeping with their bosses, distinguished-looking older men with perfect hair perched on top of empty skulls, and the pushy up-and-comers fighting to gain legitimacy by getting their first big scoop.

The reporters started off with the typical setup questions designed to lull their prey into thinking they were caring people only interested in getting the facts.

"Captain Smith, you've been through quite an ordeal. How are feeling?"

"Fine."

"Our condolences to the families of your copilots. Both the one that didn't make it and the one still in the hospital."

"Thank you."

"Are you glad to be home?"

"Yes."

"Weren't you terrified during your flight?"

"I wouldn't be much of a pilot if emergencies *terrified*

me."

Dispensing with the softball questions, the reporters asked the ones they had truly come to ask. After all, facts didn't get ratings. Manufactured conflict and gotcha questions got ratings. So many questions were shouted out by the reporters that they all mixed together.

A tall blonde wearing a red, full-length wool coat bullied her way into being heard above her competition. Waving a document, she yelled, "Captain Smith! Captain Smith! The transcript from the cockpit voice recorder was released by the NTSB this morning. Have you read it?"

"No."

"It shows in the transcript you weren't even in the cockpit when your plane went off course. How can that be?"

Mark wanted to head off this line of questioning before it got taken out of context. "I was out of the cockpit only because I was taking my required break. The FAA requires pilots on long international flights to take rest breaks in order to ward off fatigue."

She flipped the NTSB report to a page she had highlighted. "Captain, how is it you figured out that your plane was off course when your two copilots didn't even notice?"

Something about the look on the reporter's face set off alarm bells in Mark's brain. "It should all be in the transcript. I'm sure if you read it in its entirety, you'll find the answer to your question."

The noose tightened slightly. "I *have* read the entire report, Captain. It says once you returned to the cockpit you used your knowledge of celestial navigation to determine your plane was off course. Very clever of you, I must say. Your copilots were in the cockpit for three hours alone that night while you were taking your break. Yet during all that time they didn't realize the plane was headed out into the middle of the Atlantic Ocean? Do you have any explanation why that might be, Captain?"

Beads of perspiration formed on Mark's upper lip. "As

you can tell from my gray hair, I've been a pilot for a long time. When I first started flying, pilots were required to learn how to navigate by the stars in case of just such a situation. Unfortunately, that's not the case anymore. My copilots on that flight might be young, but they are professionals. They did the best they could with the training they had. I stand behind them 100 percent."

"Let's cut the crap, *Captain*. If you had been in the cockpit instead of sleeping, this accident never would have happened. You would have noticed your plane was drifting off course and done something about it right away. Those poor passengers on your plane wouldn't have spent hours thinking they were going to die."

Mark couldn't contain his anger anymore. "What the hell do you know about—"

Noelle squeezed his arm hard, digging in her nails. Mark bit his tongue and took a breath. "My crew and I did everything by the book. For you to stand here and imply we could have prevented the accident is Monday-morning quarterbacking at its worst."

She smirked. "So, you stand by your copilots? One hundred percent?" The noose synched up tighter.

"Absolutely."

The reporter thrust the transcript at Mark. "You might want to read what was going on in the cockpit while you were gone, Captain. I've highlighted the important parts for you."

Mark scanned the highlighted text. His face went ghost white.

"Allow me to tell the viewing public what the report says. One hundred terrified passengers came within inches of losing their lives that night because you were nowhere to be found, sound asleep in the bunk room. And do you know what those *professional* copilots of yours were doing? It's no wonder they didn't notice anything was wrong. One of them was reading a newspaper, then he took a nap himself. The other copilot played video games on his phone."

CHAPTER 20

IT DIDN'T TAKE LONG. WITHIN a week, four class-action lawsuits were filed in federal court based on the revelations from the cockpit voice recorder. Reporters constantly harassed Mark and Noelle with calls to their home phone, cell phones, even calling Mary's cell phone. Every phone number their family had was changed to stop the onslaught of calls.

The following week, Mark received a call from the national headquarters of the pilot's union. Jacob Shapiro, chief counsel, didn't mince words after introducing himself. "The shit has really hit the fan around here. That bombshell in the transcript has created a feeding frenzy. Every two-bit plaintiffs' lawyer in New York is trying to find a way to get in on this. Don't get me wrong. I'm in no way implying you were at fault, of course. You had no way of knowing what those boneheaded copilots of yours were doing. You weren't in the cockpit. The FAA regulations are very clear on that. Hell, you'd think you deserved a little gratitude after what you pulled off. It's just that the optics on this aren't very good."

"Are you saying I might get sued?"

"It's possible, yes. But it doesn't matter if you do."

"It matters to me," he retorted.

"They can sue you all they want. The union contract clearly states that Alpha Airlines will indemnify its pilots from any and all litigation stemming from operation of their aircraft. You're covered for up to one billion dollars.

If anyone *does* try to include you in any lawsuits, you will have the full resources and support of your union backing you up. My legal team and I will be with you every step of the way. Nothing to worry about."

"Easy for you to say. I expect to be notified immediately if you hear anything new."

"Absolutely, Captain."

Mark hung up and glared at the screen on his phone. He plopped down on the couch and clicked the TV remote. When the screen came on, some perennially cheerful talk show host was fawning all over Hollywood's latest hunk du jour.

Noelle and Mary walked in with an armload of packages after a day of shopping. Noelle dispensed with a greeting so she could share her finds with Mark. "Wait until you see what we bought."

If there was anything Mark enjoyed less than shopping with women, it was listening to them talk about what they bought during their shopping trips. He changed the channel.

"Mary found this periwinkle-colored knee-length dress for the rehearsal dinner."

Mary could hardly contain her excitement. "It's super cute. Wait until you see it." She pulled the dress out of the bag and held it up in front of herself. "What do you think, Dad? Do you like it?"

Mark shook his head. "Why do you need another one? Don't you already have enough dresses?"

The two females looked at each other and rolled their eyes. Noelle said what both of them were thinking. "Enough dresses? Why can't men think more like us? It would make life so much easier."

Mary pointed to a yellow-and-white-striped bag. "Show him the shoes."

Noelle pulled out two pairs of high heels. "I can't decide if I like the pink ones or the teal ones. Which one do you like, Mark?"

Mark threw the remote down on the couch. "If you two don't stop spending money like it grows on trees, there won't be a wedding!"

They stood there speechless as he pushed past the happy shoppers and stormed out.

Mary whined, "What's gotten into him? All you asked was which color he liked."

Noelle's motherly wisdom kicked in. "It's not the shoes, sweetie."

"What is it then? Dad's been such a grouch the last few days."

She sat her daughter down on the couch and tried to explain the workings of the male mind. "It's important for us to be supportive and patient with your dad. When men retire from a career they've worked at all their adult lives, they can feel lost at first. Like they're not needed or contributing to something worthwhile anymore. The transition can be hard. Not to mention he went through not one, but two, very traumatic experiences in the span of a week. That's difficult for anyone to deal with."

Mary's youth showed itself. "Well, so did you. And you're not a bear to live with."

She put her arm around her daughter and gently explained. "I know, sweetie, but it's different for me. I've got you to talk to. I've got Charlotte. Uncle Tommy. You guys have been so great. Dad is more of a loner. He doesn't really have anyone to talk to. Just us. We need to be as understanding as possible, okay?"

"Okay, I'll try." Mary gave her mom a hug. Pulling back, she said, "But I'm still not going to change my mind." She pointed at the footwear. "Definitely the teal. You gotta go with the teal shoes."

Noelle feigned being wounded. "*Really*? The teal? But I really *love* the pink ones."

CHAPTER 21

MARK STOMPED DOWN THE FRONT steps of the apartment building and onto the crowded sidewalk. He wandered aimlessly around Queens for hours in a foul mood with no particular destination in mind—other than getting away. The scene from the apartment replayed over and over in his mind. *What the hell is wrong with me? They just wanted to show me what they bought. Money doesn't grow on trees? How lame was that. Sounds like something my old man would have…"* Mark's head drooped. *"That's just great. Like father, like son."*

He walked up to a sidewalk newsstand, hoping to find a temporary diversion.

The owner asked, "Can I help you find anything?"

Mark scanned row after row of newspapers and magazines jammed into the racks. It seemed as if every one of them featured a picture of his angry face along with a damming headline. Even before the investigation into the accident had begun by the FAA, the press decided he was at fault for what happened. The public had been turned against Mark. Being tried in the court of public opinion was far harsher and swifter than having your day in a real courtroom. The fact that the media companies were making a fortune by spinning the prematurely negative narrative surely had nothing to do with their editorial decisions.

The man behind the counter narrowed his gaze. He pointed at Mark and said, "Hey, wait a minute, aren't you that pilot who…"

Mark dashed off before having to hear the same question from a total stranger for the hundredth time this week. He stopped at the corner of Sixty-Ninth and Exeter and pushed the button on the pole to signal the crosswalk light. The sounds of muted laughter and music floated through the air behind Mark. He turned around to see a neighborhood bar with the clever name of Jerry's spelled out in bright red neon. Mark stood there taking in the sounds of cheerfulness coming from the bar. A slight nostalgic grin formed on his face. Suddenly, thoughts of the pain of withdrawal from alcohol during rehab popped into his brain. He recalled how proud he had been to graduate from the program and be officially declared sober. Mark turned his back on the bar. He repeatedly stabbed at the crosswalk button as if the timing computer would all of a sudden have sympathy for his impatience and halt all traffic.

Of course, it didn't. Mark was forced to wait. The sounds coming from the bar were like a persistent drunk tapping you on the shoulder from behind, asking for a light. Mark turned back around and faced Jerry's bar. The noise acted like a siren's call. It was both repulsive and seductive at the same time. Mark pulled open the door and walked in.

He planted himself on a barstool in front of a long, well-worn bar then turned and looked around the dark, smoky room. Couples were huddled in booths, kissing and fondling each other. Drinking buddies toasted to whatever crossed their minds in order to justify another round. Music blared from the jukebox. Mark cringed at the noise coming from drunken patrons who tried to sing along.

The familiarity of it all triggered a suppressed craving in his brain. When Mark looked back, the bartender swept his arm behind himself and asked, "What'll you have, mister?" The mirrored back wall was filled with shelves containing bottles of every kind of liquor imaginable. The options were overwhelming—like his life at that moment. So many choices. So many problems that would temporarily disappear into the bottom of a shot glass. So much progress that would be thrown away for a sip of cheap whiskey. So much to lose that he'd recently regained. Mark came to his senses and decided to leave.

When Mark stood up, the bartender remarked, "Hey, you're that guy. Aren't you that pilot who…" He yelled over to his boss, "Hey, Jerry, you gotta see this! The pilot who fell asleep while his plane ran out of gas is standing right here in front of me!"

Something inside Mark snapped. He grabbed the bartender by the shirt and hauled him up against the bar. Whether it was the erroneous comment on what happened the night of the accident or Mark finally reaching his limit, he was livid. He screamed, "If you don't know the facts about what happened, keep your damned mouth shut! It wasn't my fault! I was on a required break!"

The end of a baseball bat contacted Mark's right cheek. Not hard enough to break any bones but enough to get the message across. Dazed, Mark released his grip and backed away.

The owner, Jerry, brandished a Louisville Slugger in Mark's direction. "Get the hell out of my place, and don't ever come back!"

Mark wisely heeded Jerry's "request" and fled the bar.

Numerous patrons had filmed the entire episode on their cell phones. Within ten minutes, video of the supposedly recovered alcoholic pilot getting in a bar fight was all over the internet.

CHAPTER 22

MARK SNUCK BACK INTO THE apartment later that night. He hoped to go unnoticed as he grabbed an ice pack for the knot on his cheek and slip quietly back out. That plan quickly went south.

Mary rushed out of her bedroom, holding her phone. "Mom! You're not going to believe this. Dad's on YouTube!" She looked over at Mark as he held a bag of ice against his cheek. "Dad? What in the world happened? You're all over the internet. Videos of you have gone viral on YouTube."

At his age, Mark wasn't exactly sure what that meant. "Is that a good thing or bad thing?" he genuinely asked.

"Are you kidding me? For some people in my generation, that's their life's goal." She scrunched up her face. "In your case, though…I'm going to go with it's a bad thing."

Noelle came out of her bedroom, spoiling for a fight. "Mark, I've been worried sick about you. Where the hell have you been?"

"Dad got in a bar fight! It's on YouTube," Mary blurted out.

Mark wished his daughter hadn't been quite so eager in responding to Noelle's question.

"What?" Anger flashed across Noelle's face. She crossed her arms and glowered at Mark. "You were in a bar?"

"Let me explain."

Noelle held up her hand like a stop sign. "I am not going through this again, Mark. The first time was bad enough."

You promised me you were never going to drink again."

"Noelle, you have to believe me. I didn't have a drink."

"Mark, stop! Do you think I'm a fool? You got in a fight—in a *bar!*"

Mark racked his brain, searching for a way to prove his innocence. "Look, I admit things got a little out of hand, but I swear I didn't have a drink. This loudmouth bartender started spouting off about how I was at fault, and..." He could tell from Noelle's face she wasn't buying any part of his explanation. Then it came to him. "Wait, I can prove it. Mary, play the video from the tube channel."

Mary rolled her eyes. "It's YouTube, Dad."

"Whatever. Play the video." Although a humiliating way to prove he didn't have a drink, Mark had his daughter play the altercation from the beginning. The video was surprisingly clear for being shot in a dark bar. Mark watched it carefully then yelled, "Stop! Pause it right there!" He pointed at the screen. "Do you see it?"

"All I see is a guy losing his temper because some bozo behind a bar was giving him a hard time."

"Look in front of me." Mark squinted at the small screen. "Mary, can you make the picture bigger?" She put two fingers on the screen and spread them apart. The picture zoomed in on the bar. Mark pointed. "What do you see?"

"Nothing. I see a bar."

"Do you see a drink on the bar in front of me?"

Noelle leaned closer to the phone and carefully examined the picture. Despite every effort to hold it back, a smile formed on her face. "No, I don't. You *were* telling the truth." Noelle shook her head and went over to Mark. She gave him an exasperated, playful push. "You make me so mad, Mark Smith. What am I going to do with you?" She lifted the bag of ice away from Mark's cheek. "I'll bet that's going to leave a mark." Then she wagged a finger at him. "If I ever *do* catch you in a bar again, I'll give you a matching one on the other side."

Mark figured the wisest thing to do was to eat a little humble pie. He came to attention and saluted. "Yes, ma'am. Captain, ma'am."

"That will be the day when you let *me* be the captain," she joked. Noelle felt this was the right time to have a heart-to-heart talk with Mark. "Mary, would you please go to your room? I want to have a talk with your dad."

"Go to my room? I'm twenty-four years old, Mom. I think I'm old enough to deal with adult subjects."

That period in life when kids transition from children to adults could be challenging for parents. It was hard to think of the person whose diapers you once changed as being old enough to get married. Old habits died hard.

"Mary, do as your mother asked."

Mary stomped away in a huff. "Ugg! I'm not a child anymore! I'll be so glad to go back to school!" She slammed her bedroom door.

Her parents rolled their eyes. Old habits died hard for kids, as well.

Noelle and Mark walked over to the couch. She picked up the day's paper off the cushion and threw it across the room. They sat down—two feet apart. Mark looked straight ahead with his arms crossed.

She began. "Mark, you don't deserve all that crap the press is saying about you. You're a hero, not a villain. Why can't they see that? It's just not fair." She rested her hand on his shoulder. "I know things are rough right now, but you'll get through this. You are stronger than you think."

Mark's head drooped.

Noelle moved closer. She put her fingers under his chin and lifted Mark's head until his gaze met hers. "I'm trying to be sympathetic—I really am—but you have to open up a little more. You haven't said two words about what happened since we got back. I can't help if you won't talk to me."

Mark pushed Noelle's hand away and stood up. "Look, I

know I lost my cool in the bar. But the bartender started shooting off his big mouth and…and I don't know, something just snapped inside." He was used to having absolute control over his crew and every movement of enormous airliners. Now Mark's life was careening out of control, and he felt powerless to stop it.

Noelle reached up for his hand. "It's not just what happened today, honey. You've lost your appetite, you're having trouble sleeping, you have nightmares, you're grouchy all the time. Talk to me. Tell me how you're feeling."

Mark saw the concern written on her face and took her hand. "Don't worry about me. I'm fine."

"You're *not* fine, Mark. I think Dr. Sullivan from the Coast Guard boat might be right. I think you might be suffering from PTSD."

Mark pulled his hand away. "Now you're a psychiatrist?"

Noelle ignored the hurtful jab. She got up and opened a side drawer in the rolltop desk next to the kitchen. She pulled out the card Dr. Sullivan had slipped her and showed it to Mark. "I've got the psychiatrist's number. We could go together. The doctor said she is really good at fixing people like you."

"Fix? I don't need *fixing*. I just need a little time to sort everything out. I've got a hell of a lot on my plate right now. Just give me some damned space."

Noelle winced at her poor choice of words. "Okay, I'm sorry. I didn't mean to say you are broken. I just think you would benefit from—"

"Look, if you are expecting me to sit in front of a fireplace and braid your hair while I talk about my feelings, forget it. Ain't gonna happen. That's just not me. And I'm damn sure not going to spill my guts to some stranger. I told you I'm fine. Now drop it."

Noelle's frustration finally boiled over. "Mark Smith, you can be so pigheaded!" She threw the card in the trash and stomped off to her bedroom, slamming the door. Old habits did indeed die hard.

The next day when Mark was out, Noelle pulled dusty bottles of Jack Daniels and Grey Goose out of her kitchen cabinet. She eyed the bottles for five minutes as they sat on the counter. Then she poured their contents down the drain.

CHAPTER 23

A week later

A KNOCK CAME AT THE APARTMENT door. Being in the middle of a phone call, Noelle put her hand over the end of the handset and looked expectantly at Mark. He looked back over his shoulder at Noelle and shrugged. She shot him an exasperated look—the universal sign that she expected him to answer the door since he was closer.

Mark put down the remote, plucked himself up off the couch, and opened the door.

April Parker stood in the hallway smiling. "Hi, Uncle Mark, how are you today?"

"Wonderful," he said sarcastically. Mark waved her in. "How 'bout you?"

"I'm great, thanks." April had seen his infamous YouTube video and wisely decided not to bring it up.

Noelle waved silently at her niece as she waited on hold to make a doctor's appointment. The cord tethered Noelle to the phone/answering machine like a leash. Mary had pestered her mother for months to get rid of the relic from the past, but Noelle wouldn't budge. She liked the idea of having the simple, reliable machine. It felt comfortable—unlike her complicated, zillion-function smartphone.

"Is Mary ready?" April asked her uncle.

At the same moment, Mary emerged from her bedroom. The cousins hugged and complimented each other on their outfits.

Mark plopped back down on the couch. "Where are you off to today?"

April excitedly replied, "We're going shop—"

Mary cut her off. "A museum. We're going to a museum."

April looked confused.

Mark cocked his head. "Really? What museum?"

Mary looked up at the ceiling. "Um…the museum of… history. The history museum."

Mark's suspicion grew. "You're going to the *history* museum?"

"That's right. It's very cool. They have a lot of old stuff there to look at." Trying to make the falsehood sound more convincing, Mary added, "All the kids go there."

Mark gave up and waved toward the door. "Okay, get out of here. Have fun looking at all the old stuff."

Mary gave Mark a quick peck on the cheek. "Bye, Dad." She steered April toward the door before her father could ask any more questions.

The two almost collided with Charlotte as she appeared in the doorway. "Whoa, slow down, girls. I'm too old to play bumper cars."

Mary and April ducked under her arm and disappeared from sight.

"Where's the fire?" she rhetorically asked.

Noelle hung up and waved her friend into the kitchen. "Hi, Charlotte, thanks for coming over."

Charlotte looked over and saw Mark sitting on the couch. She shot him an icy stare.

Mark crossed his arms and mumbled, "My day just keeps getting better."

Charlotte heard him. She couldn't resist the opportunity to get in a jab. "Mark, I'm surprised to see you here. I thought you'd be down at Madison Square Garden training for your next fight."

His faced turned crimson as he glared at the TV screen.

Hurricane

He uncharacteristically bit his lip rather than strike back.

Pleased with herself for getting the last word, Charlotte took off her coat and planted her sizable backside into a kitchen chair.

Noelle shook her head in resignation. "You two…"

Charlotte was perspiring heavily after trudging up three flights of stairs.

Noelle got up and retrieved a cold pitcher of iced tea from the refrigerator. She poured a glass and handed it to her friend.

Charlotte took a sip then spat it right back into the glass. "What in the world? This isn't sweet tea."

Noelle had a confused, deer-in-the-headlights look on her face.

"Don't tell me you don't know how to make sweet tea." Charlotte imitated a pouring motion with each hand. "You pour in tea and lots of sugar. It ain't that complicated."

Noelle still looked confused, having been raised in Connecticut.

Charlotte shook her head. "You Yankees. How about a beer? Can a lady get a beer around here?"

Noelle's face was aghast. She gave Charlotte the *cut* sign by waving her fingers in front of her throat, hoping Mark wouldn't notice.

Charlotte smacked her forehead with her palm. "I'm sorry, darlin'. I forgot. I'm really sorry." Hoping to divert attention away from her gaff, Charlotte hurriedly asked, "Sooo…how's retirement treatin' ya?"

"It's good. Great. It's really good. It's taking a little getting used to, being home all the time. Still a work in progress. But no, it's great. I love it." Noelle's answer was less than convincing.

Charlotte sat back in the chair and crossed her arms. "Honey, your answer had more waffles in it than an IHOP. It's me, your best friend. You can level with me. How's it going having you know who"—she nodded sideways—"around again?"

Noelle looked over at Mark. He was engrossed in an NBA game on TV. Mark yelled at the refs for making a bad call. Not surprisingly, the referees ignored his advice and continued to make calls the way they saw fit.

Noelle leaned closer to Charlotte. "He's bored. If he isn't sitting on the couch, he's following me around pointing out spots I missed when I'm cleaning. Last week, he rearranged everything in my kitchen cabinets. Said things weren't arranged *logically*. Now I can't find anything I'm looking for." Noelle bobbed her head sideways toward Mark. "Can we talk about this later?"

Charlotte winked in acknowledgement. "Okay, sure."

"Tell me about your new job. How do you like it?" Noelle asked.

Charlotte groaned. "Just peachy. Who wouldn't want to work as a waitress for a pimple-faced boss less than half my age. I tell you what, our last flight wasn't much fun, but I sure do miss being a flight attendant."

Noelle nodded ruefully in agreement.

Charlotte chuckled. "Worst of all is having to sleep with ol' Bubba every night. That man snores like a damned freight train."

Mark gave up trying to watch basketball with all the talking going on behind him. He clicked off the game and headed outside for a run. Jogging helped Mark forget his troubles, and the release of endorphins into his bloodstream improved his mood.

After descending the steps outside the building, Mark leaned against the railing and stuck one leg back to stretch his calf. At his age, exercising without warming up and stretching first was guaranteed to pull a muscle. A young courier pulled up nearby on a ten-speed bicycle. The teenager got off and came face to face with Mark. "Hey, aren't you Mark Smith, the pilot?"

Mark's head dropped. *Here we go again.* He put his hands

up like stop signs. "Yes, I am. But look, whatever it is you have to say, I'm not interested. I just want to go for a peaceful run, okay?"

The courier shrugged. "No problem, man. That's cool."

Mark started to walk away when the kid stepped in front of him. "Before you run off, I've got something for you." He pulled an envelope from his satchel and handed it to Mark. The courier grinned and said, "You've been served. Have a nice day." He jumped back on his bike and sped off.

Mark warily opened the official-looking envelope from the law firm of Meyer, Simpkins, and White. In it was a subpoena compelling Mark to appear at a deposition. He quickly scanned through the legal boilerplate. When he reached the meat of the letter, Mark gasped. He was named as a codefendant in a class-action lawsuit because of the accident. Mark was being sued for ten million dollars.

CHAPTER 24

MARK RACED THROUGH QUEENS AT a blistering pace hoping to outrun his troubles. The sidewalks were like an obstacle course. He dodged deliverymen wheeling dollies stacked with cardboard boxes, mothers pushing baby strollers, and apartment dwellers walking their dogs.

Regardless of how fast Mark ran, he couldn't escape the feeling of an ever-tightening noose around his neck. *Is the pounding in my chest from the torrid pace, or am I having a heart attack?* he pondered.

Mark slowed to a walk to give his weary body a break. He rested his hands on his hips and gulped down as much air as his lungs could hold. The ringtone of an old rotary dial telephone emanated from his front left pocket. He pulled out his cell phone.

"Mark, Jacob Shapiro here from your union legal department in DC."

"Mr.…Shapiro…I'm glad…you called." Mark was breathing so heavily he could barely carry on a conversation. "Give me a second, Shapiro." Mark kept the phone to his ear as he bent over. He supported himself with his free hand planted on his knee.

"Why so out of breath, Mark? Oh God, please tell me you haven't gotten into another fight!" Alarm permeated Shapiro's remark.

Mark straightened up. "No, Shapiro, I didn't get in another fight. I've already caught enough grief about that.

The last person I need piling on is my own lawyer."

"As your union lawyer, that's precisely why I brought it up," Shapiro replied. "We heard about you being named in the lawsuit. That's why I called. This is serious, Mark. It's no longer about what the press is saying about you or public opinion. You are going to be hauled into federal court and grilled like you've never been grilled before."

Mark listened in silence.

"Every time you end up on the front pages or on the internet for something stupid you've done, you're giving the other side free ammunition to use against you. You need to understand juries are made up of ordinary people. People who trust that their pilots are calm, dependable professionals. Not hotheaded bar brawlers. So, knock off the juvenal delinquent shit, okay?"

Mark's head drooped. "I hear what you're saying."

"Good. I'm not trying to pile on here, Mark, I'm telling you this as your lawyer. Regardless of the fact that you are indemnified by Alpha Airlines in this case, if you lose in court you stand to lose a lot more than just your reputation. Plaintiffs can then turn around and sue you for a whole list of other claims. I'm sorry, but the union's legal department can't get involved in civil matters. You'd be on your own."

Mark pinched the bridge of his nose and slowly shook his head. "Shit!"

Shapiro continued. "We need to meet as soon as possible to start drafting our legal strategy. My team and I will be in New York next week for a conference. Set aside some free time in the evenings to meet with us."

◆

The following week

Mark sat alone at a table by the window at Romano's. Regardless of how the meeting went, at least he'd get to enjoy their fantastic chicken spiedini. Mark picked at his meal as he wrestled with a thought that popped into his head: *This could be one of my last meals as a free man.* He quickly replaced it with another: *Knock it off. Stop being so dramatic. Everything will turn out fine.*

Three men, each wearing thousand-dollar suits, walked up and sat down. The leader of the pack handed Mark his business card. "Jacob Shapiro, chief counsel. It's nice to meet you in person, Mark." Shapiro didn't extend his hand in greeting.

A young, attractive waitress walked by their table, scribbling in her order pad.

Shapiro extended his arm, blocking her progress. "Sweetie, can we get a round of Johnnie Walker Red for the table? And keep them coming." He slipped her a twenty-dollar bill.

Mark looked at Shapiro with bewilderment. He looked at the waitress and said, "Make mine a Coke." She tucked the twenty in her apron, chomped on a wad of gum, and walked away. Mark looked back at his lawyer. "You do know that I'm a recovering alcoholic, right?"

Shapiro's associates looked at their boss.

"Shit. Sorry. I knew that. Long day," he muttered.

◆

Charlotte walked up to the bus stop outside of Romano's. She rubbed her sore neck after a long shift at the diner then checked the bus schedule on the shelter to see when her ride home would roll up. A ten-minute wait. Charlotte turned and noticed something unusual in the restaurant window. Three very well-dressed men sat facing her, talking to a man wearing jeans and a sweatshirt. His back was to the window. A waitress walked up balancing a tray of drinks. She put down three tumblers of booze in front of the suits and a can of Coke in front of the other man. He turned his head to thank her.

Charlotte immediately fished her cell phone out of her purse. She scrolled through the contacts app until reaching the list of names starting with N.

CHAPTER 25

THE PILOT UNION CHIEF COUNSEL leaned forward and spelled out the next steps for Mark. "Your deposition is scheduled for Tuesday at 10 a.m. You will be the last person on the list to be deposed. I'll be there representing you. Let's meet fifteen minutes beforehand to go over any last-minute changes."

"Where should I meet you?" Mark asked.

"To save time, let's meet in the lobby of Meyer, Simpkins, and White."

Mark pulled out his phone and pulled up the Google Maps app. "What's the address?"

"Fifty-Second and Park Avenue," one of the associates answered.

Mark looked up and shrugged. "Fifty-two...what? What's the full address on Park Avenue?"

The lawyers looked at each other, confusion evident on their faces. Shapiro clarified. "Trust me, you can't miss it. Meyer, Simpkins, and White is the largest transportation law firm in the country. Their building spans the entire block."

Mark's jaw dropped. Park Avenue was one of the most expensive streets in America. Their location indicated the caliber of law firm he was up against. *Just great*, he thought.

"They've represented plaintiffs in practically every major transportation accident for the last thirty years," Shapiro said. "Hell, their moto might as well be '*If it moves, we sue it.*'"

His associates chuckled at the bad joke.

Mark wasn't laughing. "What's your strategy? What should I expect?"

Shapiro's face turned more serious. "We've represented pilots against them before. Unfortunately, Ben Meyer himself has taken lead counsel on this case. The bastard was shrewd enough to get all the other firms that filed lawsuits to consolidate their cases under his wing. For a fee, of course."

Mark's normally calm demeanor began to show signs of cracking.

"Be prepared, Mark. Meyer is going to come at you from every angle with guns blazing. Choose every word you say very carefully. You'll see at the deposition, Ben Meyer is not someone to be taken lightly."

Mark's anxious expression changed. He sat up a little straighter. "Neither am I."

The lawyers looked between themselves and nodded.

Shapiro pulled a yellow legal pad and thick folder out of his briefcase. "This is my strategy…"

◆

Mr. Simpson stared, arms crossed, as Mark passed by him in the building foyer and bounded up the stairs. The building superintendent craned his neck and looked up the stairwell as Mark climb each of the three flights.

He walked into the apartment at 8:30. Noelle was waiting. She held a newspaper in one hand and the subpoena in the other. Fire burned in her crystal-blue eyes.

Evidence in hand, Noelle didn't utter a single word as she scowled at Mark. The long, drawn-out silence felt like a form of torture.

Mark decided the best thing to do was break the ice by speaking first. "Hello?"

Noelle's scowl intensified.

Mark had never felt so unsure about what to say next.

Unfortunately, he chose his words poorly. "How's the wedding planning going?"

Noelle looked like she was about to explode. To her credit, she walked over to the kitchen table and calmly laid out the damning evidence. The contents of the subpoena letter and a front-page story in a week-old *New York Times* had ratted Mark out. Noelle tapped the article, hard. "It says here you've been named as a defendant in a lawsuit."

"I thought you stopped reading the newspaper." Another poor choice of words.

Noelle finally let loose. "I did! Mr. Simpson has been intercepting the paper every day before it reaches our door." Now she was pacing. "But he thought it was important I read this article about you. He brought it over while you were out."

Figures. The fat bastard, Mark thought to himself. He tried to explain, but Noelle cut him off before a single word could pass his lips.

"We are going to be married soon, and I have to find out from other people that my husband-to-be is being sued? When were you planning on telling me? *Were* you planning on telling me?"

"I swear I was going to tell you. I was just waiting for the right time."

Noelle was incredulous. "The right time! What were you going to do? Stroll into the apartment one day and casually say, 'Hi, honey. How was your day? Oh, by the way, I'm being sued for ten million dollars. What's for dinner?'"

Mark looked like a kid with his hand caught in the cookie jar. "Well…actually…I thought it was a good idea, until…until you said it out loud."

"Mark Smith, don't you dare try to joke your way out of this one. This is serious. Ten million dollars!"

Mark walked up to Noelle in hope of getting back in her good graces. He reached out and tried to put his arms around her waist.

She jumped back. "Don't you touch me."

Mark might have had the solemn responsibility of protecting the lives of thousands of passengers during his career as an airline captain, but the child in him couldn't resist. He just had to do it. He reached out and touched Noelle.

She swatted his finger away. "I said don't touch me."

Mark did it again.

Again, Noelle swatted his finger away. She tensed up every muscle in her face, determined not to crack a smile. "Mark, I'm serious. Stop it."

Mark did it again.

Noelle tried desperately to look mad, but it was too late. The fire had left her eyes. "I'm going to call the police if you don't stop it. I'll have you arrested."

"For what, being stupid? There'd be a lot of lonely women in this world if they called the police every time their man did something dumb." Mark hoped self-deprecating humor would get him out of the doghouse. Then he said, "I'm sorry."

Those two words so rarely passed Mark's lips, she was caught completely off guard. It worked. Her remaining anger evaporated.

Mark led her to the couch. "I should have told you. You're right. It's just that I didn't want to worry you. I'm the one being sued, not you."

She moved closer to him. "Mark, we're a team now. Our wedding is only a few months away. If we can't trust each other, what's the sense in getting married? I have to know that I can completely trust you. No more secrets, okay?"

Mark nodded. "Okay, no more secrets. I promise." He leaned in and hugged Noelle.

She wrapped her arms around him and rested her head on Mark's shoulder. Noelle looked down and quietly said, "No secrets."

CHAPTER 26

THE NEXT MORNING, NOELLE WAS unusually quiet at the kitchen table. Normally, she was full of energy at that time of day. A morning person.

Mark decided that the less he said, the better. He concentrated instead on finishing his usual breakfast: oatmeal, made a little more palatable with brown sugar and a splash of skim milk. After he finished eating, Mark grabbed a light jacket and kissed Noelle on the cheek. "I'm going for a run." He disappeared out the door.

Noelle stabbed at her eggs but wasn't in the mood to eat. She got up, dumped them in the trash, then rinsed off her plate. Mark's bowl sat on the kitchen table right where he left it. Noelle went to retrieve it when she heard a knock at the door. She muttered, "Did he forget his keys again?" She flung open the door, ready to tease Mark about his unreliable memory.

Two menacing-looking men stood shoulder to shoulder in the hall. They both wore dark sunglasses and had short-cropped hair. The taller one said, "We're looking for Mark Smith. Is he here?"

Noelle looked him in the eye. "Who's asking?"

The men reached inside their jackets. Noelle's heart skipped a beat. They pulled out badges.

"DEA. I'm Special Agent Torres." He pointed to the shorter man. "This is Special Agent Miller." Torres opened a file he was carrying. "Are you Noelle Smith?"

"Parker. My last name is Parker."

"Parker, sorry." He poked at the file. "That's right, it says right here you and Smith are divorced. I should have read it more closely. I apologize." Of course, he already knew that. Part of the game. Torres looked up. "So, is Mark here? We'd like to speak to him."

Noelle's knees suddenly felt weak. "No, he's not here."

"When will he be back?" Torres's voice no longer had a friendly lilt to it. Agent Miller attempted to look around Noelle into the apartment.

She moved to block his view. "He didn't tell me when he would be back. Do you have a card? I'll let him know you stopped by."

Torres pulled out his business card and handed it to her. "We also need to speak to you, Ms. Parker. Since we're already here, do you mind if we come in?"

Noelle nervously cleared her throat. "Of course not. Please, come in." She ushered them to the kitchen table. "Can I get you gentlemen anything?"

"Coffee, if you already have some made," Torres responded. "We didn't get a chance to grab breakfast."

Noelle's hands trembled slightly as she poured two cups of coffee. The agents scanned the apartment while Noelle's back was turned. They observed that Mark was absent in every family picture.

She put a cup in front of each man then sat down. Neither agent touched his coffee. Noelle noticed. "So, what is it the DEA wants to talk to me about? My world-famous coffee recipe?" Both men shifted uncomfortably in their seats and quickly took a sip.

Torres tried strategy number seven from the DEA interrogation handbook. He showed concern for the subject in order to get her to relax. "How's the arm? Is the cast coming off soon?"

"Fine. Yes."

"Good. Good to hear. You had one hell of a week a while back. How are you holding up?"

"Fine."

Torres forced a laugh and looked at Miller. "With all these one-word answers, we'll have time to get some breakfast after all." Strategy number four—humor.

Noelle crossed her arms and glared across the table.

Torres quickly tired of playing by the book. He went with his gut. "Ms. Parker, why did you and your ex-husband decide to sail to New York on the *Lynda Ray* rather than fly home?"

"Wouldn't you, after that flight?"

"No, I wouldn't," he bluntly replied. "Frankly, I'm surprised a veteran pilot and flight attendant would be scared to get on a perfectly good airplane. Very curious."

Agent Miller opened a folder and laid it in front of his boss. Torres ran his finger down the page, then stopped. "It says here…you, Mark, and First Officer Whitaker were the only survivors. Did anyone bring anything with them into the lifeboat?" Torres looked directly at Noelle.

She swallowed hard. "Not that I recall."

"Then, somehow…" Torres dragged out the second word, "Whitaker died in the lifeboat. Do I have that right?" He studied Noelle's face for any twitching or rapid blinking—anything that indicated she was lying.

Noelle fidgeted in her chair. "No, you don't."

"I don't have it right?" Torres questioned.

"We've already explained all this to the authorities. A shipping container rammed our lifeboat, and Whitaker suffered a severe blow to the head. Not long after that, he passed away." Noelle pointed at the folder. "Check your notes. It should be in there."

Torres's cell phone vibrated. He pulled it out, held it below the tabletop, and scanned the incoming text message: "No sign of subject S yet. Will stay with car." He put his phone back in his pocket then nonchalantly asked Noelle, "What time did you say Mark would be coming back?"

"I didn't say. I don't know."

Agent Miller put another folder in front of Torres. He flipped it open. An old picture of Mark was clipped to the inside cover. Torres smiled and asked, "By any chance, do you have a current picture of your ex-husband? The one we have from his previous dealings with the agency is quite old."

Sweat trickled down the back of Noelle's neck. "I'll look around after you leave and see what I can come up with."

"Thank you. Any help you could provide would be greatly appreciated by the DEA, Ms. Parker. *Greatly* appreciated."

Agent Miller finally spoke up. "Ms. Parker, we've done a little digging. It appears Mark is receiving a small pension from Alpha Airlines. Was he hoping to get a large sum of money soon? To help make ends meet? Maybe an inheritance from a rich aunt? Something like that?"

Noelle cocked her head. "Why would you ask that?"

"It's just that in this city his pension won't go very far. Especially since he has almost no money in the bank. But of course, you already knew that. What with you two getting married soon, as you mentioned."

Noelle's eyes narrowed. "I never mentioned we were getting…Wait a minute. What the hell are you insinuating?" She jumped to her feet, knocking her chair over on its back, and pointed at the door. "I would like you to leave. Now."

Torres spoke. "I couldn't help but notice. You've been very nervous during our visit."

Noelle clasped her hands together in an effort to mask their shaking. "Mark and I are innocently minding our own business, then suddenly I'm getting interrogated by two DEA agents. Wouldn't you be nervous?"

"Not if I was telling the truth." Torres stood up and closed the folder. "Ms. Parker, do you know what the penalty is for lying to a federal agent?"

If the DEA agent thought he could intimidate Noelle, he'd picked the wrong person. "Let me guess." She tapped her finger on her lips. "I'd be forced to buy my wardrobe at Sears, like you two?"

Agent Torres was not amused. "Thank you for your time, Ms. Parker. We'll see ourselves out." He opened the door and let Miller exit first. Torres turned back as he stood in the doorway. "Ms. Parker, I'm confused. You said you and Mark are innocently minding your own business. What is it you are innocent of, exactly?"

CHAPTER 27

MARK ROUNDED THE CORNER AT the end of his block after running five miles. He was engrossed in his phone, checking last night's scores. Suddenly, Mark was tackled from behind.

He wrestled free from his attacker and jumped to his feet. "What the hell is wrong with you, Simpson?"

Mr. Simpson looked up from the sidewalk and reached out toward Mark. "Help me up, Smith."

Mark grabbed his hand and hauled Simpson to his feet. Then Mark lit into him. "What was that all about? Have you lost your mind?"

Simpson dusted himself off. "You are not going back to the apartment."

Mark clenched his jaw. "Look, Simpson, I know you are very protective of Mary and Noelle, but like it or not we are getting married. I have every right to live there. Deal with it."

Simpson shook his head. "It's not about that, dumbass. I'm glad Ms. Parker is getting married. Why she picked you is beyond me, but it's obvious she's in love."

"Then why the hell did you just attack me?"

Simpson steered Mark into the recessed doorway of a nearby shop. "The feds are looking for you."

Mark stole a look around the corner at the car parked in front of his building. He turned back to Simpson and whispered, "Crap, it's the DEA." Chivalry overtook self-preservation. "Noelle is in the apartment!" Mark broke out of the shadows, ready to sprint back to the apartment. Simpson grabbed his arm and pulled Mark back. "Don't be an idiot. Wait till they leave."

A blue sedan with the words "US Government Property—Official Use Only" stenciled on the side pulled away from the curb and drove straight for them. Mark and Simpson melted back into the shadows. The car slowed to a crawl as it approached the shop. Simpson jiggled the knob on the shop door. Locked.

The light at the intersection turned green, and the feds sped away.

They waited in the shadows for a moment then stepped back out onto the sidewalk. The men walked silently back to their building.

In the foyer, Mark finally spoke up. "Thanks, Simpson. I owe you one."

He pointed at Mark. "I didn't do it for you. I did it for your family. If you ended up in the slammer, it would break their hearts. Mary is a great kid, and Ms. Parker is the best tenant I've got. I'd hate to see them hurt." Simpson gave Mark a dismissive look. "Hell, if you weren't in the picture"—he slapped his belly—"and I was a few years younger...I'd throw my hat in the ring for Ms. Parker's hand."

Mark cracked a smile. "If you were a few years younger, I'd be worried." He extended his hand. "Thanks, Simpson."

Mr. Simpson waved off Mark's hand. "Put a Band-Aid on that injury. I don't want you dripping blood all over my floors."

Mark rotated his arm and looked at his right elbow. A red stain saturated the torn fabric on his jacket. Mark cupped his left hand under the bloody elbow and started up the stairs. After a few steps he turned back. "Hey, Simpson. I think I misjudged you. Tell you what. I'll keep the secret you really do have a heart just between us. Not a word to the other tenants."

Simpson grunted. "Get out of here, dumbass." With that, he went into his apartment and slammed the door.

———◆———

The second Mark entered the apartment, Noelle attacked him with a hug. She embraced Mark tightly, relieved to have him back. "The DEA was here. I think they're onto us!"

Mark pried Noelle's arms off of him. "We didn't do anything, remember? We're innocent. If the DEA had any proof otherwise, you'd be at their headquarters right now with a bright light shining in your eyes. Why don't you sit down, catch your breath, and tell me what happened?" Mark gestured with his right arm toward the kitchen table.

"You're bleeding." Noelle yanked his arm up to examine the injury. "What happened?"

"It's a long story." Mark's face suddenly had a look of concern. "But if I mysteriously disappear one day, tell the cops to question Mr. Simpson." He was only half joking.

CHAPTER 28

Tuesday 9 a.m.

MARK CAME OUT OF HIS bedroom wearing a new charcoal-gray suit. Dark circles hung under each eye. He pulled and tugged at the ill-fitting garment. Mark had long ago "outgrown" the ability to pull off wearing a slim fit cut suit.

"Look at you." Noelle stepped back to admire her recent purchase. "How do you like the suit?"

Mark lied. "You did a great job. I love it." He pulled at the shoulders when Noelle turned her head.

Mary stepped out of her bedroom, yawning and rubbing her eyes. She looked at Mark, then diplomatically said, "Wow, Dad, you look terrible. Couldn't sleep last night?" She hadn't taken the class on bedside manner yet in med school.

Noelle scolded her, "Be nice to your father; his deposition is this morning."

Mary joked, "Oh right. Don't be nervous, Dad. It's only ten million dollars. No big deal." Like father, like daughter. Mary had inherited Mark's sarcastic sense of humor.

Noelle walked up to Mark. "Let's do something about that tie."

He looked wistfully at her with his seafoam-green eyes as she fixed the sloppy knot. "I wish you were coming."

Noelle frowned. "I know, sweetie"—she banged her cast on the table—"but I can't wait another day to finally get this darn thing off. I've got the appointment for my physical and mammogram at the same time as your deposition." Her frown gave way to a look of rebuke. "Which reminds me…"

"I know, I know. I'll make an appointment for a physical as soon as things settle down." Mark held up his right hand in a Boy Scout salute. "I promise." He checked his watch. "Time to go."

She gave him a peck on the cheek. "You'll do fine. Don't worry."

Mary looked up from her cereal bowl and waved. "Kick some ass, Dad."

Noelle wagged her finger at her. "Language, young lady."

Mark winked in approval at Mary's inspiring remark and gave her a thumbs-up.

Mark took the M-Line train, packed with pushy commuters, from the Jackson Heights station directly to the Fifth Avenue/Fifty-Third Street stop in Midtown Manhattan. He walked the last two blocks.

As he approached the entrance to Meyer, Simpkins, and White, Jacob Shapiro stepped out of the back of a long black limousine. Looking refreshed, he said, "Good morning, Mark. Are you ready?"

"Ready as I'll ever be," he tepidly replied.

As they walked up, the doorman—wearing the traditional black long coat and top hat—pulled open the door. "May I see some ID, gentlemen?"

Mark looked sideways at his lawyer.

Shapiro just shrugged.

The doorman gave a superficial glance at the IDs then handed them back. "A security guard will escort you to the conference room." With that, he turned his back and closed the door.

The law firm's lofty reputation was reinforced by the

striking lobby. It was decorated with marble floors, crystal chandeliers, and a team of young, attractive receptionists. Security guards were discretely deployed around the perimeter. Even the smell in the lobby was impressive.

A muscular, bald-headed man with an earpiece stuck in his ear approached. "Follow me." With his frosty personality, the guard seemed eminently qualified to mentor DMV employees. He led them across the expansive lobby and into the elevator.

Mark noticed a small bulge under the security guards' jacket. Apparently, screwing people out of a lot of money created plenty of enemies.

The elevator doors opened at the eightieth floor. Mr. Personality turned left and walked down the hallway without saying a word.

Mark and Shapiro assumed they were to follow.

The guard pulled opened the door to the conference room and waved them in.

Mark took a deep breath. He strode confidently in like a gladiator entering the Colosseum to do battle. Regrettably, the room was empty. The sparring would have to wait.

Designed to impress, the opulent conference room did just that. Dominating the center of the room was a long, dark table flanked by a dozen chairs on each side—the battlefield, as it were. Modern art adorned the walls.

Mark stopped and looked at one strange piece. It appeared as if the artist had used the canvas to clean the floor, mounted it in a gilded frame, then declared his creation art. Mark smirked inside at the gullibility of the art crowd. He reached out toward the piece.

"Don't touch the artwork!" the guard admonished.

Mark felt lucky to still have all his fingers after that warning. Interspersed between the artwork were pictures of Ben Meyer standing next to important people. In one, Meyer stood next to former president Bill Clinton. In another, the lawyer gripped the hand of a Supreme Court justice. On the opposite wall, Meyer was pictured standing on the back deck of a yacht next to the world's richest tech titan. The lawyer proudly held up his prized catch of the day.

Mark wandered over to the window. He was rewarded with a spectacular view of Manhattan. The chaotic noise of the city faded to silence at this lofty height. The south end of Central Park was visible to the right. Rockefeller Center stood out below. The Hudson River loomed in the distance. Mark's eyes lingered on the river, recalling the miracle that took place there years earlier. He shook his head. *At least I made it to land. Doesn't that count for anything?*

Shapiro came up beside Mark. "Don't be impressed. This firm is known for doing anything to gain an advantage. It's all part of the game. We've seen it before." He guided Mark to a chair in the middle of the table and sat down. Shapiro waved away the guard. "I'd like to talk to my client."

The guard crossed his arms and stood firm.

"In private!" Shapiro barked.

He reluctantly acceded to Shapiro's request and walked away.

"Mark, remember to keep your answers short and simple. Don't add anything or try to educate them on what really happened. You'll have time to do that at the trial."

Mark nodded.

"Okay, here's my strategy. The other parties in the lawsuit are pointing fingers—most of them at you—trying to deflect blame. Their goal is to reduce the legal liability they're facing by making you the scapegoat. Alpha Airlines is saying you are at fault, not them. Tech Aerospace Corporation is trying to divert attention away from the poor design of the computer flight control system on their new plane."

"Figures," Mark replied.

"Can you blame them? Tech Aero spent seven years and thirty-two *billion* dollars developing the Tech-Liner. If the flying public thought any geek sitting next to them could hack into the plane's computers, their backlog of orders would disappear overnight."

"What's your plan?" Mark asked.

"The FARs. The federal aviation regulations clearly state you can't be held liable for the actions of your crew when you are not present."

"That's it?"

Before Shapiro could defend his mediocre strategy, a small, mousy woman walked into the room. "I'm Ms. Hartman. I'll be the court reporter for today's proceedings." She dropped a stack of papers on a desk in the corner. "Which one of you is the defendant?"

Mark raised his hand like a schoolboy.

"I'll be administering the oath now, so we don't waste time during the deposition. Raise your right hand and speak clearly into the microphone in front of you. No need to look at the camera."

Of course, Mark looked up. A camera was mounted at the top of the opposite wall—its unblinking eye pointed directly at him. Mark rambled through the standard oath then suddenly had a sinking feeling in the pit of his stomach. He queried the court reporter, "Has my microphone been on this whole time?"

Ms. Hartman nervously looked down and suddenly became very interested in the paperwork on her desk.

An army of lawyers marched into the conference room. They each stood silently on the opposite side of the table from Mark, leaving the middle chair open. The junior partners had Ivy League written all over them.

Ben Meyer strode in, trailed by his executive secretary. He was a short, chubby man with a thinning head of silver-gray hair slicked tightly down to his scalp. His suit cost more than Mark's car. Meyer's executive secretary pulled out his chair for her boss. The founding partner took his position at the center of the table. Only after he sat did the other lawyers dare to sit. Interestingly, his chair was higher than all others. No greetings were exchanged.

Ben Meyer looked disdainfully at Mark. "Let's begin."

CHAPTER 29

MEYER SCRIBBLED ON A LEGAL pad as his secretary put a cup in front of him. "Here's your coffee, sir. Venti, half caf soy latte."

He didn't bother to look up. "Thank you, Noelle."

She swallowed hard. "Um...It's Nicole, sir."

Meyer turned toward her with a puzzled look on his face. "Nicole? Oh right. Why did I think your name was...?" He snapped his fingers as it came to him. "That's where I've heard it before. Captain Smith, your lovely ex-wife's name is Noelle, isn't it?"

Mark's blood pressure shot up a few points.

Meyer looked directly at him. "How's her right arm doing? Is the cast coming off soon?"

The sparring had begun.

Mark didn't blink. He sat back in his chair and crossed his arms. "Bull shark." His odd reply silenced the room.

Anger began to smolder in Meyer's eyes as he sized up his adversary. "I beg your pardon?"

"Bull shark. How apropos." Mark pointed at the picture of Meyer standing on the back of the yacht holding his catch. "Classmate of yours? The shark, that is."

Meyer's pen snapped in half, splattering ink onto his custom-made suit. His secretary scurried over with a napkin and dabbed at the stain.

Meyer waved her away. He focused his ire on Shapiro. "Counselor, I wouldn't want to be in your shoes. You have quite an uphill battle on your hands. In the court of public opinion, your client has already been tried and convicted. The press is crucifying him daily. Frankly, I'm appalled at the media's behavior. I want to assure you, we go to great lengths at my firm to make sure that what's said in this room is never leaked to the media."

Shapiro glared back at Meyer. "As does the pilot's union," he slyly retorted.

"I'm glad you brought up your esteemed union, Counselor. It's always been known as a staunch advocate for safety and professionalism. Consider the damage that would be done to its fine reputation by fighting this unpopular case in court. For that matter, I'd hate to see *your* reputation and career tarnished."

"I appreciate your concern for my reputation, but can we get to the matter at hand?" Shapiro replied.

"Of course." Meyer smiled—the way a man-eating shark bares its teeth before attacking. "Captain Smith, I assume you are familiar with Federal Aviation Regulation 91.3?"

"Yes." Mark stuck to his lawyer's advice and kept his answer short.

Meyer turned and spoke to the junior partner on his left. "For the benefit of our court reporter, would you please tell the room what the regulation states?"

Eager to impress his boss, the man replied, "Yes, sir. FAR 91.3 unequivocally states that the pilot in command—Captain Smith, in this case—is directly responsible for, and is the final authority as to, the operation of their aircraft."

Shapiro raised his pen in the air. "If only your diligent intern had done his homework and continued reading."

The junior partner glowered at Shapiro.

"If he had, he would have come to the part in the regulations covering the reasonable reliance defense. It permits a pilot in command to avoid liability if he or she reasonably relied on a second-in-command who errs." Mark's lawyer sat back triumphantly and tossed his pen on the table.

The junior partner handed his boss a piece of paper.

Meyer didn't need to read it. "Are you aware that a recent ruling by the NTSB has resulted in the regulation being amended?"

Shapiro straightened up.

He tapped the paper for effect. "The change severely tightened up the ability of captains to blame others for their mistakes."

"My client is not at fault. I'm confident the jury will agree with me."

"Counselor, it's always the captain's fault. You know that. If you think you'll find a jury anywhere that is sympathetic to your client, good luck."

Shapiro shot back, "Meyer, what's your objective here? You know as well as I do that Captain Smith is indemnified by Alpha Airlines. You will never see one dime from him. Why insist on tarring his reputation?"

Meyer raised his voice. "My objective is to extract as much justice as possible for my poor, deserving clients."

Mark couldn't help himself. "How noble of you. I assume that means your firm will be donating its share of the *justice* you extract back to your clients."

Meyer tilted his head down and peered over the top of his reading glasses at his adversary. Mark felt like slapping the condescending expression right off Meyer's face. The lawyer continued. "Speaking of indemnification. Captain Smith, were you aware that Alpha Airlines CEO Mike Andrews had his deposition yesterday?"

"No, I wasn't."

"He testified that at the time of the accident you were no longer an employee of the airline."

Mark shot a sideways glance at Shapiro. The union lawyer just shrugged.

"Mr. Andrews said he fired you during the flight because he strongly disagreed with a very dangerous action you were about to make. I believe it was"—Meyer shuffled through his papers—"opening a cargo door in flight in an attempt to reduce the plane's weight."

Shapiro practically yelled his response. "Heat of the moment! Everyone, including Mr. Andrews, was under tremendous stress at that time. Surely, his rash decision against my client can't be viewed as legal and binding today. This is just a feeble attempt on Alpha Airlines part to escape their indemnification obligation."

Incensed at the Monday-morning quarterbacking going on, Mark defended his decision that fateful night. "What I did kept us from ditching in the Atlantic Ocean."

"How convenient for you to remember it that way," Meyer replied, sarcasm dripping from his voice. "Are you *positive* your plane wouldn't have made it without such a reckless act on your part?"

"Both the black boxes are intact. Plug the data from them into the simulator. You'll see," Mark retorted.

"Oh, I assure you, Captain Smith, we intend to do just that." Meyer had that smarmy look on his face again. He pointed over at Shapiro. "Did your crack lawyer tell you he's gone up against my firm many times in the past?"

"Yes, of course he did," Mark answered.

"Did he also mention he's lost 100 percent of the time?"

Shapiro leaped to his feet. "If you intend to impugn my reputation, then we are done here."

"Then I guess we are done." Meyer slapped the file in front of himself closed. "Ms. Hartman, you are free to go."

She quickly packed up and left.

Meyer stood, rested his fists on the table, and leaned toward Mark. "Captain Smith, I am saying this with your best interests at heart; I really am. Your best option is to take responsibility for what happened and settle quietly out of court. It would be better for everyone."

Mark stood as well and leaned toward Meyer. "Your concern for my welfare is touching, but you can go to hell. I'll see you in court."

"Have it your way," Meyer responded. As he walked away,

a tone came from his cell phone. He pulled it out and read the text message. A huge grin spread across his face. Meyer turned back and said, "You know that indemnification you are counting on, Smith? I feel terrible having to break the bad news to you first. I assumed your lawyer would have the same reliable sources at the federal courthouse that I have."

Shapiro's cell phone suddenly went off.

Meyer continued before Shapiro could answer it. "Alpha Airlines just declared bankruptcy. As of tomorrow, your airline is out of business."

CHAPTER 30

Noelle, Charlotte, Mary, and April Parker were gathered around the kitchen table. The remains of a box of chocolates and a nearly empty box of Kleenex sat in the center. They all shared the same melancholy expression.

Mark walked in, dragging his suit coat.

Noelle rushed over and embraced him with all her might. She looked up at her ex-husband with tears in her eyes. "It's all *gone*. Everything we were counting on is *gone*."

Everyone looked anxiously at Mark as if he had some sort of magic wand that could make the bad news go away. Or, although unspoken, he wondered if the looks reflected their true feelings that this was all his fault. He fumbled out an unconvincing response. "It'll be okay."

Noelle pushed away in frustration. "It's *not* going to be okay. At midnight we lose our medical insurance, your life insurance, and your pension."

Mary walked up and reluctantly asked, "I know this is not the best time to be asking, but what about medical school?"

They had no answer. Neither of her parents could bear the thought of crushing their daughter's dream of becoming a doctor. They just shrugged.

Mary's head drooped as she covered her face with her hands and stumbled off to her bedroom, sobbing. April trailed behind her cousin, hoping to provide some consolation.

Charlotte spoke up from the table. "Well, that pretty much settles it. I guess I can forget about getting that tummy tuck." She popped another chocolate into her mouth.

Later that evening

Mary had gone over to April's to escape the funeral-like atmosphere in the apartment. Mark and Noelle picked at the cold food on their dinner plates. Noelle got up and scraped the remaining food off her plate into the trash. Then she threw her entire plate, fork and all, into the can.

Mark went to her and held Noelle's quivering body. "It's okay, I'll figure something out. The trial isn't for a couple of months. By then we will be married. I'll find a job doing…doing something."

Noelle blindsided him with a verbal gut punch. "There isn't going to be a wedding."

He recoiled back. "What? I thought you—"

"We can't afford it right now. Not with what just happened."

Mark was determined to fulfill his promise to Noelle. "I said you were going to get a big wedding, and that's exactly what's going to happen."

"Mark, I know about your financial situation. The DEA told me."

His head sank. Mark felt an overwhelming sense of guilt and embarrassment. He'd let his family down again.

"We need to save every penny we have now. No more shopping trips. I doubt we can even keep the apartment." Noelle's eyes misted over. "The wedding is off." She disappeared into her bedroom.

Mark stood alone in the middle of the drab apartment. He felt a crushing pressure on his chest as he walked over and plopped down on the couch. Searching for a mindless diversion to calm his frayed nerves, he clicked on the TV. Mark suddenly started beating on the cushions with his fists. Blow after blow, he pummeled the innocent couch until the cushions began to tear, sending stuffing into the air. When his arms tired, he stopped the assault then slammed his head back against the couch, spewing profanities. Mark was dizzy with confusion. *That superstitious old cook was right,* he told himself.

Mark stabbed at the remote until landing on a sports channel. A heavy-set, balding ex-jock, who still ate like he was playing, beamed at the camera. "Be sure to tune in on Sunday for an epic Super Bowl. During the pregame show I'll be interviewing the commissioner's special guests of honor—a family who lost their beloved family dog, only to find it in a neighboring town two months later. You won't want to miss it."

Mark fired the remote at the TV, shattering the screen.

He buried his head in his hands, kicking at the batteries on the floor from the destroyed remote. He abruptly lifted his head and peered back over his shoulder in search of something. Mark bounded up off the couch and ran to the kitchen. He flung open every cabinet door in search of it. *Where are they?* he asked himself. Failing to find the liquor bottles, he tried the refrigerator as a last resort. Kale and moldy Chinese takeout were all he found. Neither would satisfy the intense craving he had. Mark slammed the door shut in frustration. Still stuck on the refrigerator door was the faded newspaper article about the accident. Mark glared at the awful picture of himself. In his mind, the title Capt. Hero now seemed to be mocking him. He tore the article off the door and ripped it to shreds.

As he was walking out of the kitchen, Mark's cell phone rang. He tried to ignore it, but the ringing wouldn't stop. He pulled the phone from his pocket and checked the caller ID. The call came from the pilot union headquarters in Washington, DC. He quickly tapped ANSWER. "Shapiro, is that you? We are going to have to completely change our—"

A female voice cut him off. "Captain Smith, this is Marjorie Watson. I'm the executive secretary for the union."

"Where's Shapiro? Put him on the line."

"Captain, I need to speak to you in complete secrecy about something." By now, her voice had lowered to just above a whisper. "Are you alone?"

"Um…yes." Mark began to worry.

"I just had to call you. It's not right."

"Marjorie, what happened?"

"I just heard the bigwigs around here saying the union can't afford to get involved in your case."

"Afford? The union has millions of dollars in its coffers."

"That's just it. You see, now that Alpha Airlines is out of business the union has just lost the dues income of twelve thousand pilots. Hell, my job is probably going to be eliminated. Anything to protect their cushy million-dollar salaries, those greedy SOBs. It's not just about the money, though. They said representing you would create a PR nightmare for the union. They are planning on saying since you are now retired, technically you are no longer a member of the union."

Mark was livid. "How can they do that? I faithfully paid my dues for over thirty-five years. And I certainly was a member of the union the day of the crash!"

"It's downright shameful, abandoning you like that. Making up excuses so they can get out of representing you."

Mark scowled. "Then I'll sue them. Force the union to represent me."

"Be realistic, Captain. They can drag out a lawsuit for years. You can't afford that."

He knew she was right. Mark pounded his fist on the table. "Shit!" After taking some deep breaths, he asked, "Then why did you call me, Marjorie? Is this your way of getting revenge on the bastards before you get laid off?"

"No, screw my job. I'm already vested with my pension. I'll be fine."

"Why then?"

There was a pause, then Mark heard sniffling over the phone. "My husband was on your plane. He's alive today because of you. You don't deserve this, Captain. I'm sorry."

Click.

Mark slammed his phone on the floor, shattering it to pieces. His mind screamed, *Why the hell is this happening? Just once, can't the world give me a Goddamned break?!* Mark stumbled across the kitchen floor, reeling from the traitorous news.

Regardless of how bad things got when flying, Mark always had his instruments to rely on to help guide him to a safe landing. Now, standing solo in the apartment, he felt like his world was spinning out of control with no parachute.

He held on to the rolltop desk to steady himself. Resting on top of it was a picture of Noelle and Mary arm in arm in front of the Empire State Building. They beamed like a couple of tourists. He picked up the picture and examined it closely. Mark came to a depressing conclusion. Without him in the picture, Noelle and Mary were happy and carefree.

The storm raging deep within his soul was more painful than any hurricane. A look of complete sorrow slowly washed over his face. Life had finally overwhelmed him. A fateful decision was made at that instant. Mark looked back at the closed bedroom door where Noelle could be heard crying. With his eyes beginning to mist up, he took his keys out of his pocket and laid them on the desk. He strode slowly to the apartment door, head bowed. Mark briefly considered grabbing his new jacket then reasoned, *Why ruin it?* He walked out of the apartment his ex-wife and daughter lived in and quietly closed the door.

CHAPTER 31

Mark stumbled down the sidewalk, nearly knocking over a young couple strolling hand in hand. When he reached the corner, he looked back up at the apartment with a pained expression. Noelle was standing at the bedroom window. She drew the curtains.

Mark stopped at the deserted corner and waited. Despite the chilly temperature, the only thing he felt was soul-numbing regret.

The number seven express bus barreled toward the intersection, trying to beat the light. Mark looked to his left and saw it coming.

He stepped closer to the edge of the curb.

The driver's shift had just ended, and he wasn't wasting any time getting his forty-thousand-pound bus back to the barn. A cold beer waited for him at Kelly's.

Mark's body began to tremble. He closed his eyes.

The bus driver perched his phone on top of his right leg where he thought no one could see it and took his eyes off the road, scrolling through his text messages.

A single tear trickled down Mark's cheek. Like a cliché, his life flashed before his eyes. In his mind, Mark saw himself at ten years old pleading with his dad to stop hitting his mom, receiving his wings on graduation day from Air Force pilot training (which both parents failed to show up for), ripping up the officers club that night in a drunken rage, Noelle's joyful face when holding Mary in her arms after giving birth, and after numerous tumultuous years later, Noelle ripping off her wedding ring and throwing it at him. Finally, Mark saw an object, a spirit, floating behind his body. The spirit shrieked like a banshee as Mark stepped off the curb.

CHAPTER 32

MARK'S BODY SUDDENLY CATAPULTED BACKWARD. He fell flat on his back onto the wet sidewalk. Disoriented, Mark looked up to see Andy Wilson, his crash pad roommate, standing over him yelling.

"Mark, what the hell are you doing? You almost stepped in front of that bus. What were you thinking?" Andy had dropped by for a visit and had seen Mark standing dangerously close to the street. Oblivious to his warning calls, Andy had grabbed Mark by the collar and pulled him out of the path of the bus. "Pay attention, big guy. That bus would have killed you."

Ashamed at what he had contemplated doing, Mark stood up and dusted himself off without saying a word.

"I heard what happened with Alpha Airlines. Sorry, man; that really sucks."

"If you only knew."

"That's why I stopped by. My last employer is looking to hire new pilots and flight attendants. I figured with the bankruptcy and all…maybe you'd want to apply. Of course, only if you feel like flying again after what happened."

Mark looked back up at the apartment window then shook his friend's hand. "Thank you, Andy. You have no idea how much I owe you."

"That means you'll apply then? Let's head back to your place, and I'll tell you all about the job."

Noelle threw open the door. Tears stained her eyes. She had seen what happened at the corner through a crack in the curtains.

Andy stood next to his friend. "Hi, Ms. Parker. I believe this knucklehead belongs to you." Andy gave her a look indicating he was fully aware of what just happened.

"Thank you, Andy. You're a good man." Noelle led Mark into the apartment.

Andy looked around expectantly. "By any chance is Mary here?"

"Goodnight, Andy." Noelle closed the door on the would-be suitor. Mark sulked away toward the kitchen. Noelle spun him around and smothered him—with a hug. Then she broke down. "I can't believe you'd even think about…how could you…" Noelle pounded on Mark's chest in a furious yet affectionate way. "I need you. We need you. Don't you know that?"

Mark grabbed her fists and clutched them tightly to his chest. He pulled Noelle close as she sobbed uncontrollably. Mark listened as Noelle poured her heart out.

Minutes later, she pulled back, streaks of mascara running down her cheeks. "Why would you even consider doing such a thing?"

Mark's head sagged. "I…I thought you guys would be better off without me around. At least you'd have the insurance money. You could stay in your apartment."

"My apartment? Mark, this apartment is *our* home. Without you, it's just a lonely room. It wouldn't be the same without you in it."

"Tell that to the rest of the world. They hate me. Everybody thinks I screwed up."

Noelle's expression instantly changed to one of excitement. She held up one finger. "Hold on; don't move." She opened the hall closet and dug out five paper grocery bags hidden behind some coats. The bags overflowed with letters and postcards banded together into bundles.

"Everyone hates you, huh?" Noelle eagerly dumped the contents of a single bag on the floor.

"What's all this?" Mark asked, confused.

Noelle knelt beside the pile and held up bundle after bundle. "This one is from people that were on our plane. This one is from family members of passengers on our plane." She dumped out another bag. "And these are from total strangers."

Mark sat down next to her on the floor. "I don't understand."

Noelle pulled the rubber band off a bundle and handed it to him. "Take a look."

He shuffled through the stack. All the letters were addressed to him. They had return addresses from every corner of the globe. He opened a few of the letters and read them. The authors expressed profound gratitude to Mark for saving them, a family member, a coworker, even saving their belief in the goodness of humanity. Many letters included supportive statements like *keep your chin up* and *you'll get through this*. One letter writer excitedly proclaimed that she and her husband decided to name their baby Mark, if it was a boy.

Mark looked up with tears in his eyes. "Why didn't you tell me?"

"I wanted to, but you've been so fragile lately. I wasn't sure how you'd take the letters. I know how uncomfortable you are with being called a hero. But you are. To these people. To me." She pointed at the stack. "This proves the public isn't against you. Regardless what the press says. The people don't blame you for what happened."

Mark leaned over and tenderly embraced Noelle. "I'm such an idiot. What did I ever do to deserve you?"

Noelle lightened up the mood. "Great, where's a tape recorder when you need one? I want proof you said that so I can play it back the next time you get mad at me."

He cringed. "Sounds a little like blackmail."

"Yes. Yes, it is." For the first time that evening, Noelle cracked a smile.

He took Noelle's hand. "You still have the number for that shrink?"

Mark eventually read every single letter and postcard. They proved to be an unexpected and welcomed source of catharsis for a lifetime of repressed emotions.

CHAPTER 33

THAT SAME NIGHT, AFTER SEEING so many letters and postcards, Mark had vowed to leave his past behind. A week later, he made good on that vow. He rolled into the parking lot at Teterboro Airport with Andy in the right seat.

Andy briefed Mark on what to expect as they walked to the front door. "Marty is a crusty old Navy man, but don't worry: His bark is worse that his bite. He runs a safe operation and has a nice stable of planes." Andy pulled open the ornately carved oak door of Luxury Jet Charters.

Mark stopped in his tracks. "Wow" was the woefully inadequate description for what Mark observed. Polished teak floors, Swarovski crystal lighting, a fully staffed espresso bar—and that was only the lobby.

Andy elbowed Mark. "A little nicer than flying out of LaGuardia, huh?"

Marty came around the corner, chomping on an unlit cigar. "Andy! How the hell are you? Come to beg for your old job back now that you've had a taste of flying for the airlines?" He was dressed in an ill-fitting thirty-year-old suit that hadn't gotten any bigger as Marty put on a few pounds. The hair on his balding head was the only thing thinner than when he first bought the suit.

They exchanged a vigorous handshake. "Same old Marty. No, you old fart, I came here to do you a favor. You desperately need pilots, and my friend here is more than qualified." Andy pointed to Mark. "Marty Dawson, meet

Mark Smith."

Marty cast a suspicious eye toward Mark. "Your friend is a little old for this job, isn't he?"

Mark answered for Andy. "I just retired from the airlines. But I figure if I'm lucky I'll have one or two more good years left in me before I croak."

Marty didn't appreciate Mark's irreverent sense of humor. "Funny. What I need are pilots with clean records and lots of jet time. What have you flown?"

Mark rattled off his flying resume. "I've flown the T-37, T-38, Gulfstream IV, C-141, DC-9, 727, 737, 757, A-320, DC-10, triple seven, and I have a handful of hours in the—"

"Fine, fine. You've got more than enough jet time." Marty was duly impressed but hid it from his face. "How 'bout your record? Any accidents? My insurance rates are bad enough. I don't need to give those jerks any reason to jack them up any higher."

Mark answered honestly. "I do have one accident under review by the FAA right now, but other than that, a clean record."

Marty cringed. "An accident? Okay, thanks for coming in Mr. Smith. Best of luck with the FAA."

Andy jumped to Mark's defense. "Hold on Marty, hear the man out."

"Like I said, I don't need my insurance rates to—"

"Mark was the captain on the Tech-Liner accident. Maybe you heard about it?"

Marty pulled the unlit cigar from his mouth. "You're *that* Mark Smith? You did a dead-stick landing in the Azores, right? That was some piece of flying."

Mark nodded.

Marty looked off in the distance and began to reminisce. "Hell of place, the Azores. We were sailing there on the carrier *Forrestal* one day when we ran into a bitch of a tropical storm. All flight operations were ceased. We were restricted below deck for two days straight. Nothing to do but watch movies and play cards."

Marty had no idea how much sarcasm Mark intended with his response. "Must have been hell for you."

Andy choked trying to hold in his laugh.

Almost fondly, Marty said, "Never forget it as long as I live." Back to the present, he asked, "You a Navy man, Smith?"

Now Mark almost choked. "Hell no. I was in the flying branch of the military, the Air Force."

Marty squinted and chomped back down on his cigar. "Oh, you mean the Air Farce. The country club branch. Golf courses, O clubs, two-mile-long runways that don't move around while you're trying to land on them."

Mark took the rivalry-based jabs in stride. He didn't let them bother him—much.

"Air Farce, you and me are going to get along just fine. You're hired." Marty stuck out his hand.

Mark left his hand at his side. "Mr. Dawson, I accept your offer on two conditions."

Marty warily eyed Mark. "Conditions? Go on."

"One, you hire my wife and her best friend as flight attendants. They are very experienced."

Marty waved away that small demand. "Done. That was an easy call. I can always use more flight attendants as often as they quit around here. And number two?"

"Number two, I'll fly for your operation as long as I don't have to listen to any more of your lame-ass Navy stories."

Marty nearly bit his cigar in half. Then he burst out laughing. "Air Farce, you drive a tough bargain. You got yourself a job." Marty slapped Mark on the back. "Come on, let me show you around."

An hour later Marty got down to business. "Smith, I run a tight ship around here. I got two rules: Never be late and treat the passengers like they pay your salary. This ain't the airlines. I'll have my chief pilot start your checkout in our new Gulfstream 500 Monday morning. Be here at 9 a.m. sharp."

CHAPTER 34

STRAPPED TIGHTLY INTO THE LEFT seat, Mark took a deep breath to calm his nerves. The Gulfstream 500 still had that new car smell since coming off the assembly line in Savannah only three months prior. Cleared by tower to take off, he advanced the throttles to the forward stops. The forty-five-million-dollar jet quickly accelerated down runway one-nine at Teterboro Airport and leaped into the air. This stallion was ready to run. Mark raised the landing gear then banked the plane into a wide, arcing turn to the west.

Just as he was about to check in with New York departure control, both engines sputtered and died. The jet was barely one thousand feet above the densely populated New Jersey landscape. Panic-stricken, Mark looked to his copilot for help.

He folded his arms and whined, "Don't look at me, it's your check ride."

The plane was dropping out of the sky like an extraordinarily expensive rock. Mark swallowed his fury at his worthless copilot and tried to prioritize the flood of computer-generated warnings blaring in his headset. The scenery out the windscreen rapidly grew larger. With no experience in this model, time unfortunately ran out before Mark could fix his dire emergency. The jet slammed into the ground, sending a mushroom-shaped fireball billowing into the air.

Noelle stretched and yawned as she came up behind the man in her bathroom. She rubbed his back and asked, "Another nightmare?"

He scooped up a handful of cold water under the running tap and splashed it on his face. Mark looked in the mirror and was shocked to see the fear in the eyes of the man staring back at him. He nodded and replied, "Same dream as last night."

Noelle wrapped her arms around Mark from behind and rested her head on his back. "I know it's hard. The thought of flying again after what happened. I get it." She released her embrace and wheeled Mark around until they were face to face. "But we really need our new jobs. Another check bounced yesterday." She looked at him with a mixture of compassion and pleading. "You need to get back on the horse, Mark. I love having you around, and I hate to admit it, but your place is in the air. It's time to pilot up, flyboy."

Monday morning, Mark walked through the doors of Luxury Jet Charters ten minutes early to begin his training. A guy barely older than his daughter walked up and asked, "Are you Mark?"

"Yes." Mark looked around the lobby. "I'm looking for the chief pilot. Can you show me where his office is?"

"Absolutely, follow me." He escorted Mark past the receptionist's desk and down a long hallway. He opened the door to an office marked Chief Pilot and sat down behind the desk. Then he enthusiastically announced, "Nice to meet you, Mark. Johnny Williams, LJC chief pilot."

Mark looked each direction down the hallway then looked back at Johnny. In a hushed voice, he said, "You'd better get out of his seat before he cans your ass."

Johnny laughed. "Oh yeah. Right. Because I look so young. I get it." He kicked his feet up on the desk. "No joke. I'm the chief pilot." Johnny turned his freshly made name plaque around on the desk and proudly added, "Going on two months now."

"Two months?"

"Turnover has been a real bear around here ever since the airlines started hiring again. As soon as our pilots gets the minimum flight hours to apply to the airlines, it's adios. Last guy in this job only hung around six months."

Mark started to wonder what he had gotten himself into.

Johnny pointed to a chair. "So, Mark, tell me about yourself. You have much flight time?"

Mark began to recite his extensive aviation background when Johnny cut him off.

"I'm just pulling your leg. Marty told me all about you. Very impressive. We're glad to have you on board." Johnny dropped his feet back on the floor and leaned forward. "Hey, maybe you can teach me a few things during your checkout."

Two weeks later

Mr. Simpson parted the curtains on his front window. The same nondescript black car sat idling at the curb again. He picked up a baseball bat and went to investigate. Simpson slowly approached the mysterious car from the rear. The dark tinting on the windows prevented him from seeing how many people were inside.

Tapping the front passenger window with the knob on the end of the bat handle, Simpson barked, "Hey, buddy. You've been hanging out in front of my building on and off for two weeks now. What's your problem?"

No response came from inside the car.

He tapped harder. "Hey, I'm talking to you."

Nothing.

Then he heard the unmistakable sound of a pump-action shotgun being readied.

Simpson immediately backed away. The car jerked away from the curb and sped off. He didn't have time to get the license plate.

Noelle had Mark sit on her suitcase while she struggled to zip it closed. "Do you really need to bring *everything*?" he questioned.

"Of course. It's our first overseas charter trip." She tickled him as Mark got up off her suitcase. "Get excited, Mark. We're going to Paris. It'll be like old times. You, me, Charlotte. The Three Musketeers ride again." Her eyes sparkled with anticipation as she spoke.

Mark couldn't mask the concern on his face. "Obviously, you know that means we have to fly over the North Atlantic."

"I know what you're thinking. Everything will be fine. You'll see." She ramped up the tickling. "Besides, we don't have any other option. I called France, and they flatly refused to move their country any closer to New York."

Mark ignored her teasing and grabbed both suitcases. "Come on, we don't want to be late."

Noelle verbally ticked off her travel checklist. "Passports. Cell phones." She yelled, "Do you have the euros?"

"Yes! Can we go now?" Mark waited impatiently out in the hallway with the bags.

Noelle looked back one more time then closed the apartment door. "Thanks for carrying my suitcase." She gave Mark a peck on the cheek. "You'll get the rest of your tip when we get to Paris." She punctuated her promise with a flirtatious wink.

Just as they started down the stairs, the phone rang in the apartment. Noelle turned back to answer it. Mark spread his arms out while holding the bags to create a barricade. "Let it go; we don't have time."

"But—"

"The recorder will get it. Let's go."

Mark and Noelle disappeared down the stairwell.

Back in the apartment, a female voice left a message after the beep. "Ms. Parker, this is Dr. Cooper from Oncology Specialists. Sorry it took me so long to get back to you with the results of your mammogram. I thought it best to send your films out for a second opinion. I need to talk to you right away. Please call my office as soon as you get this message."

CHAPTER 35

MARK AND NOELLE WALKED IN wearing their sharp new LJC uniforms. Charlotte had arrived earlier and stood outside Marty's office, trading dirty jokes with him.

With awe in her voice, Noelle looked around and said, "Damn, I think I could get used to this. Flying rich people all around the world to exotic destinations."

Mark smiled. "Sure beats the airlines. No smelly hippies wearing tank tops and Birkenstocks in this crowd. I don't think we'll be bumping into any of our passengers at Walmart."

Marty saw them coming and waved at them. "Hey, rookies, over here."

When they walked up, Charlotte gave Noelle a big hug. "Hey, darlin'." Then she turned to Mark. "Thanks for getting me this job. One more minute at that diner, and I was fixin' to strangle my boss." She reached out her hand in peace. "Truce?"

Mark's eyes narrowed as he folded his arms across his chest. Then he cracked a smile and shook Charlotte's hand. "Truce."

"Ain't this sweet. Quick, someone grab me some tissues before I start bawling."

"You're all heart, Marty. Just give us the flight details so we can get going," Mark said.

Johnny Williams walked up and joined the group. Marty looped his arm around his neck. "Johnny will be your copilot. He's never flown overseas. Mark, you show him how it's done."

The anticipation in Johnny's voice was evident. "This is going to be so cool. We get to fly over the Atlantic Ocean."

All three Tech-Liner survivors shot the young pilot a nasty look.

Marty continued. "You're flying some rich guy from France. His Gulfstream is broken, so he's chartering ours to get home. When I say rich, I'm talking about three-comma-club rich. I heard he inherited his family's business empire. Take good care of him; he's very particular. When his people booked the charter, they insisted everything be done exactly the way *Mr. Billionaire* wants it—right down to the brand of olives in his martinis."

"Typical first-class passenger. We got this," Charlotte assured.

The crew walked out on the ramp toward the waiting jet. The Gulfstream 500, of all the flashy planes out there, was the most coveted among the world's rich and powerful.

The sleek aircraft stood tall on its sturdy landing gear. There was an actual red carpet leading up to the stairs. With a charter rate of eight thousand dollars per hour, customers expected nothing less. For its passengers, the term *flying in style* seemed like a gross understatement.

Luxury yacht owners would have felt right at home in this plane. The roomy cabin was stunning. It was appointed with twelve gold-trimmed, buttery-soft leather seats, a full-size divan that turned into a bed, silk carpet, and a bathroom in the rear that a normal-size person could stand upright in.

The spacious cockpit was the part that excited Mark. It reminded him of the Tech-Liner. All the latest technology was there: fly-by-wire flight controls, wall-to-wall touch screens, even an Enhanced Vision System (EVS). This special infrared camera mounted on the nose could see through darkness, fog, rain…anything that prevented the pilots from seeing the view ahead.

While Mark and Johnny programed the flight computers in the cockpit, Noelle and Charlotte readied the cabin for their important guests. A van from New York's most elegant and expensive French restaurant pulled up to the plane. The deliveryman brought the order into the plane and left just as quickly.

Noelle unpacked the box. In it were fresh baguettes, escargot, *poulet basquaise* (a fancy term for braised chicken), four different types of cheese—enough food to feed ten people. Oddly, the order also included a hamburger. She brought a warm baguette up to her nose and drew in a long, nostalgic breath. The smell transported her back to her days in Paris as a wide-eyed twenty-year-old model. "I used to love these. Every morning, I would get them fresh from the bakery. It was all I could afford back then." She looked desirously at the long, thin loaf. "You just can't get bread like this in America."

Charlotte ripped off the end of a loaf and handed it to Noelle. "Take a bite. I won't tell." She slowly savored every morsel.

Before Noelle could swallow the last bite, a silver Rolls Royce drove through the security gate and pulled up to the red carpet. A man wearing all black and the requisite dark sunglasses stepped out. He wore his hair in a short military cut. Wearing a tight-fitting tailored suit, his muscular build was obvious—as was the bulge under his jacket from his shoulder holster. He scanned the area around the plane with a deadly serious look on his face.

Satisfied it was safe to exit the car, the bodyguard open the back door. A fluffy, snarling papillon dog was shoved at him. He dutifully, but grudgingly, accepted it. The guard extended his free hand into the car. An impeccably dressed woman in her late thirties took it and stepped out. She wore a skintight bright yellow dress that looked like it would split open at any moment. The plunging neckline was specifically designed to entice the male eye. The woman snatched her prized pooch back without a word and started for the aircraft stairs.

Noelle and Charlotte double-checked their uniforms as they waited at the door to greet their passengers. Looking down on the scene from the plane, the woman's face was hidden under a large, decorative hat that would have fit right in at the Kentucky Derby. When the woman reached the top of the stairs, she brushed right by without bothering to look at them or return the greeting extended to her.

She removed her ornate hat and thrust it at Charlotte. "Be careful with this." Long blonde locks tumbled down across her shoulders, framing her attractive face. Fire-engine-red lipstick covered her plump, surgically augmented lips. Even before sitting, the demands began. "I'm parched. I won't last another minute without a glass of champagne." She stroked the purebred Papillion's manicured fur. "And Princess would like some water. Bottled only, of course." Despite her obvious attempt to appear sophisticated, a trace of a Brooklyn accent slipped out. She was an American.

"Well bless your little heart, Princess. Bottled water it is," Charlotte mockingly replied, addressing the dog, not the woman. Back in the galley, Noelle and Charlotte quietly snickered at their pompous passenger. Charlotte whispered, "Can you believe all that fake jewelry hanging off of her? The dollar store must have had a half-off sale."

Noelle shook her head. "It's not fake. Our salaries combined wouldn't even pay for the necklace."

Noelle opened a bottle of champagne, while Charlotte returned with a bowl of water. She put the bowl on the floor and said, "Here you go, Princess. Bottled of course, Your Majesty." Charlotte had gotten the water straight from the sink faucet.

Outside, an angry conversation could be heard inside the Rolls Royce. The bodyguard hurried around to the other side of the car and opened the door. A trim, debonair seventy-year-old gentleman sporting a pencil-thin mustache stepped out of the car. He was screaming into his cell phone. Despite speaking French, there was no doubt to anyone listening that profanity was a large part of his tirade. The silver-haired man angrily stabbed his finger outward as if the caller's chest was the intended target. Still furious after hanging up, the man adjusted his bespoke suit and stormed up the stairs into the plane.

Noelle handed the demanding woman a flute of champagne from a silver platter. She turned around with a big smile to greet the approaching customer who'd paid the sizable bill for this trip. At the sight of him, Noelle clasped her hand over her mouth and dropped the tray, shattering the glasses.

The startled man took a step back. "Noelle? *Mon amour!* Is that you?"

CHAPTER 36

"I'M SO SORRY. I'LL CLEAN this up right away." Noelle had a mortified look on her face as she knelt down to pick up the broken pieces.

Girard Benoit knelt down beside her. "Please, let me help you."

The blonde woman crossed her arms and asked, "Girard, do you two know each other?"

"Oui," Benoit replied.

"No," Noelle simultaneously blurted out.

Benoit had a confused look on his face. "*Ma chéri*, it is me, Girard."

Noelle apologized again, brushed past Benoit, and hurried back to the galley. She turned to Charlotte. "I've got to get off this plane."

"What? And leave me all alone with that witch? Why?"

Noelle motioned toward Benoit. "It's him."

Charlotte peeked around the galley wall at the man. "Who?"

"It's Girard," Noelle clarified.

Charlotte looked again and just shrugged.

Exasperated, Noelle said, "Girard! The guy I had a...the guy from Paris I told you about. The older guy I met when I was a model."

Charlotte looked again. Her face turned ashen. "Oh my lord. Honey, you need to get off this plane."

The ground crew had finished loading the baggage onto the plane.

Marty stood on the tarmac at the foot of the stairs, impatiently tapping the face of his watch. "You're late! Get going." He opened a small access panel on the side of the fuselage and flipped an exterior control switch, retracting the boarding stairs. Once the stairs were tucked away, the front door locked closed like a jail cell door.

The engines started, and the plane taxied away, bound for Paris.

The bodyguard took a seat in the back so he could have a clear view of everyone on the plane. Benoit and his lady friend sat opposite each other. She wasn't speaking to him. A total of three passengers (and one dog) filled the sixteen-seat Gulfstream as it climbed on a northeasterly heading over Long Island Sound on its way to its final cruising altitude.

Charlotte and Noelle were tightly strapped into their jump seats at the front of the cabin when the woman waved at them. "Excuse me, yoo-hoo, I'd like a drink." Charlotte bravely volunteered to go back. When Charlotte approached the woman, she dismissively waved her away. "Not you, the other one."

Noelle got up, inhaled deeply, and steeled herself for more annoying demands from the woman. "Yes ma'am. What would you like?"

"An explanation." She looked over to Benoit. "Girard, it's obvious you two know each other. I believe a formal introduction is in order."

Benoit was not a person to be cornered, but he had no choice. "Noelle, meet Priscilla Winthrop."

Priscilla extended her right hand. "So nice to meet you." On the left was a sparkling ten-carat diamond engagement ring. "I'm Girard's fiancée. Our wedding is next month. And you would be?"

"Noelle Parker. I'm just an old friend, ma'am."

She withdrew her hand and raised an eyebrow. "Just? I doubt that."

Benoit glared at her with his piercing blue eyes. "Enough, Priscilla. Noelle and I knew each other many years ago. Now drop it and let her do her job. I would like a martini with two olives."

Priscilla had no intention of playing nice. But she was clever enough to know when to back off. "That sounds delightful. I'll have one as well." She picked up her dog, Princess, and stroked its fluffy fur. The dog snarled at Noelle as she walked away.

"Shut that mutt up, or it goes back in its carrier," Benoit threatened.

Priscilla tried to calm down the pint-size beast, but it turned and barked at Benoit.

That was it. Benoit's volatile temper showed itself. He snapped his finger and summoned his bodyguard, who appeared on command. Benoit ordered, "Put that mutt back in its carrier, and stow it in the baggage compartment. I'm not going to listen to that damned thing yap all the way to Paris."

Priscilla pouted and grudgingly relinquished her pet to the bodyguard, who promptly stuffed it in the carrier.

Despite being angry, Benoit spoke English reasonably well. A skill honed when sent away to the finest boarding schools by his socialite parents.

When Noelle walked up with the drinks, Priscilla chided Benoit. "Girard, how thoughtless, you neglected to introduce Jean-Luc to our *servants*." Noelle bit her lip, refusing to be baited by the bimbo dressed like a banana.

"Noelle, this is Monsieur Arseneau. He's my trusted assistant," Benoit said casually.

Priscilla corrected him. "Assistant? Please, that title hardly does justice to his many talents. Jean-Luc is our personal bodyguard. He was a member of the elite French special forces before the scandal. We were lucky to get him."

"The scandal?" Noelle questioned.

Benoit clarified. "A few years ago, after the attacks in

Paris, Monsieur Arseneau was somewhat overzealous while interrogating one of the vile terrorists. He was about to be made a scapegoat by the politicians for their failures to protect their citizens before I stepped in and put a stop to it. He's been with me since."

"I feel completely safe with him around," Priscilla added.

Arseneau wanted no part in this conversation. He told Noelle, "Show me how to access the baggage compartment."

Noelle dispensed the drinks then pointed to the rear of the plane. "Follow me." She opened the door to the bathroom at the back of the cabin and went in. Noelle turned a latch on the aft wall and pushed. A hidden door built into the wall of the bathroom opened into the baggage hold. The small compartment was pressurized to allow in-flight access in case passengers wanted to get something from their luggage. Located between the engines and lacking the same soundproofing as the cabin, a loud roar greeted Noelle when she opened the door to the compartment. On a side wall were a circuit breaker panel and various gauges reflecting the health of the aircraft systems. There was a small porthole in the aft wall allowing the crew to see the auxiliary power unit (APU) in the tail cone.

Noelle stepped back out of the small doorway to give Arseneau access to the compartment. "Latch the door closed when you're done," she instructed, then went back to the cabin. Out of spite, Arseneau put the carrier for the annoying dog on the cold floor and covered it with one of Priscilla's many suitcases.

———

The autopilot smoothly flew the plane on its prescribed course toward the Canadian side of the Atlantic. After answering a million and one questions from Johnny on the unique procedures for flying over the ocean, Mark felt comfortable leaving his copilot alone for a few minutes.

He decided to go back and greet his charter passengers, making sure to latch the cockpit door in the open position before leaving.

Mark started down the aisle toward his passengers. Arseneau saw him, jumped up, and sprinted forward. He blocked Mark with his hand and ordered, "Go back to the cockpit. You are not allowed here."

Mark nearly exploded with fury. "Who the hell do you think you are? Don't you *ever* tell me what to do in my airplane. I'm in charge, not you."

Arseneau started for his gun when Benoit grabbed his elbow. "It's okay." Looking at Mark, he said, "I'm so sorry, Captain. Monsieur Arseneau is very protective of me. I expect your sudden presence startled him. He must have assumed you were meaning me harm."

"You tell your bodyguard if he ever does anything like that again, I will immediately land this plane and have him removed." Mark's threat was somewhat hollow seeing as how most of the flight would be over water.

"My deepest apologies, sir. It won't happen again." Benoit's personality could be very disarming when it benefitted him.

Arseneau grudgingly went back to the aft part of the cabin. The overpaid thug stood with an alert posture, facing Mark rather than sitting down. His cold, soulless eyes communicated the extent of his deadly skills without saying a word.

"Captain, my name is Girard Benoit." The billionaire gestured to his left. "This is Priscilla Winthrop, my fiancée."

"Welcome aboard. I'm Mark Smith." He kept one eye on Arseneau as he spoke. "Our arrival time in Paris will be 3 p.m. I'm expecting a smooth ride over the ocean today, but be sure to keep your seat belts fastened just in case we—"

Noelle came up beside Mark and draped herself on him. "Oh good. You've met our captain. You are very lucky to have Mark as your pilot today." Noelle planted a big kiss on his cheek. "And I'm very lucky to have this handsome pilot as *my* fiancé."

"Is that right…" Priscilla slyly said.

"Is that so…" Benoit snarled.

The tone of their responses could not have been more different.

CHAPTER 37

After greeting his passengers, Mark followed Noelle forward to the galley. He pulled her aside. "What was that all about?"

"What, darling?" she replied, feigning ignorance.

"You were hanging all over me back there. What's up?"

Noelle and Charlotte each took deep breaths and exchanged peculiar looks.

Their strange behavior aroused suspicion. He narrowed his eyes as he looked at each of them. "What was that… that *look*?

"What look? Noelle said nervously.

All right, what's going on? What are you two hiding?"

"Honey, it's time you tell him," Charlotte advised. "You two need to talk. Not in the galley, though. Y'all are going to want some privacy." She shooed them toward the cockpit. "Go. I'll keep an eye on things back here."

Mark and Noelle stepped into the cockpit. Although spacious for a business jet, it lacked the room to comfortably fit three people. Plus, Mark didn't want his copilot hearing what Noelle had to say. "Hit the road, Johnny," Mark diplomatically ordered. He pointed his thumb back toward the cockpit door. "Go ask Charlotte for sightseeing tips for our layover in Paris."

Johnny got up and eagerly left the cockpit, thinking Charlotte would be excited to play the role of tour guide. Johnny didn't know Charlotte very well.

After closing the door, they sat: Mark in the left seat,

Noelle in the right. Mark turned toward his ex-wife and said, "Well?"

"Where would you like me to start?"

"The truth would be a good place."

She paused for a moment, cleared her throat, then blurted it out. "Girard and I were lovers."

Mark was rocked back in his seat by the blunt admission. After a moment, he regained his composure. "Go on."

"It happened a lifetime ago, Mark. Long before we met. I was young. He was a dashing older man from a wealthy family. I was homesick and lonely." Noelle's head drooped. "What can I say, it happened."

"Then?" Mark asked, assuming there was more to the story.

"It all became too much. I left him. I went back home and enrolled at Yale. I never heard from Girard again." Noelle reached out for his hand. "But then the best thing to ever happen in my life happened. I met you." A single tear rolled down her cheek.

Mark ignored her hand and lifted Noelle's head to look into her eyes. "Should I be worried?" he asked.

"No, of course not. He's engaged. We're engaged. You have nothing to worry about."

CHAPTER 38

BENOIT AND PRISCILLA SAT ON opposite sides of the cabin. The empty seats in front of them were arranged club style, facing aft.

After hours in the air, Charlotte figured their passengers must be getting hungry. "Would you care for dinner now?"

"Yes, I'm famished," Priscilla replied. "Do you have my special order? I couldn't bare the idea of eating another bite of that dreadful French food."

"Yes, ma'am, the caterer included your hamburger in the order."

Benoit sniffed at Priscilla's unrefined American palate.

Charlotte reached over and pulled hidden tables up out of each sidewall and extended them across in front of each seat. She laid white linens on the tables then came back with the catered French feast, spreading it out in front of Benoit. He tucked his napkin into his collar and dove in.

Charlotte put the hamburger down in front of Priscilla.

She raised a finger. "Wait, there aren't any fries. Where are my French fries?"

Charlotte planted her hands on her hips. "Missy, this ain't McDonalds. What you see is what you get."

Benoit snickered under his breath.

"Then bring me another martini," Priscilla demanded. "You have those, don't you?"

Charlotte clenched her jaw and went back to the galley.

Johnny was patiently waiting for those tourist tips, but as soon as Noelle walked out of the cockpit, Charlotte grabbed her. "Well? How did it go? Did you tell him everything?" Before Noelle could answer, Charlotte looked over at Johnny. "Beat it, kid. Adults are talking here."

Johnny obediently went back into the cockpit.

Noelle shrugged. "Yes, I told him. He's hurt. I can tell. No husband wants to learn his wife was with another man, no matter how long ago it happened. Mark just needs some time to process the bomb I just dropped on him."

Charlotte put her arm around Noelle. "If you need to talk, you let me know."

She nodded gratefully.

"Hey, I know what will cheer you up. The witch of Brooklyn wants another martini. Why don't you take it back to her?" Charlotte joked.

"I'm sure that will make me feel *much* better."

Charlotte grinned and handed Noelle the martini. "What are friends for? Go."

Noelle put the drink on Priscilla's table. "Is there anything else I can do for either of you?"

Benoit looked concerned. "I noticed you haven't had anything to eat yet." He gestured at the empty seat facing him. "Please, join us. Priscilla and I would be honored to have you dine with us."

Both women were taken aback by the unexpected invitation.

Noelle combed her mind for an excuse to decline. "I'm sorry, but eating with the customers is against the rules." That was the best she could come up with on short notice.

"We understand, dear. Girard, you wouldn't want her to get in trouble for breaking the rules, would you?" Priscilla was hopeful he would agree.

Benoit's anger flared. "I make the rules. I am paying for this flight." He quickly caught himself and reeled in his volatile temper. He took a breath and regained his composure. "I meant if Noelle explains that I specifically requested she join us, her boss will certainly understand." He gestured toward the empty seat again. "Please, won't you join me? I have far too much food for one person here. I would hate for it to go to waste, what with all the starving children in this world."

Noelle cast a skeptical eye at his supposed compassion for the world's less fortunate.

Benoit pointed at Charlotte. "I'm sure your coworker won't mind if you take a short break."

"Don't you need my help in the galley?"

Unfortunately, she didn't catch the hint. "Honey, one time I served two hundred passengers a full dinner between New York and Detroit. I think I can handle this tiny crowd on my own for a few minutes."

"It's settled then," Benoit announced. "Please, join me."

Noelle relented. "Certainly, sir."

He stiffened in his seat. "Sir? Noelle, we know each other far to intimately for you to call me sir. It's Girard from now on. I won't hear of anything less."

Priscilla silently fumed at the thought of her perceived rival sharing a meal with her fiancé.

CHAPTER 39

BENOIT WAVED HIS HAND ACROSS the feast. "It's a pleasure to share a meal with you again after all these years. Please, enjoy."

Noelle didn't waste any time as she savored a mouth full of the poulet basquaise. She closed her eyes and smiled. "This tastes just like it did at that small café on the Seine we used to go to. Remember?"

"Yes, I do. But I'm surprised you remember eating anything from those days. You ate like a bird. I was worried you'd waste away to nothing."

"Such is the life of a model. Starve yourself for the camera." Noelle patted her flat stomach. "Luckily, I don't have to obsess over every calorie anymore."

"Nonsense, *ma chérie*. You could go back to modeling tomorrow." Benoit looked her up and down as he gushed. "If I didn't know better, I'd guess you were in your thirties."

Priscilla pursed her lips. "Just how old are you, dear?"

"I'm fifty," Noelle confidently replied.

"My, you do look wonderful for such an advanced age."

Holding back his temper, Benoit turned toward his fiancée. "I believe I hear Princess barking. She must miss you terribly. Why don't you go back and see how she's doing?"

Priscilla perked up at the prospect of seeing her beloved mutt. She ripped a large chunk of meat off her hamburger with her fingers and hurried off to the back of the plane.

Benoit turned back to Noelle. "Finally, some peace. We

have so much to catch up on. How has life been for you since Paris?"

"It's been good. It's great. Life always has its ups and downs, but I'm happy." She gave a *Reader's Digest* summary of the past thirty years. "Mark and I met when I became a flight attendant. Unfortunately, we fought a lot, and things didn't work out. He had a lot of issues to work through. We split up five years ago. But now he's a completely different man. I'm proud of the progress he's making. We *had* planned to remarry soon, but…"

"What happened?" Benoit asked with apparent concern.

"It's a long story. He's being sued. Our airline went bankrupt. Now money is very tight. It's been pretty rough lately."

"Because of the accident in the Azores?"

Noelle cocked her head. "You heard about that?"

"How could I not? The press covered it for weeks."

"Trust me; we saw the coverage. With all that is going on, I decided it's just not the right time to get married."

"Do the two of you have any children?" Benoit inquired.

Noelle's face beamed with pride. "We have a daughter. Her name is Mary. Smart as can be. She's going to be a doctor. Top of her class at Duke with only one semester to go until she graduates." The pride on her face shifted to sorrow. "Unfortunately, the bankruptcy has forced us to change plans. We can't afford to send her back to finish. She's just heartbroken about it." Noelle forced a smile. "So, tell me about your life. Obviously you've done very well."

"Yes, I have." Modesty was not one of Benoit's traits. "As you can see"—he swept his hand across the cabin—"I have jets at my beck and call. I would never dream of flying on airliner."

His not-so-subtle swipe at her previous profession stung.

He continued. "As a young man and the only heir, I took over Benoit Industries from my father after he passed away. With ambition and tenacity, I turned the struggling company around after years of mismanagement by him. It's grown considerably since then. We've expanded into military weapons production, pharmaceuticals, shipping, mining precious minerals, and many other areas. Soon, my company will rival the largest US companies."

Noelle looked back at Arseneau. "That explains the bodyguard. I imagine by achieving that level of success, you've made a few enemies along the way."

"My dear, the business world is a cutthroat place. If a man doesn't make some enemies, he is not succeeding. Fearlessness is a must. At this stage, many more fear me."

He ominously added, "For good reason."

Noelle took in Benoit's words and nodded. She changed the subject. "And now you're engaged. I'm happy for you. Priscilla seems nice." Noelle was surprised her nose didn't grow after saying those last two sentences.

Benoit looked back down the aisle. "Her? We shall see. Maybe the third time things will work out."

Noelle sat back and crossed her arms. "That's right. You were married when I was in Paris. Something you conveniently neglected to tell me."

Benoit scoffed at her remark. "You prudish Americans will never understand French customs. A married man is expected to have a paramour. Someone to make life more stimulating."

Noelle smirked. "Does Pricilla know about your French customs?" She thought for a second then glared at Benoit. "Wait a minute. Is that all I was to you? A source of *stimulation?*"

Benoit clasped Noelle's hands. "*Mon amour,* how could you say such a thing? You were so much more than that to me. When you left without any explanation, I was heartbroken." He caressed her hands. "Now look at me."

Of course, Girard looked different all these years later. What hadn't changed was the intensity of his blue eyes. When angry, his glare was so intense it could cut through granite.

As he confided in Noelle about his life, that intensity was replaced with sadness. "All these years later, I sit here an old man with two failed marriages and no children or grandchildren. Not a single heir to carry on the proud Benoit name." He looked wistfully into Noelle's eyes. "I would give my entire fortune to find a woman such as you."

Priscilla walked up to the table at the same moment that Mark stepped out of the cockpit. They were surprised at what they saw.

Noelle immediately let go of Benoit's hands.

CHAPTER 40

"WHAT THE HELL IS GOING on here?" Mark demanded.

Priscilla echoed his concern. "Why were you holding her hands, Girard?"

"It meant nothing. We were only talking," Girard indignantly responded.

"It means something in my country," Mark shot back.

Benoit nodded knowingly. "Ah, I see the misunderstanding. You are Americans. That is the problem. People in your country are so uptight about any physical contact. In France, acquaintances innocently holding hands while talking is quite common."

Mark's expression told Benoit he wasn't buying the excuse.

Nonetheless, he continued. "For example, if I were to meet you on the streets of Paris, Monsieur Smith, it would be rude of me to not give you what we French call *faire la bise*. I suspect you wouldn't approve of that either."

"Speak English, Benoit."

"It means to give you a kiss on each cheek. Perhaps I could just demonstrate for you," Benoit cleverly offered.

Mark took a step back at the thought of Benoit getting his lips anywhere near him. "Noelle is fluent in French. If I need any translating done, I'll get it from her."

"As you wish, Monsieur." Benoit turned to Priscilla. "So you see, my dear, this was all a simple misunderstanding. I meant nothing by it."

She wasn't buying his excuse either but made a big display of pretending to forgive Benoit with a kiss—for Noelle's sake.

"Noelle, I need to speak to you," Mark firmly said.

She got up and walked into the cockpit with Mark.

Johnny got up before being asked. "I know, I know. Beat it." He closed the door as he left.

Mark pointed to the cabin. "So, I *should* be worried about you two. And don't give me *the French are very demonstrative* line. I'm not buying it. That man still has feelings for you."

"You're right; he does." Noelle's surprising response left him speechless. "I have a past, Mark. A past before, us. But I love *you*, not Girard."

"Then why aren't you holding *my* hands right now? The same way you were with him. We're talking, aren't we?"

Noelle blew out a long breath in frustration. "Men and your stupid jealousies. What are you going to do next, grunt?" Noelle reached out and forcefully grabbed Mark's hands. "There, I'm holding your hands. Are you happy now?"

Mark tried to pull his hands back, but Noelle had an anaconda-like grip on them. His real reason for being jealous came out. "Damn right, I'm jealous. He's a multibillionaire. I'm a broke, retired pilot being sued for ten million dollars."

Then Mark added the most important difference between him and Benoit (from a pilot's perspective, of course). "Hell, he even has his own Gulfstream. How am I supposed to compete with that?"

Noelle let go of his hands and sighed. "You're right. You can't. It's not even a fair fight. It's over, Mark. I'm leaving you for Benoit the Billionaire."

Mark glared at Noelle and tried his best not to laugh. "It's not funny. Stop trying to joke your way out of this."

She looked directly at Mark. "You're right; I'm sorry. I'll go open the door and throw him out right now." Noelle started toward the cockpit door with an impish smile on her face.

There was no way Mark could stay mad at Noelle when he looked into her beautiful blue eyes.

And she knew it.

"Very funny. Instead of throwing him overboard, how about this? The next time you talk to Benoit, no holding hands, no kisses on the cheek, none of that French crap. Just talk." Mark felt like getting in a little dig of his own. "Or is my request too *jealous* for you?"

"Okay, I agree: No more of that French crap." Noelle's impish grin returned. "Touché, Mark."

He sighed and rolled his eyes. "Just tell me what you talked about."

"We talked about our lives since…since we were together. That's all. I told him all about us, about Mary, about getting remarried. Then he told me about his life. To be honest with you, I feel sorry for him. He's a lonely old man. He has two failed marriages and no children."

"Don't feel too sorry for him. He's got billions of dollars to keep him company. Be careful, Noelle. Men like him don't get to where he's at by being nice. You have no idea what he's capable of."

CHAPTER 41

Noelle returned to the cabin. Benoit was waiting outside the cockpit door for her. "If I have caused any trouble between you and your ex-husband, I apologize."

"It's just a misunderstanding. Let's drop it and move on."

But Benoit wouldn't let it go. "Allow me to make up for the trouble I've caused." He pointed at Noelle then the cockpit. " I would be honored to have you both as my guests during your stay. I have a small property outside of Paris called Château Paradis. You would be more than comfortable there."

Charlotte snorted, "*Chatoo Paradish,*" badly mangling the pronunciation. "Sounds pretty comfy to me."

Noelle translated for her Southern friend. "It means Heaven's Castle."

Priscilla hissed an expletive under her breath at the thought of Noelle joining them.

Benoit turned and shot her a withering look that silenced any further challenges to his decision.

Although not interested, Noelle couldn't resist the opportunity to stick it to Priscilla. "That sounds lovely. How nice of you to offer. Is it far?"

"Not at all. We would fly there in my helicopter to avoid the miserable Parisian traffic," Benoit assured.

"What about Charlotte and Johnny? Are they invited?" Noelle asked.

"I'm afraid not. There isn't enough room on the helicopter for everyone on your crew."

"We can't leave them—"

Benoit quickly cut off any reasons for declining his invitation. "To make up for having to exclude them, I will have them stay in my apartment on the Champs Elysées. It is much more elegant than a hotel. They will have my entire staff at their disposal. Maids, cook, driver, butler."

That last part definitely got Charlotte's attention. "Did you say butler?"

"At your beck and call."

"Someone serving *me* for a change? Hell, that works for me."

Noelle shot her friend a reproachful look for that unhelpful comment. "No, I can't accept your offer. Mark would never agree to leave his crew."

Charlotte elbowed Noelle. "No harm in asking him, is there?"

Benoit poured on the pressure. "I remember how much you loved to visit the botanical gardens in Paris when you were young."

Noelle could see the image of the gardens in her mind. "The *Jardin des Plantes*. Yes, I remember. The flowers there were magnificent. And the fragrant smells…"

"You'd get lost for hours wandering the paths, admiring all the beautiful flowers."

"Could we visit the gardens before going to your place?"

"No need. Years ago, I hired their director to design the grounds at my estate. I believe he outdid even *le Jardin*."

Charlotte implored with her eyes. "A butler, honey. I'd get my own butler! Just ask."

Benoit tried to help close the deal. "Your wise coworker is right. There is no harm in asking, is there? If he declines my invitation, then so be it."

Noelle was out of excuses, out of allies, and more than a little intrigued. "Okay, I'll ask." She pulled open the door to the cockpit, stepped in, and closed it behind her. When

Noelle came back out after only eleven seconds, the verdict was obvious. "Mark said"—she decided to clean up his response—"thank you for the offer, but no."

Benoit bowed his head in defeat. "As he wishes. It's a shame you won't get to see my magnificent gardens." He went back to his seat and sat down across the aisle from his gloating fiancé.

With a downbeat look on her face, Noelle checked her watch. "We will be landing at Le Bourget airport in forty-five minutes. Is there anything else I can get you?"

Priscilla started to ask for something, anything, just to make Noelle wait on her.

Benoit cut her off. "*No*. We don't need anything else."

Noelle and Charlotte stepped into the galley to stow all remaining food and drink in preparation for landing.

Benoit tapped his fingers on his table in frustration then checked his diamond-encrusted wristwatch. He unbuckled and stomped off to the back of the plane.

Arseneau stood as Benoit approached. The two had a hushed conversation, after which Benoit returned to his seat. The bodyguard disappeared into the bathroom.

Five minutes later, Arseneau reappeared, holding Princess at arm's length. He walked up and deposited the mutt in Priscilla's lap.

"Princess, you're back! Mommy missed you so much." She snuggled with the dog then turned to Benoit as if seeking permission to keep it with her during the arrival into Paris. "Girard?"

With an irritated look on his face, Benoit explained. "I didn't want Princess to be alone in the dark during the landing. It might frighten her." He pointed at the mutt. "But I expect you to keep it quiet."

Priscilla drew the tips of her fingers across her lips like a zipper. "Not a peep. Princess will be a good girl."

The remainder of the flight, each time the dog looked Benoit's way it let out a low growl.

CHAPTER 42

JOHNNY PREPARED THE JET FOR landing at Le Bourget, the spot northeast of Paris made famous when Charles Lindbergh landed there after flying solo for thirty hours across the Atlantic. He programmed the autopilot to fly the approach, but Mark waved off his efforts. He rarely got a chance to hand-fly an approach with the airlines, and he wasn't about to pass up on this opportunity to show off his flying skills to the rookie pilot sitting next to him.

After being instructed to contact the tower by Paris approach control, Johnny switched frequencies. "Le Bourget tower, Gulfstream Two-Seven-Lima-Juliet is ten miles out for landing." He identified the plane by its tail number, speaking the last two letters, *L* and *J*, phonetically for the French controller. *L* and *J* were the last two letters of every tail number at Luxury Jet Charters.

"You are cleared to land on runway zero-three," the controller replied.

"Roger, cleared to land on runway three."

"Gear down," Mark commanded.

Johnny grabbed the gear handle sticking out from the instrument panel and pushed it down. The landing gear hydraulically lowered into place with a loud clunk.

At the sound of the gear coming down, Benoit looked out the window at the sprawling city. Arseneau got out of his seat and came up to Benoit, covering the speaker of his cell phone with his hand. He handed the phone to Benoit, who listened for a moment then thrust it back at Arseneau.

Benoit jumped out of his seat and went up to Noelle as she buckled into her jump seat. "Tell the pilot not to land."

Surprised by the last-minute demand, Noelle implored, "Girard, you need to sit down right now. We're about to touch down."

Sounding homesick, Benoit explained. "Change of plans. I want to fly over Paris. It's a beautiful day. A rare day without smog. I want to see my beloved birthplace from above before landing. Tell the pilot not to land."

"Please," he added.

Noelle raised an eyebrow but complied with his request. She picked up the intercom handset and punched the COCKPIT button. "Mark, the customer would like you to fly over Paris before landing." She listened, then threw up her hands. "I know, I told him!" She listened for a few seconds more, then said, "Thanks."

The engines suddenly increased to full power. The landing gear banged back up into the gear well as the nose pointed skyward. After a moment, the plane leveled off and began flying a lazy circle around Paris. This little sightseeing tour would tack on another two thousand dollars to the charter bill.

Back in his seat, Benoit beamed as he took in the sights. The afternoon sun gave the city a warm glow. He motioned to Noelle. "Come, look."

She debated the safety of getting out of her jump seat at such a low altitude. Noelle looked up to see Priscilla glaring right at her. She unbuckled and sat across from Benoit, pressing her face against the large panoramic oval window.

As she looked down on the city, fond memories came flooding back. From a distance, it all looked so innocent and beautiful. She drank in the sights of Paris. Noelle clearly saw the River Seine as it wound through the city's arrondissements. Tears welled up in her eyes at the heartbreaking sight of the fire-ravaged Notre Dame cathedral on the Île de la Cité. Flying westward, Gustave Eiffel's engineering marvel poked up above the din of the city, dominating the scenery as it had for more than a hundred years.

After fifteen minutes of flying lazy circles around the city, the flight attendant call chime went off in the cabin. Mark was signaling Noelle to pick up the intercom. She reluctantly left the window and answered. Noelle covered the handset with her hand and turned to Benoit. "Mark says he's getting low on fuel. He must land now."

Benoit turned back to look at his bodyguard.

Arseneau lifted his cell phone from his ear and nodded his head.

"I've seen enough," Benoit said.

"It's okay; we can land now," Noelle said. She hung up and strapped back in.

———◆———

The delay in landing had allowed a thick cloud bank to drift over the area, greatly reducing visibility at all nearby airports. The tower called on the radio, directing Mark's plane to go into a holding pattern until the visibility improved.

Mark grabbed the microphone. "Negative, Le Bourget tower. Gulfstream Two-Seven-Lima-Juliet is unable to accept holding. We are too low on fuel. We need to land now."

The unsympathetic controller in the tower brusquely replied, "Negative. Enter holding pattern as instructed."

Johnny nudged Mark. "Tell him we have EVS."

Mark nodded gratefully. *Maybe this kid isn't so green after all.* He clicked the transmit button. "Tower, we are equipped with an enhanced vision system. The weather at the airport will be no problem. Request landing clearance."

"Ah, oui, Monsieur. In that case, you are cleared to land on runway zero-seven."

"Cleared to land runway seven." Mark turned to Johnny. "Activate the EVS."

Johnny tapped a few buttons on the instrument panel then gave Mark a thumbs-up. They each folded down a glass screen from the ceiling, similar to how a driver pulls a sun visor down into his field of view. Readings from the plane's vital instruments were projected onto the glass heads-up display (HUD). In addition, a grayish-green picture representing the real world hidden below the clouds was also displayed on the glass. The EVS computer had integrated a number of different inputs from the plane, including the infrared camera in the nose, to create a crisp, virtual picture for the pilots.

The bad weather at the airport was now immaterial to Mark. On the HUD he could see the runway, taxiways, even the traffic jam on the A1 motorway. They caught a brief glimpse of the approach lights as the jet broke out of the clouds seconds before the main wheels kissed the runway. Aircraft without EVS were left doing circles in the sky.

As they slowed, Johnny radioed the tower. "Two-Seven-Lima-Juliet requesting taxi instructions to customs."

"Two-Seven-Lima-Juliet, taxi to the Benoit Industries hangar ahead at your two o'clock."

Mark interceded on the radio. "Negative, tower. We are an international flight. We need to clear customs first before dropping off our passengers."

The tower controller barked, "Taxi now to the hangar!"

Johnny looked over at Mark. He just shrugged. Despite the sizeable monetary fine and paperwork hassle that violating customs laws can have on a pilot, Mark had no choice but to comply. He taxied his plane up to the hangar with the massive Benoit Industries logo painted on the doors.

The ground crew was waiting. A man in white coveralls

waived his orange wands in unison over his head to direct the plane to its parking spot. After stopping, Mark shut down the left engine then directed Johnny to start the APU (auxiliary power unit). It was needed so the plane would have electric power after shutting down the right engine.

Johnny pushed the START button for the APU on the overhead panel. Nothing happened. He pushed it a second time. Again, nothing. He advised Mark, "Something's wrong with the APU; it won't start."

Irritated, Mark pushed the button himself, as if his magic captain's fingers would somehow start the stubborn APU where Johnny's hadn't.

It didn't start.

The ground crew clamped their hands over their ears. Even with only one engine running at idle, the noise was deafening. Mark gave the crew the hand signal alerting them he would need an external power cart plugged in. They hustled one over and plugged it in to a receptacle under the nose of the plane. As designed, the electrical system shifted over to the power cart. Mark flashed a thumbs-up to the ground crew. It was now safe to shut down the remaining engine.

Just then, a government vehicle sped up to the jet. French Customs was painted on the side of the car in both French and English. A stern-faced man in a dark blue uniform and round, flat-top cap stepped out of the back seat and glared at the cockpit.

Mark saw him. "Shit. I knew we should have told the tower to go to hell." He pointed toward the ramp for Johnny's sake. "Customs is here." Mark grabbed his passport out of his suitcase, left the cockpit, and asked Noelle to help him interpret his way out of this mess. He opened the door and lowered the boarding stairs. The customs official waited at the foot of the stairs with his arms tightly crossed. Two armed agents flanked him.

Once in front of the official, Mark tried to explain. "I'm sorry, I don't speak French. There must have been a misunderstanding on the radio." Mark held out his passport. "I never meant to—"

The man in charge raised his hand, signaling Mark to stop. In passable English, he said, "Passports won't be necessary, Captain Smith. I've taken care of everything."

Mark turned to Noelle. "How does he know my name?"

She shrugged, confused as he was.

The official looked over Mark's shoulder to the top of the aircraft stairs. He smiled broadly and gushed, "Monsieur Benoit, welcome home! It is a pleasure to see you again."

Benoit stepped on to the ramp, embraced the official, and exchanged a kiss of greeting on each cheek. "Director Brassard, how kind of you to meet my flight."

The official gave a slight nod. "It is no bother at all."

Benoit turned to Mark. "Captain, this is Monsieur Brassard. He is in charge of customs."

Mark nodded. "I apologize for the confusion, sir. I assumed we would be clearing customs the normal way. There was no need for the head of customs for Le Bourget airport to go to the trouble of meeting our plane in person."

The official sniffed at Mark. "You are mistaken, Captain. I am not the head of customs for this airport."

"But..." Mark's expression showed he was completely lost now.

"I am the director of customs for France."

CHAPTER 43

DIRECTOR BRASSARD TIPPED HIS HAT and left the scene as quickly as he had arrived.

Benoit and Priscilla acted as if this sort of thing happened every day.

A mechanic walked up to Mark. "How much petrol will you need?"

Mark shook off his confusion from the customs incident. "I'll determine that later. We have a bigger problem: our APU won't start."

The small engine in the tail cone was capable of powering most of the systems on the plane, but per FAA regulations it had to be operational to legally fly over the ocean in case of an emergency.

Mark shook his head. "We can't go anywhere until it's fixed."

Benoit spoke up. "My mechanic would be happy to take a look at it. If necessary, he will repair it as well." In French, Benoit instructed his mechanic to find out what the problem was.

The mechanic came back after only a few minutes. "Captain, your crew needs to be more careful. The reason it won't start is because the circuit breaker for the APU has been pulled out and somehow broken off."

Mark looked suspiciously over at Benoit's bodyguard.

Arseneau crossed his arms and sneered at Mark with a self-satisfied look.

Mark held Arseneau's cold stare, long enough to communicate his lack of fear of the thug. Then he turned and asked the mechanic, "How long to fix it?"

"At least two days, Monsieur. I would need to order a new part, then have my men install it."

Benoit barked at his mechanic, "You are to repair Captain Smith's plane as soon as possible. Park his plane in my hangar until the new part arrives."

The doors to Benoit's large hangar parted. A Gulfstream 500 sat on the pristine floor of the hangar next to a brand-new Airbus H225 Super Puma helicopter. Both aircraft had the Benoit Industries logo proudly painted on their tails.

Benoit addressed Mark and Noelle. "That settles it then. Since you are stuck here, you should join me at my estate." He gestured toward the helicopter. "Mark, you are welcomed to fly it if you like."

Mark wasn't fooled by Benoit's attempt to buddy up to him by addressing him by his first name. Still, he salivated over the prospect of flying the gleaming, twenty-eight-million-dollar craft. He watched as it was towed out of the hangar onto the ramp right in front of him. Mark's gut was telling him that there was something suspicious about the broken APU circuit breaker. Without any proof, he didn't want to pass up this once-in-a-lifetime opportunity. Even if it was Benoit's helicopter. Mark tried to sound hesitant. "Okay, we can stay. But only until the plane is fixed."

"Wonderful." Benoit directed the attention of his chauffeur to Charlotte and Johnny. "Take these two to my apartment. Tell my staff to pamper them with anything their hearts desire."

The chauffeur grabbed their suitcases and tossed them in the trunk.

Johnny turned to Charlotte. "Since we have time, I'd like to go to a museum while we're here. Which one do you recommend?"

Charlotte flashed a devious grin. "I know just the place,

kid. You ever heard of the Moulin Rouge?"

"Is that a museum?"

"A very special museum," Charlotte replied. "It's only open at night. I'll take you there myself."

They hopped in the limo and sped off.

Noelle shook her head and rolled her eyes when Charlotte looked back with that same grin on her face.

While Charlotte was busy making plans to corrupt the morals of his young copilot, Mark had wandered over to the Gulfstream parked in the hangar. He walked to the back of the plane and looked up at the tail. Next to the company logo was the aircraft registration tail number. Aircraft registration numbers in France started with the letter *F*, followed by a dash, then a maximum of four letters.

Mark flinched when he read it. "That's creepy." The tail number was F-NOEL. Mark noticed heat waves raising up from the back of the engine. He reached up and touched the engine nacelle. It was hot. He flagged down a nearby mechanic. "Excuse me, do you speak English?"

"Yes, Monsieur, I do."

"How many jets does Benoit have?" Mark asked with a puzzled look on his face.

The mechanic looked confused as well. "Only one. Why do you ask?"

"I thought…I thought his plane was broken back at Teterboro?"

"You are mistaken!"

Mark spun around to find Arseneau standing right behind him.

The mechanic scurried away with a frightened look on his face.

"Go back to your own plane," Arseneau ordered.

Mark momentarily considered taking on Benoit's lapdog then and there. He changed his mind when he saw the butt of a pistol sticking out of Arseneau's coat. Mark wisely walked away. As he neared his plane, Mark noticed

Benoit and another well-dressed gentleman standing off to the side of the hangar, having a heated argument. Benoit repeatedly poked the man in the chest as he shouted at him. The man slapped Benoit's hand away and stormed off to his nearby Mercedes. The car left a black streak of hot rubber on the tarmac as it sped off.

Arseneau went up to Benoit to investigate the altercation. The helicopter engines had started, preventing Mark from overhearing the conversation. Shortly after speaking to Benoit, the bodyguard drove off in the same direction as the angry man.

CHAPTER 44

THE SLEEK HELICOPTER LIFTED OFF and quickly climbed above the cloud bank into clear skies above. The pilot turned to Mark and offered to let him fly.

Mark nodded tentatively and gripped the stick and collective. He scanned the high-tech panel for help guiding the unfamiliar craft. An offering of instruments comparable to any modern jet lay in front of him. Mark jerked the stick side to side, doing his best to keep the helicopter straight and level. He failed miserably. The aircraft bucked and weaved through the afternoon sky. Little wonder: Mark had never flown a helicopter before. His sizeable ego had prevented him from mentioning that small detail to Benoit.

To prevent his demanding boss from getting airsick, the helicopter pilot diplomatically recommended he resume flying.

Mark happily relinquished the controls to the pilot, sat back, and enjoyed the short flight.

The clouds eventually dissipated, giving the pilot the opportunity to fly low over the rolling French countryside for the benefit of his American guests. Twenty minutes later, they arrived.

Benoit's "small" property turned out to be a massive estate perched atop a flat plateau with a breathtaking view of the countryside. A single road led up to the front gate. An ornate golden gate was set into an impenetrable stone wall modeled after the protective barrier that had once surrounded ancient Rome. Like so many rich and powerful before him, Benoit had an infatuation with seeing himself as an equal to emperors and kings. That conceit didn't stop at the wall. The entire estate was designed to resemble the historic palace of Versailles and its grounds. Manicured lawns, easily equivalent to a dozen football fields, surrounded the castle-size house on all sides.

Benoit picked up the intercom handset next to his seat and instructed his pilot to fly slowly around his estate before landing. The impromptu tour was obviously meant to amaze his middle-class guests.

As the helicopter circled, Mark noticed a formidable security force guarding the perimeter outside the wall. Armored Humvees with roof-mounted machine guns prowled the area. No one made it inside these grounds without scrutiny from the guards.

Two ordinary-looking buildings, presumably housing the staff, were tucked away out of sight behind a row of trees.

The helicopter touched down next to the main house and shut down its engines. A dozen servants rushed up retrieving luggage and offering glasses of champagne. Priscilla grabbed two, certain she would need those, and more, to endure the next few days.

Benoit led the way to his home.

Staff pulled open the front doors for him as he strode in.

Benoit stretched out his arms in wonderment. "Welcome to Château Paradis, my humble home." Greeting them in the center of the foyer was a two-thousand-year-old marble statue of a voluptuous Greek goddess.

Mark and Noelle rotated, gawking at a level of opulence beyond anything they'd ever imagined. Their mouths hung wide open as they took it all in. The original artwork, museum-worthy furnishings, hand-carved woodwork, and imported Italian marble floors were breathtaking. Benoit enormous wealth didn't put him in the top 1 percent. No, he was in the top 0.00001 percent—and it showed.

Château Paradis was so over the top, rather than giving off the impression of class and refinement, the excess of it all reeked of insecurity and narcissism.

"I would be happy to give you a tour of the more impressive rooms in my home after you get settled in," Benoit said. "My staff will show you to your separate rooms now. Please join me in the Grand Hall after you've had a chance to freshen up."

Mark sneered at Benoit. "We won't be staying in separate rooms."

He gave a slight bow. "My apologies. I assumed being Americans and not yet married, it was customary for a man and a woman to sleep in separate bedrooms. My understanding of your culture must be out of date." His apology lacked any hint of sincerity.

They entered their bedroom on the second floor. This one room was bigger than three of their apartments back in New York. The staff trailing Mark and Noelle began to unpack their suitcases for them. Mark raised a hand to put a stop to it. "Chill out, guys. We got this."

The staff stared blankly at Mark.

Noelle stepped in and interpreted his slang-filled instructions.

They shrugged and left the room.

Noelle walked to the window and flung open the drapes. "Can you believe this place?"

"It's okay," Mark grunted.

Noelle knew exactly where that gargantuan understatement was coming from. She walked over, pressed her body up against him, and clasped her hands around the back of Mark's neck. "I told you not to worry about where my affections lay, and I meant it. Even if Benoit is still carrying a torch for me after thirty years, I'm not interested. I've got you, Mary, and our lives back in New York. What more could a gal ask for?"

She cupped Mark's shoulders and pushed him back to arm's length. "Let's just enjoy the time we're here, okay? We'll drink a bunch of his expensive champagne, then it's *au revoir*." That mischievous grin reappeared on Noelle's face as she teased Mark. "Au revoir is French for—"

"I know what it means," he shot back in mock anger. "Keep up that French crap, and I'll leave you behind when we fly home." Mark smiled.

Noelle was more than a match for returning Mark's good-natured jabs. She pulled the duvet off the bed, draped it over her shoulders, and sauntered around the room in a regal fashion suitable for a coronation. "If you leave me here, France will just have to crown me their new queen, like Marie Antoinette."

Mark's voice turned serious. "Be careful what you wish for."

CHAPTER 45

A STOIC DOORMAN TIPPED HIS HAT as he opened the door leading to the Grand Hall. He stepped back, ushered Mark and Noelle in, and shut the door behind them. The room certainly merited its name. The massive space was lined with rich, dark paneling. Overhead, crystal chandeliers hung from an elaborately painted vaulted ceiling. Like silent sentinels, suits of armor stood at attention around the room. Swords, pistols, and muskets adorned the walls. The weapons were meticulously arranged in uniform starburst patterns. Taking in the view, Mark guessed the room had at one time served as a medieval armory for a powerful land baron.

Benoit looked up from his computer screen and rose from an enormous antique French Provincial-style desk at the far end of the room. "Ah, come in. I hope you've found your accommodations to be suitable?"

"They'll do," Mark deadpanned back.

"Enjoy some champagne while my staff prepares dinner."

A butler holding a silver tray appeared.

"Feel free to roam the grounds if you like. I have some business to attend to, but I will join you at dinner." Benoit turned around and disappeared through a small door behind his desk, which led to his private study.

Mark surveyed the room. "Damn, this guy has enough weapons and security guards to start a war. Seems like a lot for a legitimate businessman. Even for a billionaire."

Noelle tugged eagerly at Mark's hand. "Let's go see the

gardens."

They walked out of the house into acres and acres of perfectly manicured landscaping arranged with military precision. Not one blade of grass was taller than the next. Not one leaf dared to deposit itself on the ground. They strolled for an hour on crushed stone paths that wound through trees of every variety and flower beds filled with a rainbow of colors. The calming sounds of water flowing from baroque fountains down into long crystal-blue pools lent a tranquil ambience to the garden.

Noelle bent down and gently touched the petal of a perfect white rose. She drew in a deep breath. The fragrant smells of the garden were gently edged aside by the aroma from the meal being prepared by the kitchen staff. Noelle stood, turned toward the house, and drew in another deep breath. The smells of simmering gourmet foods wafting from the kitchen acted like an invisible hand pulling Noelle back to Château Paradis.

When they entered the house, Mark and Noelle were led into the dining room. It was adorned with vibrant tapestries alternately hung between crystal light fixtures. Heavy maroon-colored fabric, edged with golden fringe, draped the windows. On an impossibly long table lay an extravagant banquet fit for a—well, fit for a billionaire: a cornucopia of gastronomic delights topped with rich sauces, paired with the best French wines, and followed by a variety of artisan-crafted desserts, covered the table.

At the far end sat Benoit and Priscilla. Although next to each other, they weren't speaking.

Mark passed on the strange foods and helped himself to one of Priscilla's hamburgers.

―――◆―――

The next morning there was a rap on their bedroom door. Noelle sat up in the four-poster bed, drawing the covers up to a more modest level before answering. "Come in!"

A butler opened the door and rolled in a cart topped with an assortment of fresh pastries, fruit, cheese, and hot coffee. He spoke in English as a courtesy to his guests. "Good morning. I hope you slept well. Shall I serve you now?"

She responded, "Bonjour. Leave the cart, *s'il vous plait*. We will serve ourselves."

His smile showed that the butler appreciated Noelle speaking in his native tongue. He reciprocated by speaking in hers. "As you wish. Master Benoit is indisposed this morning, but he would like you to join him at the stables later for an afternoon ride." The butler pointed out riding gear, perfectly sized for each, hanging in the closet. "Enjoy your breakfast." He nodded. "Bonjour, Mademoiselle."

After the butler left, Mark and Noelle donned plush robes left at their bedside and eagerly headed for the breakfast cart. She looked at Mark and gushed, "I could get used to this. A butler delivering breakfast every morning. No more slogging out of bed every morning in the dark to start up the coffee maker." Noelle bit into a plump strawberry, savored the sweet taste that was absent in most store-bought berries, then joked, "I wonder how much a butler would cost in New York City?" She looked at Mark and inquired, "How much are we making now flying charter flights?"

He pointed at the cart and sniffed, "About enough to afford one of those silver spoons."

They walked in to the stables that afternoon and found Benoit standing next to three beautiful purebred Arabian horses with chestnut coats. The stable boy had the horses saddled up and ready to ride.

Noelle feigned concern. "Only three? Where's Priscilla? Won't she be joining us?"

Benoit shook his head. "She drank too much wine last night. She's feeling *under the weather*, I believe you Americans call it. She won't be joining us."

Arabians have a reputation of being a high-strung, skittish breed. Noelle approached the majestic horses and reached out to pet one. The stallion reared back its head and pulled against the reins. She grabbed a carrot from the feed cart then grasped the reins halfway up. Noelle gently pulled the reluctant horse closer until it got a whiff of the carrot. "That's right, boy, come on; I've got something for you." Her calm, soothing voice enticed the horse to accept the peace offering from Noelle's hand. She stroked its muzzle while the horse devoured the carrot. Her kindness was rewarded with a lick on the cheek from the horse. "I want this one," Noelle announced.

The stable boy helped each rider mount their steeds. Off they went for an afternoon ride around the sprawling estate. Benoit led the way. A light westerly breeze animated the leaves on the trees as they cut a path through a forested area of the estate. Ribbons of sunlight that made it through the foliage illuminated the path.

Midway through the ride, they stopped at a small pond. The three dismounted and stretched their legs while the horses drank.

Taking in the grandeur of it all, Benoit took the opportunity to boast about his success. "My father would never have dreamed his son would someday own an estate such as this. He thought hard work and living a frugal life was the only path to success."

"And you don't?" Mark asked.

"No, Monsieur, I don't. My father was a fool. This world gives a man nothing." Benoit balled up his fist. "A man *takes* what he wants. He doesn't let anyone, or anything, get in his way." He waved his arm across the landscape. "That is how I came to own this magnificent estate. At first, the previous owner balked at my offer to buy it. He told me to go to hell. Said he would never leave Château Paradis. But eventually, I prevailed."

A sly grin formed on Benoit's face as he pointed out a headstone on the far side of the pond. "It turns out he was right."

The water break for the horses had been no random event. The message being communicated by Benoit resonated loud and clear.

The animals lifted their heads and waited patiently after drinking their fill. Benoit mounted his horse then stared unfocused into the distance. The cocky, arrogant look in his eyes slowly disappeared. A genuine look of pain replaced it. He let out a heavy sigh. Talking softly to himself, Benoit said, "After all I've achieved, all I've built, I have no one to pass it on to." He felt Mark and Noelle's stare from his right. Benoit cleared his throat and said, "Let's return to the house."

When they arrived at the front steps and dismounted, staff took the reins and led the horses back to the stable.

As they entered the house, a butler pulled Mark aside. "Monsieur, the aircraft mechanic called while you were riding. He asked me to inform you it will take one more day before your plane is repaired. He assured me it will be ready the morning after next."

Benoit seemed pleased to hear the report from his mechanic.

Mark shrugged in resignation. "Okay, thanks. I'll need to call back to the US then, to update my boss."

The butler guided Mark into a room off the entryway and pointed at the desk. "Feel free to use the phone here in the parlor. If you need to use the computer, it is available also." The butler closed the door as he left.

Mark picked up the receiver and began to dial. His eye was caught by the Benoit Industries logo bouncing randomly around the blank computer screen. Mark hung up and listened for any activity out in the hallway. Hearing none, he pulled the computer keyboard toward him and woke up the computer from screen-saver mode. Mark typed Benoit's name into Google. He was being nosy. He wanted to find out how much the jerk was worth.

"Four billion dollars! Holy shit!" Mark covered his mouth as if his outburst would cease to exist if he did. Mark quietly closed the Google website and reached for the phone, dialing up his boss. When he answered, Mark said, "Hey Marty, it's me. You're not going to believe how much the guy that chartered the plane is—"

"Where the hell are you, Mark? I've called your cell phone ten times," Marty grumbled.

"Hello to you, too, Marty. Lovely to hear your voice," Mark kidded. "Noelle and I are at the client's estate out in the middle of nowhere. I don't have any cell service out here. Not that I'm complaining. You should see this damned place."

"I figured as much."

Mark cocked his head. "What do you mean?"

"I mean I'm not surprised you guys ended up at his place."

"What are you talking about?"

Marty explained. "He demanded that Noelle be on his plane. When his secretary made the reservation, he said Benoit required that Noelle be assigned to the flight or he wouldn't book with us. I just assumed they knew each other."

Mark sat bolt upright in his chair. "Did the man you talked to say he was Benoit's secretary or assistant? This is important, Marty."

"Hell, I don't remember. When a billionaire shells out eight thousand dollars an hour to charter one of my planes, I give him whatever he asks for."

Mark ignored Marty asking him when his plane would return as he hung up the phone. His suspicious nature went on high alert. Mark pulled up a flight tracking website on the computer, entered the tail number of Benoit's jet, and requested a complete listing of all flights in the last two months.

Mark was dumbfounded by what came up. Benoit's plane had made numerous flights to and from New York City during that time period—the last one on the same day they flew to Paris. Benoit's plane flew the exact same route as Mark's plane from Teterboro to Le Bourget. It landed fifteen minutes before they did—the same amount of time Mark spent flying over Paris at Benoit's last-second request. He wasn't imagining things when he felt the hot engine. Benoit's plane had just flown and been put back in the hangar.

BOOM! A loud clap of thunder rattled the windows.

"Jesus!" Mark jumped out of his chair at the sound. He rushed over to the window and pulled back the curtain.

A violent storm was about to hit Château Paradis.

CHAPTER 46

MARK NEEDED TO FIND NOELLE and tell her about his troublesome discoveries. He hurried across the room, flung open the door, and ran right into Arseneau. The bodyguard was back and had been eavesdropping outside the door.

Arseneau pushed Mark back into the parlor. "What are you doing in here? Who were you talking to?"

"It's none of your damned business who I was talking to," Mark shot back. He tried to walk around him, but the bigger, stronger man blocked his path.

Arseneau looked over at the desk. The computer monitor was lit up. "Why were you using the computer?"

Mark raced back behind the desk. "I was checking exchange rates. I'm thinking about getting a little place like this for myself."

Arseneau advanced toward the desk and pointed. "Move over by the fireplace and keep your hands where I can see them."

Mark scanned the desk for the heaviest object he could use to defend himself.

"What's going on in here?" Benoit barked, standing in the doorway to the parlor.

The special forces assassin casually lowered his arm to his side and mumbled, "Monsieur Smith asked for my help logging in to the computer."

Mark grabbed the computer mouse and clicked on the settings menu, wiping out all history of recently visited websites. "No need. I figured it out myself. Turns out there is nothing interesting to see here, anyway. I think I'll go watch some TV." Mark brushed by Arseneau, giving him an intentional bump as he left.

Mark wandered around the massive house, searching for Noelle, eventually finding his way to the kitchen. When he entered, the staff froze in place. They looked as if an alien had just walked in. A guest had never ventured into the kitchen before.

"Hello. I'm looking for Noelle. Have you seen her?"

The staff muttered between themselves in French and pointed at Mark.

He tried again. "I'm looking for a woman about this tall"—Mark held his hand out chin high—"red hair, blue eyes, can be very frustrating at times."

A man dressed in a white shirt, black vest, and black pants approached Mark. "Monsieur, you wish for something?"

"I'm looking for…" Mark gave up and tried hand gestures to make up for his limited knowledge of French. He traced the shape of an hourglass with his hands. "A woman. I'm looking for a woman with red hair."

The man smiled broadly. "Ah, oui, Monsieur, a woman." He traced the same hourglass shape with his hands. But his gestures were much more exaggerated at the curved parts. He slapped Mark on the back. "*Une prostituée!*"

The females on the staff giggled into their hands, while the males grunted in bawdy approval.

Mark had no idea what the man had just said but could tell it was fruitless to continue. Assuming the man was referring to food, Mark said, "Thanks, not right now. I'm sure my hunger will be much greater later tonight."

The females giggled even louder while the males all nodded and flashed enthusiastic smiles at Mark. He left the kitchen completely confused and decided to wait for

Noelle in their bedroom.

Mark scanned the expansive grounds from the window of their room. Noelle was nowhere in sight. To kill time, he picked up the TV remote and clicked through the channels.

"Great, everything is in French," he grumbled. Mark continued to surf the channels until his ears suddenly perceived a familiar language. CNN International was broadcasting the day's news in English. He plopped down in front of the TV, waiting for Noelle to return. The anchorman blathered on in a formal British accent about some hiker who had been stranded on a Swiss mountain for two days without water.

Impatient, Mark got up and checked the window again. Since his last look outside, the clouds had opened up, and a deluge was pouring from the sky. Lightning lit up the estate grounds while thunder crackled overhead.

The CNN anchor switched to the next story. "In shocking news out of Paris, business titan Pierre Bertrand was found dead in his apartment last night."

Mark turned back to the TV. When a picture of the dead man popped up on the screen Mark dropped the remote and stood frozen. The man he had seen arguing with Benoit at the hangar was the same man on the screen.

The reporter continued. "Police found Bertrand alone with a single gunshot to the forehead. In an unusual twist at this early stage, Paris's chief of police publicly declared Bertrand's death a suicide, effectively closing the matter to further investigation."

He laid the top sheet of paper down and went on. "In related news, the death of Bertrand sent his company's stock tumbling down 75 percent today. Benoit Industries, which is engaged in a fierce hostile takeover bid for Bertrand's company, had no comment on the news."

Mark clicked off the TV and stroked his chin, worry lines creasing around his eyes. He got up and paced nervously around the room, looking out the window again for Noelle. A flash of nearby lightning illuminated his silhouette in the window as he scanned the grounds.

Out in the hallway, he could hear a couple speaking French. The sounds of laughter grew louder as they approached the bedroom door.

Noelle walked in, soaking wet.

Benoit—drenched as well—gave a gentlemanly bow outside the door and bid Noelle *adieu*. Mark turned around to see his ex-wife's wet, semitransparent clothes clinging to her like a second skin.

CHAPTER 47

BEFORE MARK COULD EVEN SPEAK, Noelle dashed off to the bathroom and closed the door. Mark stood outside the door, his temper increasing with every passing second. Noelle emerged a minute later in bare feet, wrapped in her robe, vigorously drying her tangled red locks. Her wet clothes lay in a heap on the bathroom floor.

She looked up and smiled. "You're never going to believe what happened."

Mark clamped his arms across his chest and shot back, "You've got that right."

Noelle stopped drying her hair. "What?"

"Where have you been? I've been looking all over for you." He walked over to the window and pulled back the curtain. "And don't tell me you went for a stroll in the garden. I checked."

"You checked?" Noelle let out a deep breath of exasperation between pursed lips. "Let me guess. This…this *rant* of yours is because Girard escorted me back to my room, isn't it?"

"Damn right it is. Why were you with him?"

Noelle threw the wet towel to the floor. "Are you ever going to stop with the jealousy? Nothing happened."

"It didn't look that way to me."

Her irritation at his behavior boiled over. "You want to know why you didn't see me in the garden when you were spying out that window? It's because I wasn't in the garden."

Mark threw up his hands. "I know that. That's what I just said."

Noelle's face turned the same shade as her red hair. "If you would have just asked, instead of interrogating me like some kind of criminal, you would know where I was. I walked down to the stables to get another look at those magnificent animals. Halfway back, it started pouring down rain. Like a gentleman, Girard rushed out of the house to help me. By the time we got back, we were both soaking wet. We looked so awful, all we could do was laugh at ourselves." She planted her hands on her hips. "Now, are you happy? Can we just drop it?"

But Mark's arms still hugged his chest, topped off with a self-satisfied smirk. "While Girard was being such a *gentleman*, did he happen to tell you he planned all this? This whole trip has been one big charade from start to finish. Hell, he probably picked out the food on our flight himself because he knew how much you loved it."

Noelle struggled to understand Mark's outlandish claim. "Okay, enough. You're not making any sense at all. What do you mean he *planned* all this? Until two days ago, we hadn't seen each other for three decades."

Mark grasped her by the shoulders. "Benoit booked the flight contingent on you being on it. If Marty didn't assign you to his flight, the deal was off."

Noelle pushed against Mark's chest and backed away. "Mark, stop! Just stop! Your insecurities over an affair I had thirty years ago are causing you to create absurd conspiracies in your mind. I can't take it anymore. If you refuse to trust me every time I'm out of your sight, then we have no business getting married."

As soon as the words left her mouth, Noelle regretted them. "Wait. Mark, I—"

Her words hit Mark like cannonballs. He reeled back on his heels. At that point, his anger prevented any hope of a judicious response. Through gritted teeth, Mark growled,

"Fine! If that's what you want, you got it. The wedding is off!" He stormed out of the room, slamming the door behind him. A few seconds later, the door to the adjacent bedroom opened then slammed shut.

Furious with herself for letting her temper get the best of her, Noelle flung herself down on the bed, sobbing uncontrollably.

The storm outside was nothing compared to the tempest raging in her heart.

CHAPTER 48

THE THUNDERSTORM EVENTUALLY PASSED. AS darkness gave way to the dawn, narrow rays of sunlight peeked through gaps in the curtains. There was a soft knock at the door. Noelle rolled over, still wrapped in her robe. After a sleepless night, she looked a fright. "Go away. I don't want any breakfast." She rolled back over and covered her head with a large pillow.

Another knock came, louder this time.

"Go away, I said!" The knocking persisted, despite her pleas. Noelle pulled the pillow off her head and looked up, a pulse of hope in her voice. "Mark? Is that you?" She bounded out of bed and flung the door open so fast it nearly broke off the hinges.

Noelle recoiled. "Girard?"

Benoit smiled from behind a breakfast cart. "Bonjour. I apologize for disturbing you. After what happened last night, I thought you might need some sustenance."

Noelle grimaced. "You heard our fight?"

"My dear, everyone in the house heard it."

Noelle blushed with embarrassment. "I'm sorry. We never meant to broadcast our problems out to the whole world. I just get so frustrated with him. One minute I want to kiss Mark nonstop, and the next minute I feel like I could just kill him."

Benoit arched an eyebrow at her last comment. He stood there, his face reflecting the awkward position of marital counselor he found himself thrust into.

Noelle apologized. "I'm sure the last thing you want to hear about is my relationship problems."

Benoit waxed poetic. "Ah, love. It is the best thing the gods invented and the worst thing." He gestured into the room. "May I? I'll leave you alone with your breakfast."

Noelle stepped aside. "Yes, I'm sorry, please come in. That was very thoughtful of you."

Benoit rolled the cart to the middle of the room then turned to leave. As he approached the door, Noelle reached out to stop him. "You never told me what happened."

"Pardon?" Benoit looked confused.

"Your two marriages; what happened? Why did they both end in divorce?"

Benoit's forehead wrinkled. *Such a personal question*, he thought. Predictably, he blamed everything on his ex-wives. "They were not meant for a life such as this. Inferior upbringing, I suspect."

"So, it was all *their* fault?" Noelle's tone revealed her doubt.

After a moment of reflection, he quietly said, "No, not all of it. For many years, I blamed the divorces on their unreasonable behavior, their lavish spending in search of happiness, their tempers. Eventually, I came to realize it was me who was to blame, not them."

In a rare display of honesty, Benoit bared his soul. "As I've grown older, I now see it was my controlling nature that drove them away. Well, that—and my jealousy. Every time another man looked at my wives, I would go into a fit of rage. Accuse them of all kinds of terrible things."

Noelle threw up her hands. "What is it with you men and your irrational jealousies? Mark can be the same way sometimes. Like last night. He flew off the handle just because you escorted me back to my room." She looked Benoit in the eyes. "He even accused you of planning this whole thing so you and I would be together."

Noelle's words hung awkwardly in the air.

Normally quick to defend himself from false accusations, Benoit looked down and stood mute at the bedroom door.

Noelle's eyes narrowed. "Girard?"

He refused to look at her.

"Girard? This wasn't some big charade orchestrated by you so you could get me back to Paris, was it?"

When he looked up, his eyes pleaded for understanding. "Please, let me explain." He reached out for Noelle.

She slapped away his hand. "Explain? What the hell could you possibly say that would explain what you've done?"

Benoit blurted it out. "I love you, Noelle."

CHAPTER 49

THE STARTLING CONFESSION FROM BENOIT reverberated in her head. Noelle retreated and fell back into a chair, trying to comprehend the emotional bombshell that had just detonated in her bedroom. She buried her head in her hands and took deep breaths, trying to regain her balance.

Benoit knelt down in front of her. He reached out for Noelle a second time.

She looked up and thrust out a hand to stop him. "Don't you dare touch me. I can't think straight right now. I need some space."

"Of course." Benoit backed off. He got up, quietly shut the door, then took a seat across from Noelle.

She looked at him with misty eyes. "How can you say you love me? It's been thirty years since we were together. Everything is different now. You're not in love with me; you're in love with a fantasy. A brief period of passion. Nothing more."

"I've never *stopped* loving you," Benoit said. "When I saw your picture in the papers after the accident in the Azores, I knew we had to be together again." He leaned forward. "Can you honestly say what we had meant nothing to you, mon amour?"

"Of course it did—at the time. I was young and carefree back then. I was alone in the City of Lights; you were this dashing, sophisticated man who showed an interest in a skinny, shy girl from Connecticut. It was a dream come true. But dreams aren't real."

"They can be—if you'd just give me a chance." Benoit gently clasped Noelle's hand. This time, she didn't pull away. "I know your heart."

A tear trickled down her cheek. "No, you don't. Life has changed me. I'm not that same person I was back then."

Benoit edged closer. "But I do know you. You left home after high school to escape your life and see what the world had to offer. That's why you came to Paris. That's why you chose to be with me. Don't you see?"

Noelle's silence encouraged Benoit. "I can give you a life that would make your dreams pale in comparison. Don't you want more out of life than to spend the rest of it trapped in a tiny flat in Queens?"

Noelle lifted her head high and wiped away the tear. "Of course, I do. Mark and I were planning on moving out, but then the bankruptcy happened and…" She paused in mid-sentence. A confused look flashed across Noelle's face. She pulled her hands away from Benoit. "How do you know where I live?"

He fumbled for an answer. "I must have read it one of the papers."

"That was never mentioned in any of the papers." Noelle stood up. "Have you been spying on me?"

"You must understand. A man in my position has to be careful. I can't afford to assume anything. There is too much at stake."

Noelle raised her voice. "So, you *were* spying on me!"

"Spying is such a distasteful word. I was just being prudent, that's all." Benoit stood up and dashed to her side. "I know what I did might sound frightening in your world, but I had to do it. I know everything about you and your family."

That last sentence sent a chill up Noelle's spine. She pointed at the door. "I want you to leave. Please, leave."

"Of course, I understand. You need time to think about

what I've said. Take a stroll in the gardens to calm your mind. You always loved doing that." Benoit opened the door to leave but then turned back. "I don't mean to be blunt, but we both know you would be happier with me than with Mark. I love you, Noelle. And I'm willing to do anything to prove it."

CHAPTER 50

CLANG! CLANG! MARK WAS JOLTED awake from deep REM sleep. He lifted his head. *What is that damned noise?*

In the darkened bedroom, his hand searched blindly across the top of the nightstand until landing on the alarm clock. He pulled it over and held it up to his face. Nine in the morning. Mark dragged himself out of bed and pulled back the curtain to find out what the commotion was. Bright sunlight assaulted his retinas. He squinted and shielded his eyes with his hand to block the glaring light. Rubbing his bloodshot eyes after a long, restless night, he tried to focus.

On the lawn, a group of men prepared to go to work, throwing tools and equipment into the back of a truck. A knock at the door surprised Mark. He grabbed his robe and stormed over to the door, ready for round two with Noelle.

When he opened the door, a different butler than the one who delivered yesterday's breakfast stood aloofly in the hallway with a cart. *How many butlers does this damned place have?* Mark thought.

"Your breakfast, sir. Shall I set it up for you?" he asked.

"No, I got it, Jeeves."

"It's Marcel, sir." The expression on the butler's face now had a hint of offense. It was obvious he disliked having to serve such an uncouth American in his bosses' elegant mansion.

Mark sensed that his irreverent humor didn't sit well with the butler. He tried to put together a few words of French to smooth things over. "Bonjour, sir. See voo play for my breakfast. It looks bueno."

The butler rolled his eyes and gave up. He turned to walk away.

Mark grabbed his arm. "Wait, Marcel, hang on." The butler turned back. Mark pointed down the hall at Noelle's door. "Do you know if Ms. Parker is awake? Did you bring her breakfast up yet?"

"I'm not at liberty to say, sir."

Mark looked puzzled. "You're not at liberty to say if she's awake or if you've brought her breakfast?"

"Both, sir. Master Benoit instructed me not tell anyone he brought Ms. Parker's breakfast up to her bedroom earlier this morning. Good day, sir." His intentional slip of the tongue showed that Marcel disliked his tyrannical boss even more.

Mark yanked the breakfast cart into the room and slammed the door. "That's it, I've had it with those two. I'm out of here." He hurled his robe to the floor and picked up the clothes he wore last night. Mark looked in the mirror after hurriedly dressing. The tired, drawn face staring back at him looked worse than the soiled and wrinkled clothes he had on. He marched over to the window, ripped back the curtain, and scanned the estate grounds. The truck hauling the work crew had left.

"Where the hell is it?" He flung open another curtain. "You gotta be kidding me." Mark opened the bedroom door and looked left and right down the hall. Yet another butler walked his way. Mark stopped him. "Hey, buddy, where is the helicopter? I need to get a ride back to Paris."

The prim and proper butler sniffed at Mark. "*You* need the helicopter?"

"Yes, *I* need the helicopter. I'm leaving."

"It is not here, Monsieur. It is gone."

Mark threw up his hands. "No shit, Sherlock. I can see that. When will it be back?"

The butler stiffened. "Back? I do not know this word *back.*"

Mark realized the butler was just messing with him in retaliation for barking at him. "Oh…okay, I get it. Snotty French butler dislikes all Americans. Real original. How about this? Do you understand the word *car*? How about you call me a taxi, or a cab, or whatever the hell you call them in this country." He held up his cell phone. "I'd call one myself, but unlike *America* where we have cell phone service everywhere, at this little backwater place of yours I can't get a signal. Can you do that for me?"

The butler crossed his arms. "No, Monsieur, I can't."

Mark pinched the bridge of his nose. "Jesus. Just point me to the nearest phone then. I'll figure it out myself."

"It won't do any good if you call a taxi. No car can come here. The storm last night damaged the only road leading up to Château Paradis." The butler pointed to the window were the earlier noise had come from. "The grounds keeping staff has been dispatched to fix it. They say it won't be repaired until tomorrow morning. You are stuck in this *little backwater* until then." Turns out the butler understood English just fine. He spun around and stomped off.

Mark closed the door and slammed his fist against it. "Dammit!" He shook his bruised hand as he stalked around the room, trying to figure out a way back to Paris. A check of his cell phone showed no signal. Frustrated with his predicament, Mark plopped down on the bed. The breakfast cart brought up by the butler sat in his line of sight. An unfamiliar yet enticing mixture of smells wafted from it. He could hear his stomach growling but ignored it and checked the window again. Still no helicopter.

He turned back. The aromas from the breakfast cart seemed to be following him. Mark walked over to it and peeked under the lid covering the silver tray. He didn't recognize a single food. "Ah, screw it." Mark sat down, pulled the cart up to himself, and devoured the unfamiliar food. When he had finished eating, Mark wiped off the knife, fork, and spoon with a napkin. As if Benoit were standing in front of him, Mark declared, "I'm taking the silverware, asshole."

A solid knock on the door startled Mark. He quickly put down the purloined silverware.

Mark opened the door to find Arseneau glaring at him. "Come with me. Monsieur Benoit wants to see you."

Mark pointed back toward the cart. "No can do, butthead. I haven't finished my breakfast yet. Tell your boss I'll come by and see him when hell freezes over."

Like a vicious Rottweiler that had just been called Fluffy, Arseneau cocked his head with a confused look on his face. He didn't understand Mark's slang. So, he reverted to a language Mark would understand. Arseneau gripped his pistol under his coat and barked, "Now!"

CHAPTER 51

ARSENEAU PUSHED MARK TOWARD THE Grand Hall. As they approached the door to the hall, Mark heard shouting outside. He turned to the window and saw Priscilla and Noelle engaged in a catfight in the garden. No hair was being pulled, but accusatory fingers were being thrust about as the two shouted at each other. Mark turned to go investigate, but the bodyguard grabbed his arm, preventing him from deviating from his rendezvous with Benoit. He pulled the door open and pushed Mark in.

"Ah there you are. Come in." Benoit closed the day planner sitting on his desk, clicked off his computer, and waved Mark and Arseneau into the Grand Hall. "Thanks for coming to see me, Mark."

The hairs on the back of Mark's neck stood up when he saw Benoit's unexpectedly welcoming expression. He could only remember one other time Benoit had called him by his first name. Considering Benoit had sent his goon to escort him to the meeting, Mark had a gut feeling this wasn't going to end well.

"What is so important that you had to interrupt my breakfast?" Mark demanded. He cringed inside at how nervous he sounded.

Benoit gestured toward a chair. "Please, sit down. I called for you because Noelle asked me to talk to you on her behalf." A master at billion-dollar negotiations, Benoit's face showed no indication he was blatantly lying.

Mark marched up to the front of the desk and leaned toward Benoit. "Oh really. Did she ask you this when you brought breakfast up to her bedroom this morning?"

Benoit flinched. His jaw tightened. "She's upset about the argument you two had last night and wants some time alone to think. I'm sure you'll respect her wishes." Benoit wasn't requesting; he was telling.

"And I'm sure she can speak for herself. Trust me on that one." Mark turned to leave, but Arseneau blocked him.

"Wait. Before you go, there is another reason I wanted to speak to you." Benoit pulled a thick dossier out of his desk drawer and plopped it down in front of Mark. "I want to show you something."

Mark eyed the folder. "What is that?"

"After I saw the stories about your accident, I had my assistant make a few trips to New York to gather information for me. Arseneau is a master at that. With my resources and connections, there is little I can't learn. I know everything about you, Smith. If you don't believe me, take a look."

Mark flipped open the file. Paperclipped to the inside cover was an old photo of him. The exact same picture the DEA agents had when they spoke to Noelle. Copies of Mark's DEA file made up the first five pages. Following those were confidential patient files from the facility where Mark went through alcohol rehab, his FAA file, his personnel file from Alpha Airlines, the police report he and Noelle had filed about the sinking of the *Lynda Ray*, Mary's college transcripts, and finally, court documents pertaining to the ten-million-dollar lawsuit against him.

By the time Mark closed the file, his face was ashen. "Why are you showing me this?"

"See for yourself." Benoit gestured toward the window on the far wall. Mark walked over and looked out. Noelle was sitting on a bench in the lavish garden, crying. His head sank.

Benoit continued. "We both know that Noelle is loyal to a fault. What else would explain why she stayed with you after all the misery you've brought her?" Benoit pointed at the dossier. "But is it really in *her* best interest to be with you? Since the day she first met you you've done nothing but ruin her life. Do you really want to ruin the *rest* of it? Noelle deserves to be happy for once. If you really cared about her, you'd want that as well." Benoit carefully examined Mark's eyes to see if his strategy was working.

Mark thought back to all the pain he'd caused Noelle. The arguments, the tears, the lean times she endured when he blew all their money. Then he looked around the ornate room he was standing in. Even his dreams weren't rich enough to imagine a room as elegant as this. And it was only one of dozens like it. Mark's mind was overwhelmed. He slumped down in a chair and announced, "I'm going back to Paris. When will your road be fixed?"

"Paris? I think that's a wise decision. You will be able to think more clearly there. I sent my helicopter to get the supplies needed to fix my road. My men are working as fast as they can. As soon as the helicopter returns, you are welcome to use it."

Mark stood to leave. He almost said "thank you" to Benoit but then realized how bizarre it would be to thank a man who was trying to steal Noelle away from him. Even more upsetting, as harsh as they were, the multibillionaire had made some valid points about Mark's clouded past.

Benoit did offer an olive branch of sorts. "I was about to step outside to shoot skeet. If you would like to take your mind off what we talked about, you are welcome to join me."

With nothing better to do until the helicopter returned, Mark considered his offer.

Benoit let out a barely suppressed laugh. "You do know how to shoot a gun, don't you? I wouldn't want you to get hurt."

Benoit's swipe at his manhood provoked Mark. "Yes, I know how to shoot a gun. I was in the Air Force." Mark nodded toward the dossier. "But you probably already knew that."

"Are you much of a shot, Smith?" Now Benoit was just toying with him.

"I can hold my own."

"Ever shot a 12-gauge shotgun before? They're very powerful."

Mark puffed out his chest. "Lead the way."

Benoit opened the small door in the wall behind his desk and led Mark into his private study. Arseneau trailed close behind. The study was a spacious, well-appointed room where modern weapons hung on the walls next to paintings by Renaissance masters. He pulled two exquisite, handcrafted shotguns off the rack and handed one to Mark, along with a box of shells.

Mark picked up a shell and studied the gun for a moment. He looked for the latch to unlock the breech and expose the backend of the barrel in order to insert the shell. He fumbled around examining each side of the gun while Benoit waited. Mark had never shot a shotgun in his life.

Benoit took the gun back and handed it to his bodyguard. "Why don't you let Monsieur Arseneau assist you?"

Benoit and Arseneau turned their guns upside down and loaded six shells into the magazines under the barrels. Instead of handing the gun back to Mark, Arseneau held on to it. Benoit sniffed, "Let him carry it for you, just to be safe." He opened a door leading out to the courtyard and pointed. "After you."

Mark strutted out ahead of Benoit. At the far end of the courtyard a trap machine loaded with clays sat on the lawn. As he got closer, Mark suddenly realized there wasn't another person in sight. It dawned on him that he was walking in front of two armed men that detested him.

CH-CHUNK! Both men pumped back the actions on their guns and chambered a round.

CHAPTER 52

WHEN THEY ARRIVED AT THE shooting stations set up on the grass, Mark sarcastically remarked, "What, no butler to launch your clay pigeons for you?" He pointed his thumb back toward Arseneau. "Or is that why you brought your lapdog along?" Mark wasn't interested in who got stuck launching clays; he was making a play to get his gun back from Arseneau.

Benoit pointed at the machine and bragged, "It's voice activated. When the shooter yells "pull"—a clay target shot out of the machine—"it launches one automatically." Benoit stepped up to his shooting station and invited Mark to do the same. He asked, "Do you mind if I go first?"

Mark shrugged. "It's your place."

Benoit raised his gun then yelled out the launch command. The saucer-shaped target bolted into the air. With a loud *BOOM*, Benoit turned the clay to dust. He turned to Mark and smirked. Benoit took aim again. Another clay launched. It, too, turned to dust. The third clay met the same fate. Benoit nonchalantly lowered his left hand and brushed his leg twice, like a baseball coach sending his player a sign. Then he put his hand back on his gun, raising it up to firing position.

Behind Mark, Arseneau raised his shotgun, closed one eye, and sighted down the barrel. He pointed it at the back of Mark's head.

Benoit yelled "PULL!" The clay launched. At the exact same moment, both men pulled their triggers. The clay shattered. Arseneau had raised his aim.

Mark instinctively dove for the ground at the sound of the shot coming from behind him. He rolled over in the wet grass and screamed, "What the hell are you doing? You could have killed me!"

"I apologize if my bodyguard frightened you," Benoit said. He bent over and offered him a hand up.

Mark angrily waved it off and stood on his own.

"I assure you your safety was never in jeopardy. When Monsieur Arseneau aims at a target, he never misses."

Mark considered rushing Arseneau but quickly thought better of it. The message Benoit was sending registered loud and clear with Mark. "What the hell do you want, Benoit?"

Benoit held his gun in the ready position. "I thought I made that clear. I want you to leave here without Noelle."

Mark rocked back on his heels.

"Without you holding her back, she would have a life of unparallel luxury. No more worries about money. Noelle would finally have what she always dreamed of when she first came to Paris."

Mark glared at him. "I'm not leaving Noelle with you."

Benoit shook his head. "I thought you would say that. Selfish as always, Smith. You don't care if she's happy, you only care about yourself. In that case, I have a business proposition for you."

Mark narrowed his eyes and cocked his head.

"If there is one thing the business world has taught me, it's that every man has his price. If you do what's best for Noelle, I assure you that you will be well taken care of. I will pay you triple the airline pension you lost in the bankruptcy. Any amount of money you are liable for because of the lawsuit, I will pay it." He waved his arm dismissively. "Ten million dollars, whatever the amount, done. I will pay Mary's medical school tuition for as long as she is in school. After she graduates, I will set her up in her first medical office. Park Avenue, if she likes." Sensing reluctance on Mark's part, Benoit swallowed hard before dangling the final carrot in front of him. "You can have my Gulfstream jet. All expenses will be paid to fly it for the next ten years."

Mark's jaw dropped. He was completely and utterly speechless.

CH-CHUNK! Benoit and Arseneau both pulled back the actions on their shotguns and chambered another round.

Benoit sneered at Mark. "Or, you can tell me to go to hell."

CHAPTER 53

BEADS OF SWEAT FORMED ON Mark's trembling upper lip. He had no intention of taking a dime from the son of a bitch, but he had to find a way to get out of this trap alive.

"Mark! Girard!"

They turned to see Noelle running toward them.

Before she reached them, Benoit warned, "For once in your life, do the smart thing, Smith."

"What happened? I heard gunshots." Alarm filled Noelle's voice as she took in the scene.

Benoit smiled and pointed at the machine. "Not to worry, my dear. I was just teaching your ex-husband a lesson in how to destroy a target. Hopefully, I succeeded."

Noelle looked Mark up and down. "What happened to you? You're all wet."

He shrugged. "It's nothing. I slipped on the wet grass."

She hooked her arm around Mark's waist and guided him toward the house. "Let's get you inside and into some dry clothes before you catch a cold."

He was more than willing to let her lead him safely away from Benoit's planned ambush.

Noelle grabbed dry clothes out of the bedroom closet and tossed them to Mark. "Here, put these on."

"Thanks." Mark quickly changed. As he was buttoning up his shirt he said, "Not to seem ungrateful, but a person can't catch a cold from being in wet clothes."

Noelle looked insulted. "I know that."

Mark cocked his head. "But outside you said—"

"I said that to get you out of there. When I saw that Benoit and his goon had shotguns and you didn't, I didn't believe for a minute he took you out there to only shoot skeet. I saw the fear on your face."

Now Mark looked insulted. "*Fear*? I had everything under control."

"Flyboy, I can read you like a book. Don't bother trying to put on this tough guy act with me. I can see right through it. You were scared. Oh, and by the way, you're welcome for saving your butt."

Noelle knelt down and began packing her suitcase, while Mark finished changing into dry clothes. He looked over at her. "What are you doing?"

"We're leaving. As soon as possible. I'll tell you the details later, but I had time to think about it, and I don't belong here anymore."

"Here?" Mark asked.

"Here! Château Paradis. Paris. This whole damned country. I just want to go home."

Mark walked over and stopped Noelle from packing anything else. "Go home to what? To me and all my problems? To a tiny apartment and no money? The lawsuit? We can't even send Mary back to medical school. For once, stop being so damn stubborn and think things through for a minute." Mark took in a deep breath, then announced, "I think you're better off staying here."

Dumbfounded, Noelle looked up at his seafoam-green eyes. "Mark, why are you saying this? Tell me what's going on," she implored.

He turned his back to her.

Noelle rose and spun Mark back around. "He's behind this, isn't he? What did Girard say to you out there? Did he threaten you? Bribe you?"

Mark averted his eyes. "No, he didn't."

"Then why are you doing this to me? To us?"

Mark grabbed Noelle by the shoulders. His heart was pounding. Tearfully, angrily, he shook her. "Dammit, I'm doing this for you!"

Noelle was frantic. "But I don't want to stay here. I just want to go home!"

Mark regained his composure then somberly said, "You are home." He swept his hand across the room. "This amazing place. Paris. All of it. It's what you've dreamed of since you were a teenager. You belong here. It's what you deserve."

Noelle clasped her hands on each side of Mark's face. "I don't want any of this. I want you. Can't you see that? When we get back home, we'll figure something out."

Mark gently took Noelle's hands from his face and kissed her on the cheek. "There's nothing left to figure out." With tears streaming down his cheeks, Mark turned and walked out of Noelle's life with nothing more than the clothes on his back.

CHAPTER 54

NOELLE THREW HERSELF ON THE bed, pummeling the stack of innocent pillows with her fists. As she lay there sobbing, she heard a faint thumping sound. Noelle was sure it was her heart breaking in her chest. As the sound grew louder, she lifted her head to try to identify the source. Noelle jumped up and looked out on the lawn. The helicopter was returning. The grounds crew was headed for the landing area, but Mark wasn't among them. She only had minutes to find Mark and stop him before he left her life forever.

Noelle dashed out of the room and down the sweeping staircase yelling his name. She burst into the Grand Hall. "Mark!"

Benoit looked up from his desk with a surprised expression. Arseneau stood guard to the side.

Noelle stormed toward Benoit with a vengeance. "What did you do, Girard? What did you say to Mark?"

Arseneau grabbed Noelle and swept her up in a bear hug before she could reach Benoit.

"Put me down!" she screamed. Her kicking and thrashing had little effect on the muscular bodyguard.

"Put her down," Benoit ordered as he came around the desk.

Arseneau released Noelle, standing nearby in case she decided to threaten his boss again.

Benoit flicked his hand dismissively toward Arseneau, shooing him away. "Go. Leave us alone." Before his bodyguard could voice his protest, Benoit yelled, "I said go!"

Arseneau stomped off into the study, making sure to slam the door behind him.

"Where is Mark?" Noelle demanded again.

"I have no idea," Benoit sniffed. "He told me he's decided to leave you. I imagine he's packing." His left eye twitched slightly.

Noelle's skill in reading body language helped her pick up on the slight facial tick as he told that lie. She decided two could play that game. "You said you love me, Girard. You told me you would do anything to prove it. Did you mean it?"

He looked surprised. "Yes, of course I meant it. Why would you doubt me?"

Noelle's face turned crimson red. "Are you serious? After all the deception and lies you told to get me here?"

"It was the only way to get you back. I had no other choice, mon amour."

Noelle crossed her arms and glared at Benoit. "You could have been honest with me, like Mark was upstairs."

Benoit swallowed hard. A dead giveaway. "What do you mean?"

"Mark told me everything, Girard." She confidently strode up to him. "Now I'm giving you a choice, mon amour. Why did Mark decide to leave me? Tell me everything you said to him. If even one word differs from what he told me, you will never see me again."

Benoit closely studied Noelle's face. She didn't even blink. He exhaled and gestured toward a sofa. "Let's sit. I will tell you everything."

The simple flight attendant had just outfoxed the shrewd business titan.

The fury inside Noelle burned hotter with every detail of Benoit's repugnant plan to bribe Mark. She forced herself to keep a blank poker face until he finished.

Then all hell broke loose.

CHAPTER 55

Noelle went off like a Roman candle. She jumped up from the sofa and screeched, "You son of a bitch!"

Benoit was rocked back by the rage in her voice.

"You lied to me. You manipulated my heart. Now you've driven such a wedge between us that Mark is leaving me. All so you could get what you wanted. You've ruined my life, Girard. I hate you!"

Benoit had never been spoken to like that by anyone. Unable to control the world around him now, he reverted back to the two-bit hustler in an overpriced suit he had always been. "I can give you everything your heart desires. Name it; it's yours."

Noelle shook her head in disgust. "How could I have been so blind? Mark was right about you all along. You don't love me. You are a lonely, heartless old man in love with a thirty-year-old fantasy."

Benoit shot out of his seat at Noelle's stinging insult. "You would walk away from all this! To go back to your pathetic little life with that oaf?"

Noelle glowered at Benoit. "That *oaf* you're so jealous of loves me for who I am today—flaws and all. Not some fantasy. You just don't get it, do you? What you have to offer me is not enough. I want more." Her voice softened slightly. "I want someone who loves me so much he's willing to get in a tiny little lifeboat with me during a hurricane." She shook her head slightly. "I could never marry you, Girard. You *are* the hurricane."

Benoit lashed out. "You left me thirty years ago because you were a foolish child. What you've said today proves you are still that same foolish child, unable to know what's best for her. Leave my home, I can't tolerate the sight of you."

That was the last straw for Noelle. Until that spiteful comment, years of pent-up anger and regret had driven her words. Now, spurned in such a callous manner by her former lover, she was hell bent on revenge. She poked her finger into his chest. "You bastard! How could you have taken advantage of a lost and vulnerable girl still grieving over her mother's death? You used me just like you use everyone. To you, the truth is a weapon to be wielded for your own benefit. I left you thirty years ago because I found out you were married—your biggest lie of all. Do you know how humiliated I felt knowing I was carrying the child of a married man? I felt so used, so ashamed, at how gullible I had been. Leaving you was the best decision I've ever made."

Benoit's eyes flared wide open. His anger catapulted to rage. "You were pregnant? With my child? How could you have kept this from me all these years?"

"How could I? Ever since I met you, you've done nothing but lie to me!"

Benoit forcefully grabbed Noelle by the shoulders. "What did you do with my child! You must tell me. Where is my child?"

She wrenched herself free from his grasp. "I would never let a horrible person like you anywhere near an innocent child. I gave her up for adoption to keep you from her. The records are sealed. You will never find her."

Benoit strode unsteadily over to his chair and slumped down. He buried his head in his hands and mumbled, "Her? I…I have a daughter?" He contemplated this shocking new revelation for a moment then lifted his head and pounded his fists on the desk. "I will never forgive you for what you've done! Never!" His frightening words echoed throughout the Grand Hall.

Mark and Priscilla rushed into the room at the outburst.

"Girard, what is all the yelling about?" Priscilla asked.

Benoit stood up behind his desk. His angry demeanor had completely changed. A calm veneer concealed his rage. He shouted, "Arseneau, get in here!"

The bodyguard charged out of the private study like an angry bull ready for a fight.

Benoit pointed at Priscilla. "I want you to escort Madame Winthrop back to New York City. You are to leave immediately on the helicopter then take my jet."

Priscilla came around the desk and clutched Benoit's arm. "Girard, I don't understand. What are you saying?"

Benoit pried her well-manicured hand off of his arm. "The wedding is off. I never want to see you again."

Priscilla reacted like she'd been hit between the eyes with a two-by-four. She stumbled back clutching her chest and gasping for air. "What did you say?" Then she turned and glared at Noelle. "You *bitch*! What did you do?" Suddenly, she lunged at her rival like a pouncing leopard.

Mark stepped between the women and blocked Priscilla's attack before she could strike.

Benoit sneered at Priscilla and Noelle. "American women have no place in France. You are deceitful, manipulative, and heartless." His words were an obvious case of projection, although he would never have the self-awareness to admit that. Benoit continued. "Smith, Ms. Parker, you will be taking a *taxi*. I want you out of my home tomorrow morning the instant the road is fixed."

There would be no discussion of his edicts. Benoit turned and disappeared into his private study.

CHAPTER 56

MARK TRIED HIS BEST TO console Noelle as she sobbed in his arms back in their bedroom. He sat down on the bed with her and gently stroked her long red hair. "We'll leave as soon as the road is fixed. That will be the last you will ever see of that bastard."

She looked up tearfully. "I thought you'd walked away from our life together and wanted me to be with Benoit. But now I know why you said those things. He told me everything. How he bribed you to leave me. But you never intended to take his money. You wouldn't still be here if you did."

"And let that jerk have you? Not for all the money in the world."

Noelle eked out a smile as she dabbed at the tears in her eyes with a tissue. "You forfeited millions to be with me."

"Actually, it's closer to a hundred million," Mark corrected. He grabbed another tissue and handed it to Noelle. "I've told you before, you're my lifeboat. I'm sticking with you whether it's a hurricane, a nut-job billionaire, or an empty bank account."

Noelle hugged him tightly. "We should have never come here. You were right all along about him." She looked up ruefully. "I'm so sorry. Can you ever forgive me for what I've done?"

Mark grinned, thinking a little humor would help lighten the situation. "For what? Making me eat that crap they call food here in France? I'll get back to you on that one."

Noelle pulled away from Mark and lowered her head. "No, it's not that. For not being totally honest with you all these years." She got up and walked over to the bedroom door, locking it to ensure privacy. When she sat back down on the bed there was a distance between them.

Mark's grin disappeared. He tilted his head to look into Noelle's downcast eyes. "Noelle? Look at me. What are you talking about?" He reached out and tried to lift her head so their eyes could meet.

Noelle resisted his hand. She turned away. She couldn't bear to look Mark in the eyes after lying to him since the day they first met. All those years of guilt came pouring out of Noelle in the form of tears. A torrent of regret flowed down her cheeks.

Mark had no idea how momentous Noelle's revelation was about to become. Rather than push her to talk, he embraced her and let Noelle exorcise the burden she had been carrying, one tear at a time. When her sobbing subsided, he softly asked Noelle, "Can you tell me now? I promise I'll just listen." He handed her the box of tissues.

Noelle wiped away the last of her tears. She had none left. The emotional well was empty. She tried to look Mark in the eyes but couldn't bring herself to do it. With her head bowed in shame, she said, "I lied to you."

Mark kept his promise and forced himself to stay silent.

"Before we were married, I told you about Paris. I said I left Benoit, but I lied about why. It wasn't just because he was married." Noelle drew in shallow, shuddering breaths as she worked up the courage to continue. "I left because I was pregnant with his child."

Mark rocked back on the bed at her admission. He bit down hard on his lower lip to keep from speaking.

Noelle looked up with red, swollen eyes. "I was young, unmarried. I didn't know what else to do. I couldn't stay in Paris. So, I came home. Well, not home. My dad never found out. I couldn't bear to tell him what happened. He was so brokenhearted after Mom died it would have killed him to find out his only daughter was pregnant with a married man's child. Times were different back then. I stayed with family until after the baby was born then went back home. Dad died never knowing the truth."

"What happened to the baby?"

Noelle's head sank. "I gave her up for adoption."

Mark clasped Noelle's hands. "It must have been heartbreaking giving your baby away to strangers, but it was the right thing to do. It was best for the baby."

Noelle began to sob again. The well wasn't empty after all. "That's not everything. There's more."

"More?" Mark eyed Noelle suspiciously and pulled his hands away.

Tearfully, she blurted it out. "Strangers didn't adopt my baby. Tommy and Stephanie did. April Parker is not my niece; she's my daughter."

CHAPTER 57

An hour after being unceremoniously dumped by her billionaire fiancé, Priscilla Winthrop and her snippy little dog were escorted to the helicopter by Arseneau. The staff had been pleased to pack her bags and send *her* packing as well. No glass of champagne was offered upon her departure.

She looked back at the house as she walked across the lawn. Benoit stood in the window, watching from his study. The classy broad she was, Priscilla flipped him the bird. Emotionless, he turned away and disappeared. No longer trying to hide her Brooklyn accent, she screeched, "I can't wait to leave this wretched excuse of a country and go back to America, where I belong."

Arseneau ignored the insult to his homeland and offered a hand to Priscilla as she climbed aboard. She gladly took it. The helicopter lifted off and flew away into the clear blue sky.

———

The roar from the departing helicopter snapped Mark out of his stunned silence. He slowly stood up and wandered around the bedroom, aimlessly running his fingers back through his full head of gray hair. His eyes searched the room for some semblance of understanding.

Noelle went to him and tried to embrace Mark.

He pushed her away. "Give me some space. I need a minute." He continued to pace, his face reflecting the churning emotions in his heart. After a lengthy, painful silence Mark turned to Noelle. "I don't understand. How can April be your daughter?" His head was spinning.

Noelle gestured to a chair. "You should probably sit down."

Mark sat down in the nearest chair.

She explained. "My brother and sister-in-law lived in New York City—same apartment they live in now. They'd been trying for years to get pregnant without any luck. Tommy gives me a hard time, but we really do love each other. When I told him what happened, he brought me down from Connecticut to have my baby. But after I held April in my arms that first time, I couldn't bear the idea of never seeing her again. She could've been adopted by a couple who lived on the other side of the country. We all felt it was the right thing to do to keep her as part of our family. So, they adopted her. Even though it was done as a closed adoption, now I would get to see my daughter grow up and become the wonderful person she is today."

Mark nodded slowly but didn't speak, trying to digest the unsettling information. He rested his chin on his folded hands, deep in thought.

"I'm so sorry I've kept this secret from you all these years. I should have told you." Noelle's head drooped. "You probably hate me." She walked over and pulled her suitcase out of the closet. "I'll sleep in the other bedroom tonight. When we get back to New York, I'll give Marty my notice. You'll never have to see me again after you move out." She began to gather up her things and stuff them into the suitcase.

Mark knelt down and stopped her. He lifted Noelle up and turned her to face him. She tried to apologize again, but Mark pressed his finger to her lips before the words could come out. "I won't be moving out, and you won't be quitting." He smiled that goofy grin of his. "How could we afford that pretty wedding dress you're constantly talking about if you quit your job?"

Noelle's eyes teared up. "You still want to marry me after everything I've done?"

"Please. After everything I've done in my life, I would be the world's biggest hypocrite if I expected you to be perfect. All this proves is that we are perfect for each other. Two flawed people with pasts, who've made mistakes. When I think of all the times you've forgiven me, how could I not do the same for you?"

Mark continued talking, but Noelle shut him up with a passionate kiss. She wrapped her arms around him, kissing Mark and crying simultaneously. They enveloped each other in a fervent embrace. Mark swept Noelle up in his arms and carried her over to the bed. He laid her down, lowering himself gently on top of her. An hour later, emotionally and physically spent, Mark and Noelle collapsed into each other's arms, falling sound asleep.

CHAPTER 58

THERE WAS A LOUD KNOCK on their bedroom door. Mark groaned and forced open one eye. "Who...who is it?" he said groggily. Though his vision was blurry, he saw that the room was dark. The clock on the nightstand completed the puzzle. Six in the morning. He and Noelle were so completely exhausted after all they'd been through, they'd slept for twelve hours straight.

A second knock was followed by a man's voice. "The road is passable. You must leave now."

Mark gently shook Noelle. "Get up." She protested with a few choice words and rolled over. He shook her again. "Noelle, it's time to leave. Get up." For a third time there was a knock on the door. Mark yelled, "I heard you, dammit. Gives us a minute!"

Grumbling, along with retreating footsteps, could be heard from beyond the door.

Mark turned on the stained-glass Tiffany lamp on the nightstand. Noelle rolled back and asked in a gravely whisper, "What time is it?"

"Time to leave this dump." He pulled the covers off Noelle to deny her any refuge then rousted her again. "Come on, get up." Mark crawled out of bed and lumbered off to the bathroom.

Noelle yawned loudly and rubbed her weary eyes. She sat up, stretched out her arms, and arched her back like an awoken feline. Throwing her legs over the side of the bed, she stuffed her feet into plush slippers and shuffled across the floor to the closet. She yanked clothes from the hangers then tossed them haphazardly into the suitcases. Next, she emptied the drawers in the dresser. When she pulled their clothes out of the top drawer, the dossier folder fell to the floor. Mark walked in from the bathroom as Noelle picked it up. She stared blankly at it then held it out. "What's this?"

Mark smirked. "I swiped it off Benoit's desk. That moron thought he could blackmail me into leaving you. He sent Arseneau to New York a couple of times the last few months to gather all kinds of dirt on me. You wouldn't believe the confidential information that thug was able to get his hands on. Just goes to show you how money trumps integrity in New York City." Mark took the file and tossed it in the trash. "Guess that was a big waste of money. I hope it cost him a ton, the jerk."

Noelle walked over and pulled the file out of the trash can. "Why didn't you tell me about this?"

"I was going to, but things got pretty intense yesterday. I put it in the drawer and forgot about it. What you told me about April is a lot more important than that crap." He shrugged. "Besides, you already know everything that's in there."

Noelle thumbed through the pages. Her eyes widened with every document she saw. She cried out, "Oh my God! No!"

Mark ran to her side. "What?"

"Until yesterday, Benoit didn't know April existed. Out of revenge, I told him I was pregnant with his baby and that I gave her up for adoption." Noelle shook the file. "If Arseneau can find out all this about you, he can find April!"

Mark clenched his jaw. "That shrewd bastard. That's been his plan all along after he found out. Benoit didn't send his bodyguard to New York to get rid of Priscilla, he sent him to get his daughter back. That's why he made us wait to leave. Hell, the road was probably fixed hours ago. Benoit wanted to give Arseneau time to find April!" Mark grabbed the dossier and hurled it to the floor, scattering pages across the room.

"Arseneau has April. And I handed her right to him!" Noelle collapsed into Mark's arms.

CHAPTER 59

MARK CLOSED HIS EYES AND quickly developed a plan. He opened them and pointed to Noelle. "We have to warn them. Call April. I'll call Tommy and Stephanie. Arseneau wouldn't think twice about killing anyone who got in his way."

They each dialed up the numbers on their phones. A shrill tone immediately sounded in both phones. Mark pulled his phone away from his ear and checked the screen. "Crap, still no signal out here." He stuffed his phone in his pocket. "We need to get to Paris to get cell service."

Noelle grabbed the remaining clothes and jammed them into the suitcases. Mark carried both as they raced down the dimly lit stairs, landing in the expansive foyer. Being the coward that he was, Benoit was nowhere in sight.

A lone butler stood silently at the front door. He pulled it open as they approached. A thick blanket of fog had settled over the region overnight, reducing visibility to a few dozen yards. Noelle shivered as a blast of damp, chilly air swept into the foyer and enveloped them.

Outside, a taxi sat idling in the circular drive. Exhaust sputtered lazily out the tailpipe. Its headlights cast a ghostly white glow as the light reflected off trillions of water droplets suspended in the foggy air.

The butler announced, "The fare has been paid. You must leave now."

Mark grabbed the man's arm. He was the same butler Mark had insulted the day before. "Good, you speak

English. You have to help us. It's an emergency. Call Benoit's apartment in the city and tell my crew to get to the plane immediately. Tell them to get everything ready so we can takeoff as soon as we get there."

The butler didn't answer, merely grunting his refusal to help Mark.

Noelle edged Mark aside. She spoke to the butler in French, imploring the man to help them. He appeared unmoved by her pleas. Noelle thought for a second then tried a different tactic. Again, she spoke to the butler in French.

When she finished, a devious grin sprouted up on the butler's face. "Oui, Madame, it would be my pleasure to assist you. I shall call the apartment right away." He had understood every word Mark said. Noelle and the butler exchanged plutonic kisses on each cheek, then the butler went off to the parlor to make the call.

Mark tossed their suitcases into the trunk of the taxi then jumped in the back seat with Noelle. He banged his open hand down on the top of the front passenger seat and barked, "Le Bourget airport, as fast as possible."

Noelle repeated the instructions in French to ensure the driver understood. Pea gravel sprayed out from behind the rear wheels as the driver gunned the accelerator. Heaven's Castle faded from view, swallowed up by the fog.

The small taxi sped down the mile-long driveway through the soupy fog toward the front gate. The driver leaned forward and stared intently at the winding driveway as the wipers struggled to clear the mist off the windshield. Sensing he was approaching the gate, the driver blew the horn and flashed his lights to alert the guards to open the impenetrable barrier. Suddenly, it appeared. He skidded to a stop to avoid a collision. The gate didn't budge.

Two guards armed with AK-47s materialized out of the mist. Guns at the ready, they cautiously approached the taxi and shined flashlights in the windows.

"Open the damned gate!" Mark yelled, shielding his eyes from the light.

This only served to further arouse the suspicions of the guards. Pointing their guns at the driver's head, they motioned to the back of the car and instructed him to open the trunk. One guard went to search it while the other stood in front of the taxi, barking something into his radio. Moments later, an armored Humvee rolled up outside the gate. Precious minutes ticked by while the guards wasted time with an obvious show of force. Satisfied there were no dead bodies in the small trunk, the guard gave a wave to his comrade. The man pulled a tablet computer out of a side pocket on his camouflage pants and typed in a code. The metal gates creaked and groaned as they slowly swung open. As soon as there was enough space to squeeze through, the taxi driver stomped on the gas pedal, fully intending to spray the guards with gravel as he made his getaway. Noelle looked back to see the guards shaking their fists and cursing at the driver.

Mark pulled fifty euros out of his wallet and placed the bill in the cup holder between the front two seats. He gave the driver a thumbs-up. "Good job, buddy. Thanks." The driver folded the bill and slipped it into his shirt pocket. Then he returned the unfamiliar hand gesture to Mark.

The car fishtailed and skidded sideways across the pavement as it turned from the gravel driveway onto the main road. Mark checked his phone again. Still no signal. He turned to Noelle. "What did you say to the butler back there to get him to help us?"

Noelle snickered. "I told him Benoit was a lousy lover. For a French man, that is the ultimate insult. Once the word gets around to the rest of his staff, he'll never live it down."

An hour later, the taxi driver hooked up with the A86 motorway that rings Paris. Although it was the weekend, the infamous Parisian traffic slowed the car down to a speed more typical of freeways in LA. The driver offered some uniquely French hand gestures at the other drivers and blared his horn, to no avail.

Mark looked at his phone. Finally, the signal strength bars were indicating cell service. Mark and Noelle redialed the phone numbers. Strangely, both calls immediately went to voice mail. They tried to call April and her parents a second time. The calls ended with the same result. Mark checked his watch. "It's 2 a.m. in New York. Maybe they turned off their ringers." He suggested texting instead. Messages warning them to be on the lookout for anything suspicious went unanswered.

Le Bourget airport came into view as the sun climbed above the horizon. The taxi driver skidded to a stop in front of Benoit's hangar. Luxury Jet Charters' Gulfstream was sitting on the ramp, fueled up and ready to go. Noelle thanked the driver profusely, while Mark grabbed the bags. They dashed across the ramp and up the plane's stairs. Mark thanked Johnny with a slap on the back then jumped in the captain's seat while Noelle closed the door.

With trepidation, Charlotte asked, "What's going on? What happened?"

"I'll tell you everything on the way back to New York. Buckle in."

They cinched down their seat belts, strapping tightly into their jump seats. The jet engines spewed out scorching-hot exhaust as the Gulfstream 500 roared off the runway and headed west just a few knots below supersonic speed.

CHAPTER 60

UNABLE TO REACH APRIL AND her parents to warn them about the danger they faced, Mark did everything possible to shave time off the flight back to Teterboro Airport. He flew a GPS-derived route directly to the airport at fifty-one thousand feet, far above the congested tracks airliners flew back to North America. At higher altitudes, jets switch from flying a specific airspeed to flying a percentage of the speed of sound. Gulfstream jets are known for their sturdy construction, but Mark had no intention of ignoring the maximum speed limit determined by the company's structural engineers and test pilots. He flew across the Atlantic at Mach .925, the jet's absolute top speed.

The plane ripping itself apart in flight from excessive speed would have put a horrible end to their rescue mission. Taking every shortcut, Mark's savvy piloting decisions shaved nearly an hour off the typical flight time between Paris and New York.

Convinced there was nothing more he could do to get back any sooner, Mark left Johnny in control of the plane and went to the cabin. Noelle and Charlotte were sitting in passenger seats talking. Mark joined them.

Charlotte was just finishing a story of what happened on their end. "If his staff had kicked us out of his apartment any faster, the door would have hit us in the butt."

Noelle turned to Mark and brought him up to speed. "I told Charlotte everything that happened at Benoit's estate."

Mark shifted uneasily in his seat. "Everything?"

Charlotte interrupted, "She didn't need to tell me about April and the adoption. I already knew about that. Noelle told me years ago."

Mark snapped his head back in surprise. "You told *her* but not me?" The tone of his question echoed the betrayal he felt inside.

Noelle explained. "I had to tell someone. My life was at an all-time low back then. You were having your problems with alcohol. Our marriage was on the rocks. Keeping the secret bottled up inside me all those years was killing me."

Charlotte defended her friend. "Let it go, Mark. That's all water under the bridge now. April is a great kid. Let's focus on how to protect her from Benoit's hired gun. If he hasn't gotten to her already."

Mark put his wounded feelings aside and refocused on reaching April as soon as possible. "We won't have cell phone service for most of the flight. Once we get to a low enough altitude on approach into Teterboro, we should get reception back. I'll be busy flying so Noelle you call April and find out if she's okay. Warn her to get out of her apartment immediately and don't go back. Tell Tommy and Stephanie to do the same." He reached for Noelle's hand. "All we can do now is wait and hope that psychopath hasn't found her yet."

With hours to go and a plan solidly in place, Charlotte got up and headed for the galley. "I don't know about y'all, but I'm hungry." She flipped open the doors on the cabinets. "Well looky here." It was stocked with food and drinks.

Noelle wrinkled her brow. "How did you…"

Charlotte chuckled. "I told his people at the hangar that Benoit was going to be on our plane and that he demanded it be fully catered with American food. You should have seen those bozos scramblin' around at that hour of the morning trying to find some grub." She opened the last cabinet door. "Biscuit and gravy, anyone?"

◆

At midmorning, New York City time, Mark started a high-speed descent from fifty-one thousand feet for landing. Still far too high to get cell phone reception, Noelle nervously checked the signal strength icon on her phone screen every thirty seconds, waiting to get at least one bar. The sprawling city came into view out the window but still no signal.

Air traffic control radioed their plane and instructed them to slow down to their minimum speed. When Mark questioned the clearance, they were told there was a string of aircraft that had preceded them into the New York City airspace and their plane was at the back of the line. Even on weekends, aerial traffic jams plagued the skies in this area—as any passenger who's flown into LaGuardia or JFK knew from experience. Slowing down the plane so far out from Teterboro would add over twenty minutes to the flight.

Mark hated to abuse an option designed to get priority handling ahead of all other planes, but he felt he had no other choice. He pushed the transmit button. "New York approach, Gulfstream Two-Seven-Lima-Juliet declaring an emergency."

The controller's voice went up an octave. "Gulfstream declaring an emergency, say the number of souls on board and the nature of your emergency." Covering his boom mic with his hand, the controller turned and called for a supervisor to assist him. When the shift supervisor walked up, the controller working Mark's flight told him he needed a clear path for the plane straight to Teterboro. The supervisor made it happen.

Mark knew if he said he had a mechanical malfunction so dangerous that it required him to declare an emergency it would draw too much scrutiny from the FAA. So, he replied, "We have four souls on board. A passenger is having chest pains. Requesting direct to Teterboro at this time." He figured the FAA was less likely to investigate an ambiguous medical issue than a mechanical problem.

The controller responded. "Already done, Two-Seven-Lima-Juliet. Proceed direct to Teterboro Airport. Cleared to land runway one-nine."

"Thanks for your help. We're cleared to land runway one-nine." Mark pushed the throttles forward until the Gulfstream reached red line on the airspeed indicator.

Noelle jumped when her phone rang unexpectedly. April Parker was calling.

CHAPTER 61

"AUNT NOELLE, WHAT IS GOING on? I got your voice mails and text messages."

Noelle's voice was frantic. "Are you okay? Are you at your apartment? Where are Tommy and Stephanie?"

Alarmed, April said, "You're scaring me. Tell me what's going on."

"Answer my questions, April. You and your parents are in danger."

"My parents went to Lake George for a romantic weekend. They left their phones at home and said they won't be back until tomorrow night."

Noelle exhaled. "Oh thank God. Where are you? At your apartment?"

"Um…no."

"Good. Don't go back there until I tell you it's safe. Where are you now? I'll explain everything after I come get you."

With hesitation, April replied, "Um…I'm…If I tell you, do you promise not to tell my mother?"

Noelle's eyes narrowed. "I promise I won't tell…Stephanie. Where are you?"

April came clean. "I'm spending the weekend at my boyfriend's place." Dead silence greeted her admission. "Aunt Noelle, are you still there?"

"Yes, young lady, I am. Do I know this boy? Have we met his parents yet? What's his name?"

"Um…it's Derek. I *am* an adult, you know."

"Well then you should act like one and—"

Charlotte gave her the *cut* sign and whispered, "Not now," trying to stop the motherly interrogation.

Noelle collected herself and continued with more vital matters. "We can discuss this later. The most important thing is do not go anywhere near your apartment. Something bad happened while we were in Paris, and we think a very dangerous man is in New York because of it. I'll call Mary and have her stay with you until we get there."

"I hope you have better luck getting ahold of her than I have."

April's words sent a jolt through Noelle's heart. "What did you say?"

"I've been calling her cell phone since last night, but she never answers. I went by your apartment this morning to see if she wanted to get coffee, but nobody answered when I knocked. It's like she just disappeared."

Noelle dropped her phone. "Oh God."

Charlotte grabbed her. "Honey, what is it? What happened?"

She could barely speak the words. "I...I think Arseneau has Mary."

The sound of the landing gear falling down in place signaled that the plane was about to land. Charlotte supported Noelle as the realization of what might have happened to her daughter drained the strength from her legs. She helped her best friend sit down in the nearest passenger seat and fastened the seat belt around her waist. She quickly took the seat across the aisle. A few seconds later, the Gulfstream slammed down on the runway at Teterboro Airport. Mark stopped the plane in half the normal distance and steered it toward the ramp.

Marty stood on the ramp in front of Luxury Jet Charters' hangar, waiting for their arrival. The plane screeched to a stop in front of him, and Mark immediately shut down both engines. The APU took over powering the electrical system on the plane. The door opened, and the boarding stairs unfolded.

Marty hurried up the stairs into the jet. When Mark emerged from the cockpit, Marty said, "ATC called and said a passenger on your plane had a medical emergency. I called an ambulance. It should be here any minute." Marty looked at the empty cabin then back at the four faces of the crew silently staring back at him. He narrowed his eyes. "What the hell is going on?"

Charlotte ignored him and pulled Mark aside. "Nobody has been able to reach Mary. I think Arseneau might have her. You guys get to the apartment. I'll explain everything to Marty. Go!"

Mark scooped up Noelle, helped her down the aircraft stairs, then had her sit on the concrete so she could catch her breath. She tried her best to hold it together so the dread she felt inside would not overwhelm her.

The ambulance Marty had called for roared across the ramp and skidded to a stop in front of the plane. Two EMTs jumped out, medical bags in hand, and rushed past them up the stairs.

In the middle of his headlong run to get to his car Mark looked over his shoulder at the ambulance. Its flashing red and blue lights lit up the ramp. He jerked to a stop, turned around, and sprinted back to Noelle. Lifting her to her feet, Mark helped her into the passenger seat of the ambulance and safely strapped her in. Then he jumped in the driver's seat and sped off in the stolen vehicle.

As he merged into traffic, he fell in behind a long line of cars. He flipped every switch on the dashboard until he found the one for the siren. The maddening New York traffic was no longer an obstacle.

Noelle gripped the door handle with both hands as Mark skidded around corners and dodged oncoming cars. "Mark, slow down," she pleaded.

"Call Mary!" Mark yelled, ignoring her pleas.

Noelle searched her pockets for her phone then realized it was on the floor in the plane.

He looked over and saw Noelle's confused expression as she came up empty-handed. Mark pulled out his phone and thrust it at her. She called Mary repeatedly, but all the calls went to voicemail.

Two blocks from their apartment, Mark shut off the lights and siren. He drove slowly up the street in front of his building, searching for any sign of Arseneau. The normally bustling neighborhood seemed unusually quiet.

There wasn't a soul around. Even the neighborhood dogs were quiet.

To keep from attracting attention, Mark pulled the ambulance over to the curb two buildings away from his own.

Noelle and Mark quietly entered the foyer then stopped. Nothing appeared out of the ordinary. The sounds of families living their lives wafted in the air. They crept up the stairs to the third floor. Approaching their apartment, they didn't notice anything unusual. Mark put his ear to the door. Nothing. He guided Noelle behind him with his arm, unlocked the door, and stepped in.

The apartment was in complete shambles. The phone had been ripped from the wall and smashed. Destroyed furniture and broken picture frames littered the floor. A violent fight had taken place in their home.

With Noelle safely behind him, Mark grabbed the largest kitchen knife he could find and cautiously checked each room in the apartment. Mary wasn't there.

Noelle pulled out the phone and dialed her daughter's number again. When it connected, the unthinkable happened. The muffled sound of Mary's ringtone could be heard coming from inside the hall closet. Mark looked down and saw a trail of blood leading up to the closet.

Their hearts skipped a beat. He rushed over and threw open the door.

Noelle looked inside and wailed, "Oh God, no!"

CHAPTER 62

Building superintendent and former Marine Ralph Simpson lay dead from a single gunshot to the middle of his forehead. Mary's cell phone had been placed on his chest. His bloodied hands and torn clothing indicated he'd put up a hell of a fight before succumbing to his assailant.

Noelle buried her head in her hands, weeping.

Mark had seen the killer's signature single shot to the forehead before. The French businessman who argued with Benoit at the hangar had died in the exact same manner.

He pulled up the flight-tracking website on his phone and entered the tail number of Benoit's jet. It had departed Teterboro Airport bound for Paris less than an hour ago—minutes before Mark landed.

He turned to Noelle. "Arseneau did this. He's got Mary."

"We don't know that," Noelle pleaded. "Maybe she went away for the weekend. Maybe she went for a jog." Noelle tried desperately to come up with a reason, any reason, that her daughter wasn't in the clutches of the psychopath. "I'll call April again. Maybe she's seen her."

Noelle snatched the phone back, but Mark stopped her from dialing. "People with his background don't do anything by chance. That's why he left her phone on Simpson's body. He sent us a message. He has our daughter. If Arseneau didn't intend on kidnapping Mary, she would be…" Mark couldn't bring himself to finishing his distressing thought out loud.

"Then we have to call the police," Noelle said.

He looked down at the gruff, yet brave man slumped in the closet. The man who died trying to protect his daughter. "It's too late for that." He looked back at Noelle. "We don't have time to get mixed up in all this. The police will take us to the station and have us filling out paperwork for hours. Hell, until their investigation is completed, we would be considered suspects. If there is any hope of getting Mary back alive, we don't have a second to waste."

"We have to call someone," Noelle implored.

"Think about it. Who do we call? The FBI? They don't have any interest in dealing with a missing persons case." Mark continued. "Interpol? The French police? Benoit is untouchable in his country. Getting the authorities involved over there would just tip him off." He let out a deep sigh. "We don't have a choice. His plane is on its way back to Paris. We're going to have to get Mary back ourselves."

Noelle checked her watch. "The first airline flights to Paris don't leave until tonight."

"Shit!" Mark paced back and forth across the debris-strewn floor, deep in thought. Suddenly, his face lit up. He grabbed Noelle's hand. "Come on, we're going to get our daughter."

———◆———

Sirens blaring, the ambulance tore through the streets of Queens.

Mark handed Noelle his phone. "Call Charlotte." She dialed, waited for the connection, then put the phone on speaker and held it next to Mark's mouth so he could keep both hands on the wheel. He didn't wait for her to speak after she picked up. "Look, Charlotte, I know we've had our differences in the past, but please, you've got to help us. Arseneau kidnapped Mary from our apartment, and he's on the way back to Paris with her. Simpson, the building super, died trying to stop him. Where are you now?"

"I'm still at the airport."

"We're headed your way. Leave now so you can honestly say you haven't seen us. Go to the apartment then call the police. Tell them you went there to look for us but have no idea where we are."

"Okay, but why come here?"

"We're going to steal Marty's jet."

CHAPTER 63

MARK MADE GOOD TIME RACING past the normal weekend traffic on the city streets. When they entered the Lincoln Tunnel the ambulance suddenly skidded to a stop. A road crew repairing potholes had reduced the road down to one lane, squandering the progress he'd made. Drivers in front of the ambulance tried to yield to the emergency vehicle, but they had no room to pull over. After inching along for what seemed like an eternity, the ambulance popped out on the east side of the Hudson River in dreary Weehawken, New Jersey.

Sirens off, he quietly drove into the parking lot at Luxury Jet Charters and out onto the ramp. Luckily, the Gulfstream was still sitting where Mark left it. No one was around to see them sneak on to the plane.

As they stepped aboard, a gruff voice said, "Going somewhere?"

Marty Dawson was sitting in the cabin waiting for them. He chomped down hard on his unlit cigar and got up from the plush leather passenger seat. Mark started to speak, but Marty held up his hand. "Don't bother lying to me, Smith. I know why you're here. Charlotte told me. You two thought you were going to steal my airplane, didn't you?"

Noelle pleaded for understanding. "Marty, you don't understand. Our daughter has been kidnapped."

"You're wrong," he countered. A look of remorse washed over the crotchety Navy man's weathered face. He looked over at Mark. "You remember that *lame* story I told you when we first met? The storm that made our lives so miserable was named tropical storm Edna. Same name as my ex-wife. Ironic, isn't it? When she left me, she took my kids and disappeared. I never saw them again. In all these years I've never gotten a call, a card on my birthday, nothing. I'd do anything to see my kids again for just one hour." With misty eyes, he said, "So, yes, I do understand." Marty wandered over to the door to leave. He turned and said, "I topped off the gas tanks. Galley still has lots of food in it. Your bags are on board." He reached out and gave Noelle her phone. "Go get your daughter."

Noelle grasped his hand and gave Marty a long, heartfelt embrace.

Mark shook his hand. "Thanks, Marty. We owe you."

He clamped down on Mark's hand. "You bet your ass you do, Air Farce. I had to promise the EMTs a ride in one of my jets to keep their mouths shut about you heisting their ambulance. But if the cops or FAA come looking for you after this is over, don't expect any help. From here on out, you're on your own. I was never here." He waved them away. "Now get outta here before I change my mind." He disappeared down the stairs, retracting them and closing the door with the exterior control switch. He pounded on the side of the jet twice then walked away.

Mark entered the cockpit and went to work. He fired up the APU and checked over all the systems on the plane. Satisfied everything was operating normally, he programmed the computers for the flight to Le Bourget.

Noelle hung out in the cockpit doorway, wishing she could somehow help. "Do you want some coffee?"

Mark waved her offer away without looking back. "No." He continued punching buttons and flipping switches.

"How about some food?"

"Maybe later. Please, I'm busy right now." He continued getting the plane ready but felt her gaze on the back of his neck. He turned around to see Noelle looking like the last kid picked to be on a team. He patted the right seat. "Here, you can sit up front with me and be my copilot."

Noelle gleefully hopped into the copilot seat and rubbed her hands together, ready to help. She was dying to push buttons and flip switches just like Mark. "What do I do? Talk to me, Goose."

Mark's head cocked to the right with an incredulous look on his face. "Goose? Man, you've been hanging around pilots too long. Just sit there, and don't touch anything unless I tell you to."

She slumped back in her seat with a frown that quickly morphed into a full-on pout.

Mark saw her pouty look and took pity on Noelle. "Okay, you can help by talking on the radios for me."

The pouting worked exactly as Noelle had planned.

Mark pointed to a red button at the top of the control stick on Noelle's side of the cockpit. "When I tell you, press that button and repeat what I say. No more. No less."

Noelle's mood perked up considerably at the prospect of being a real-life jet pilot—in her mind, at least.

Mark started both engines, lowered the flaps, and tuned the radio to the Teterboro ground control frequency. He pointed to Noelle's radio button on the control stick. "Tell ground control we'd like to taxi for takeoff." Just as she was about to transmit, he said, "Wait!"

She jerked her hand away from the stick.

"Ground control will want to know our tail number, route, and destination. They enter all that into the ATC computer system."

"So? Isn't that what we want?"

"It gets passed along to every controller from here to Paris."

Noelle still had a confused look on her face.

"Remember how we got special treatment from customs? They knew it was us because our radio call sign is our tail number. Benoit will know we are coming. His contacts will tip him off."

"You're right. Look how easy it was for him to find out all that confidential information about us."

A devious smile suddenly appeared on Mark's face "Of course…"

Noelle's eyes narrowed. "I know that look. What are you cooking up?"

"There's no reason to alert Benoit if they think we *are* Benoit."

"You've completely lost me."

With a self-satisfied tone in his voice, Mark said, "Tail number. When we call ground control, we tell them *his* plane's tail number, not ours. Our jets are the same model. The guys in the tower are too busy to get out their binoculars to check and see if every tail number a pilot gives them on the radio matches the ones on the side of the plane. Once it's in the system, we're good to go."

Noelle looked skeptical. "One small problem with your brilliant plan: I have no idea what it is."

Mark beamed. "I do." Mark spelled out each letter by using the phonetic alphabet. "November, Oscar, Echo, Lima. Say those words at the beginning of every radio call."

Noelle nodded. "Okay, got it." Her face showed she failed to grasp the significance of the letters in the tail number.

"You're going to love this." Mark reached across the cockpit and wrote down the first letters of each word as he said them aloud. NOEL.

Her eyes widened. "Okay, that's just downright creepy."

Mark had Noelle call ground control on the radio with all of the required flight information. After only a few seconds, the controller called back. "The computer won't accept your flight plan. An aircraft with your tail number is already in the system."

Mark slapped his forehead. "Crap, I should have thought of that. Arseneau is still airborne. He's two hours ahead of us." He thought for a moment then keyed his mic, "Sorry for the confusion, ground control. That's the tail number of my other jet. Enter the call sign Mike, Alpha, Romeo, Kilo instead."

CHAPTER 64

MARK RACED BACK ACROSS THE Atlantic Ocean at maximum speed. With the sun dipping below the horizon as they approached Europe, he did some rough calculations. Even after knocking off a significant amount of flight time, they were still going to land an hour after Arseneau.

When he explained the situation to Noelle, she demanded, "You have to fly faster, then."

"I can't. The plane is already dangerously shaking at this speed. Any faster and it will break apart."

"But we have to get to Mary before it's too late." Noelle spelled out the obstacles facing them. "Arseneau will take the helicopter back to Benoit's estate. We have to take a taxi—if we can find one at this time of night that is willing to drive that far outside the city. That puts him even farther ahead of us. And that assumes we can even find Château Paradis. I'd never been there before. It was dark when we left, and it's dark now. All I remember is that it's west of Paris. A taxi driver could spend hours wandering around looking for it out in the middle of nowhere."

"Even if we could find it, we'd never get past the guards at the gate," Mark cautioned.

Noelle's eyes teared up as she turned to Mark. "Our daughter's life is in danger, we have no way of helping her, and it's all my fault."

Mark closed his eyes and took in a sharp breath as he racked his brain for a way to save Mary. A moment later, his eyes popped open. "I have an idea." He pulled up an aviation map on his tablet that covered the Paris area. Next, he took out two low-tech items from his flight bag—a pencil and a piece of paper. "The day we arrived, we flew due west in the helicopter at 150 knots for twenty minutes." He furiously scribbled the math problem on the paper. "That means we flew fifty nautical miles." Then he went back to the tablet. Starting at Le Bourget airport, he drew a line on the screen fifty miles long on a straight westerly course. Mark wrote down the latitude and longitude of the point where the line ended, entering that location as the new destination in the navigation computer. With pride in his voice, Mark pointed at the tablet and announced, "Got it! Benoit's estate is in this area. If we fly directly there instead of landing at Le Bourget, we'll arrive only thirty minutes after Arseneau."

Noelle threw up her hands. "And then what are we supposed to do, parachute in?"

Mark flashed a wide smile. "I have another idea. Have you ever seen the *Space Shuttle* land?"

"Yes, but you aren't an astronaut, and this isn't the space shuttle."

He smiled even bigger. "No, it's not, but it *is* a Gulfstream."

Noelle shook her head and raised a palm in confusion. "So?"

Mark explained. "Astronauts can't practice landing the shuttle, so NASA uses a Gulfstream jet to simulate it. They practice hundreds of landings in the jet at idle power with the landing gear hanging down so they can simulate the extreme angle the shuttle drops out of the sky. At the last second, the pilot pulls the shuttle out of its dive and lands like a normal plane." He crossed his arms in triumph at his brilliant idea.

"I don't know if you noticed, flyboy, but there was no runway at Benoit's place."

"Ah yes, but there are acres of flat manicured lawns surrounding his house. The sturdy landing gear on our plane won't know any difference."

"Assuming we don't die playing Buck Rogers, when the guards outside the wall hear us land, we'll never make it to the house alive," Noelle warned.

Mark frowned. "Yeah, that…that could be a problem."

With both deep in thought on how to save their daughter without getting killed first, the only sound in the cockpit came from the air rushing by. Meanwhile, the plane arrived over the location Mark had programmed into the navigation computer. A tone went off in the cockpit, alerting them they had passed the new destination without landing.

Noelle gritted her teeth. "I've got an idea, but you're not going to like it."

"Hey, I'm game for anything at this point."

"Swoop down like you said"—she mimicked a plane diving with her hand—"then when we get close to the estate shut off both engines and glide in. That way the guards won't hear us land. They can't see us; it's dark. The last thing they'll be expecting is our plane dropping out of the sky."

Flashbacks of the dead-stick crash-landing in the Azores flooded Mark's mind. His hands began to tremble. "Absolutely not. It's not safe. I only get one shot if I shut down the engines. If I misjudge the landing, we die."

Noelle reached out to calm his hands. "If we don't try, Mary dies."

After flying four thousand miles, Mark was faced with a nearly impossible task. Pick Benoit's estate out of the thousands of specks of light on the ground from miles above the French countryside then glide in for a landing. On this moonless night the number of ground lights and stars were roughly equal, leading to a deadly visual illusion pilots call the fishbowl effect. Everything out the cockpit windows looked the same. The line between the sky and ground no longer existed. It was like trying to find a needle from the inside of a haystack—in the dark.

Mark's throat constricted as the grim choice they faced registered in his gut. A hurricane of conflicting emotions swirled in his mind. Mark looked out at the sea of darkness outside the cockpit windows. He lifted his chin and swallowed hard. "Let's go get our daughter."

With the engines pulled back to idle thrust, the Gulfstream jet slowed to a speed just above stalling. Mark extended the flaps then lowered the gear. The wheels locked solidly in position, creating enormous amounts of drag as planned. The plane nosed over into a hair-raising dive *seven times* steeper than an airliner on approach. Mark and Noelle fell forward against their shoulder straps. The plane's speed quickly climbed back up to the redline.

The air traffic controller jumped up from his seat and screamed into his microphone. "Gulfstream Mike, Alpha, Romeo, Kilo, what are you doing? Our radar shows you descending at a high rate of speed. Get back to your assigned altitude immediately!"

Mark reached down and turned off the radio. To prevent the controller from tracking him, Mark also turned off the aircraft transponder. The green blip representing their jet disappeared from the radar screen.

As it dove for the ground, the readout on the altimeter scrolled by so fast it was unreadable. Mark turned on the enhanced vision system to search for the estate in the blackness of night. Confused, he rechecked his coordinates on the navigation computer with the results of his crude calculations. He carefully scanned the picture on the HUD, looking for the massive estate. The plane should have been right over the top of Château Paradis. It wasn't there.

Mark yanked back on the control stick and pushed the throttles forward. The plane leveled off ten thousand feet above the ground. "It's not here. I must have miscalculated.

We can't land."

In a calm voice, Noelle said, "You can do this, Mark. You did it before in the Azores. You saved everyone's lives that day."

His hesitation didn't come from a lack of self-confidence. Mark didn't doubt his flying skills. Just the opposite. But over a career flying the most sophisticated jets in the most demanding circumstances, he'd come to learn that those who think "it" will never happen to them are the most likely to buy the farm. A healthy respect for the myriad ways to "screw the pooch," as aviators crudely put it, was the best way to die in a rocking chair at the retirement home as opposed to the bottom of a smoking hole in the ground.

She looked over and winked at him. "Come on, Buck Rogers, let's go get Mary."

Mark pressed his head back against the headrest and let out a long, deep breath. Then he looked down at the empty ring finger on Noelle's left hand. He had made her a promise, and he was going to do whatever it took to keep it. Despite the long odds, he went back to work, steering the plane through a series of turns trying to locate the estate on the EVS.

A few anxious minutes later, Mark yelled, "Got it!" He put the plane into a dive again and started the APU. With the flight path aiming crosshairs on the HUD right over the sprawling lawn next to the house, Mark did the sign of the cross. Then he shut down both engines.

CHAPTER 65

Very little was different from the pilot's perspective once the auxiliary power unit took over running the systems on the plane. Except for the fact that the view out the cockpit windows was completely void of any light and the jet was hurtling toward the ground at an ungodly speed and angle. Other than that, things were completely normal.

The ground-proximity warning system began screaming about imminent collision with terra firma. A computer-generated female voice screeched, "PULL UP! PULL UP!"

With her face turning a sickly shade of green, Noelle gripped the front edge of the glare shield above the dashboard with both hands. At only two thousand feet above the ground, Mark hauled back on his control stick. The Gs increased, pressing them down into their seats as the plane began its round out to landing. Mark had misjudged the height of the estate grounds by a mere five feet. Still descending, the Gulfstream slammed into the lawn then bounced back up into the air. He froze the controls and let the plane settle back down onto the grass. Mark stomped on the brakes, digging parallel ruts over a mile long across the perfectly manicured lawn.

The plane finally jerked to a stop two hundred yards past the house. Mark immediately shut down the APU to keep from attracting attention. Enveloped in darkness, they squinted and peered out the cockpit windows for approaching guards. Minutes passed, and no one came. Using battery power, Mark opened the door and lowered the stairs. Suddenly, bright lights on each stair riser came on. Designed to safely illuminate the path into the plane, the lights now became a beacon announcing their arrival. He dashed back into the cockpit and pushed the button on the overhead panel to disconnect the battery from the electrical system, killing the lights.

Again, they waited silently for any signs of approaching trouble. Hearing none, they crept down the stairs and ducked behind one of the large main landing gear, surveying the eerily quiet scene. Benoit's helicopter sat on the lawn between them and the house. By sheer luck they had avoided crashing into it during their clandestine landing. They crouched down and sprinted over to it.

Mark reached up and felt the underside of the helicopter engine. "Still hot," he told Noelle. He scanned the house for any signs of activity. The only light came from the windows of the Grand Hall. Together, they snuck over to the nearest window and peered in through a small opening in the curtain. Arseneau wasn't visible. Benoit sat at his desk at the far end of the room.

Noelle cocked her head when she saw him. Benoit looked different. His arrogant, cocky demeanor was gone. Head bowed down, the billionaire now looked like a defeated, tired old man. The name of his estate, Château Paradis, seemed like a sad irony. For the reclusive and lonely billionaire, his large, empty house—and life—must have felt more like hell than heaven.

If Benoit was feeling sorry for himself, Mark and Noelle had no intention of extending him the same emotion. They crept over to the large front door. It opened without a sound on its well-oiled hinges. Getting their bearings in the dark foyer, they set off on the path to the Grand Hall as quietly as possible. Arriving outside the door, Mark held up his hand. They stood motionless and listened. The only sound coming from the room was Benoit tapping away on his computer keyboard.

The ornate faceplates of all the doors had keyholes in them due to the age of the château. Mark knelt down and looked through it into the room. Nothing had changed. Benoit sat alone in the room. He turned to Noelle. "Ready?"

"Hell yes," she growled. He had never seen such a bloodthirsty look in his ex-wife's eyes.

"Go!" They burst through the doors and sprinted across the large room. The startling appearance of the two stunned Benoit speechless. His mouth hung open, but nothing came out.

With the ferocity of an attacking Hun, Mark yelled, "Where is our daughter? What have you done with her?"

Benoit stood and grasped for words as if he'd just seen a ghost. "How did you…what is going…"

"You kidnapped our daughter. Where is she?" Noelle roared.

"Your…daughter? How could I know where your daughter is?" His mind began to refocus on the situation at hand. "What are you doing in my home? How the hell did you two get past the front gate? I'm calling security." Benoit grabbed the phone on his desk and began to dial.

Mark lurched over toward the wall and snatched a spear out of the grasp of a medieval suit of armor standing on display. He reared back and aimed the spear at Benoit's heart. "Put down the phone. Now!"

The billionaire immediately complied.

Mark advanced toward the desk with his arm cocked back, ready to launch the spear. "You have two seconds. Tell me where Mary is."

Without warning, Arseneau burst through the door from the private study. In the blink of an eye he drew his pistol from his shoulder holster and shot Mark. The spear fell away as Mark collapsed to the floor.

Noelle screamed and turned to help him, but Arseneau turned his gun on her. "Don't move!" He came around the desk with his gun trained on her then glanced down at Mark. He was alive. The bullet had torn through his left thigh. Thick crimson liquid oozed across the floor from his injury. Arseneau drew a bead on Mark's forehead.

"Stop!" Benoit held up his hand. "Before you kill him, I want to know what the hell is going on." He glared at Mark. "How did you get back to Château Paradis? I sent you away only this morning."

Mark grimaced in pain as he pressed his palm on the leg wound to staunch the bleeding. He nodded up at the window.

Benoit walked over and pulled back the curtain. He recoiled slightly at the sight of a Gulfstream jet parked on his lawn. Impressed with the resourcefulness of his rival, a smirk formed on his face. Benoit wiped the complimentary expression away before turning around. Addressing Noelle, he barked, "How dare you accuse me of kidnapping your daughter! I would never do such a thing!"

"You're lying!" Noelle shouted. "Just like you've lied about everything else. You planned all of this. You couldn't find April, so you kidnapped Mary instead to get your revenge on me."

The fierce look on Benoit's face suddenly softened. He walked back over behind his desk and bent forward, planting his hands on its top to support himself. After a breath, he said, "My daughter's name is April?"

Noelle winced inside at making such a grave mistake. She had just given him the last piece of the puzzle to find his daughter.

Strangely, Benoit didn't look like he'd just gotten the ace to complete a royal flush. In fact, the new knowledge of his daughter's first name softened his expression even more. He straightened up. "On my honor as a gentleman, I would *never* do something as despicable as harming a child.

You have every right to doubt me after all that I've done, but on this you must believe me."

"Like hell I must!" Noelle pointed back to Mark. "We both saw what your goon did. He killed Mr. Simpson then kidnapped our daughter just like you told him to do. Don't lie to me, Girard!"

"If you believe I would spend my entire life yearning for an offspring of my own then kidnap another man's child over something as common as a broken heart, then you truly never did know me, Ms. Parker." Benoit slid open a desk drawer and pulled out a nickel-plated revolver. He turned to Arseneau and ordered, "Put your gun down on my desk and back away."

The bodyguard flinched at the bizarre command from his boss.

"Put it down," his boss repeated.

Arseneau laid his gun on the end of the desk and took a step back.

Benoit pushed the latch on the side of the gun and popped out the cylinder. All six chambers were loaded. With a snap of his wrist, the cylinder locked back in place. He gripped the handle firmly, lifted the gun, and aimed it directly at Noelle's heart. "There are six bullets in my gun. One is enough to kill a person at this range."

Mark looked up from the floor and begged, "Benoit, please, don't."

The billionaire's eyes misted up. "I've loved you since the day we met, Noelle. But you were too blind to see it. You were the only woman I've ever risked giving my heart to, and you broke it. But that wasn't enough for you. Even keeping my own child from me wasn't enough. You detest me so much that you would break into my home and accuse me of such a terrible thing as kidnapping your daughter. There is nothing left to say. It's over."

Trembling, Noelle closed her eyes and held her chin high. The next thing she heard was the sound of metal on wood. She cautiously opened one eye then the other. Benoit had laid the revolver on the front edge of his desk and stepped back from it.

He gestured toward the weapon. "Go ahead, take it. I won't stop you." Arseneau started for his own gun, but Benoit raised a hand. "No. You are not to interfere."

Noelle looked down at Mark with a stunned expression on her face.

"Take it! Shoot him!" he yelled.

Benoit stood tall with his hands clasped behind his back. "Go ahead. Take my gun, Ms. Parker. If you truly think I would do such a heinous thing, then shoot me. When you broke my heart a second time, my life ended anyway. All the money in the world won't heal the pain you've caused me." He raised his voice. "Go ahead, shoot me!"

Noelle snatched the gun off the desk. She stood ten feet away from the man who'd lied to her, used her, stolen her innocence. Nothing stood between her and the ultimate revenge. Anger at Benoit for harming her child bubbled up inside her so intensely that Noelle began to quiver. She raised the gun and pointed it at Benoit. "Where's my daughter!" she screamed.

He glared back at her but remained silent.

Hands trembling, Noelle pulled back the hammer. "Where is Mary!"

Benoit refused to speak.

An ear-splitting shot rang out.

CHAPTER 66

STARTLED BY THE SOUND, NOELLE dropped her gun on the floor. Benoit fell forward onto his desk—dead. Bright red blood flowed out of the bullet hole in his back.

Behind him, Priscilla Winthrop stood in the doorway to the private study. She turned her weapon from Benoit and aimed the smoking gun in her hand at Noelle. "You *whore*. I was going to be filthy rich. You ruined everything!" She tightened her trigger finger. "Now, you're going to join your pathetic lover in hell."

Arseneau snatched his pistol from the desk and pointed it at Priscilla. "Put the gun down. Now!"

Her eyes darted back and forth between the woman she desperately wanted to kill and the trained special forces assassin. Even if she got off a shot, she would surely die.

"Now!" Arseneau repeated. "Lay your gun on the desk."

Priscilla glared at Noelle, shook her head, then grudgingly lowered her gun and placed it on the desk.

Arseneau approached cautiously, never moving his aim from her center of mass. He grabbed the gun and flung it back into the study. He came around the desk and grabbed a fistful of her blonde hair, yanking Priscilla's head back. "You're going to pay dearly for that." Arseneau forced his lips to hers, passionately kissing Priscilla. She wrapped her arms around his neck and gladly returned the kiss. When their lips parted, Arseneau smiled and said, "Well done, mon amour. Exactly as we planned."

Her eyes lit up at such high praise from her normally stoic lover.

Frozen with fear, Mark and Noelle grappled for understanding at what had just happened.

Arseneau wasted no time with an explanation. He came around the desk, kicked the revolver that Noelle had dropped across the polished marble floor, then pushed her next to where Mark lay bleeding.

Assuming this was the end for him, Mark taunted Arseneau. "You're getting rusty in your old age, asshole." He tapped the center of his forehead. "You missed."

Gloating, he replied, "No, Monsieur, my aim is fine. I want you alive—for now."

Priscilla shouted, "Just shoot them, Jean-Luc! Stop wasting time. We have two billion dollars of that pathetic old fool's money to find."

Mark laughed out loud. "You idiots. Benoit has over four billion dollars. I looked it up. If you're willing to risk going to prison for the rest of your lives, at least steal all of it."

Arseneau nodded his head in admiration. "You are correct. His fortune is worth four billion dollars—the part that the French government is aware of. But we had no way of taking it without arousing suspicion. So, on the flight back to New York we decided to settle for *only* two billion."

Now Priscilla was gloating. "We know he has it stashed away in untraceable offshore accounts. Girard bragged about how he'd saved billions in taxes over the years by siphoning off money from his companies. Two billion dollars' worth." She snickered, "French men are so stupid. Pretend they are good in bed, and they become putty in your hands."

"All we need are the account numbers and passwords," Arseneau said. "Whoever has those, has the money. And no one will ever know it's missing. With Benoit dead, we will tear this place apart until we find them."

Noelle shook her head. "He *was* telling the truth. Girard didn't plan all of this; you did. But why? Why kidnap Mary and bring her back here?"

Arseneau explained. "To force you to return. You Americans are so predictable. Take something from you, and you come storming back with a vengeance on your white horse. By returning, you've not only made the dirty work of getting rid of Benoit possible; you've given us the perfect alibi. We tell the police that the depressed lovesick billionaire kidnapped your daughter in a twisted attempt to get his old flame to marry him."

He pointed at Mark. "Then the cowboy and his sidekick broke in to the house to get her back. Sadly, we arrived on the scene to find that a gun battle had left all four people dead. As the only witnesses, the police will have no choice but to believe our story. With two billion dollars in the bank, we retire in luxury to a villa in the South of France. Idiots, Monsieur Smith? Hardly."

"Shoot them, Jean-Luc!" Priscilla shouted again.

He held up his hand to quiet her. "In due time. I have an important question to ask Monsieur Smith first."

Arseneau walked over and stood in the pool of blood next to Mark's wounded leg. "In your dossier was a police report. I read the statement you and Ms. Parker gave about the ship sinking and your rescue from the lifeboat. You failed to mention a single word about something Mr. Whitaker was transporting for me. Very curious." Arseneau lifted his foot and stepped down on Mark's leg wound.

He screamed out in agony at the excruciating pain.

The assassin continued. "You stole a million dollars from me, Smith. I want it back." He pressed down harder. "Where is my cocaine!"

CHAPTER 67

"LEAVE HIM ALONE!" NOELLE PUSHED Arseneau away. "We don't have your drugs. I swear. We panicked when we found the cocaine in Whitaker's bag and threw it in the ocean."

"Cocaine? What is she talking about, Jean-Luc?" Priscilla asked suspiciously.

Able to breathe again, anger overcame Mark's pain. "Let me spell it out for you, genius. Your boyfriend here is nothing more than a common drug dealer. He paid off crewmen on ships that Benoit's company owned to smuggle his drugs for him. It's a flawless scheme. Sailors from poor countries are the perfect drug mules. They visit ports all over the world as a normal part of their job. They get a nice payday; he gets his drugs delivered—all while keeping his hands clean and never putting himself in jeopardy." He glared at Arseneau. "Do I have that about right?"

The bodyguard had a perverse look of pride on his face.

"How could you get involved in such a filthy thing as dealing drugs, Jean-Luc?" Priscilla sniffed. "And for such a meaningless amount of money. One million dollars? We are going to have billions, Jean-Luc, *billions*."

He glared at Priscilla. "No one steals from me and lives."

"You fool. Forget this obsession you have with filthy drugs. We have to find the passwords to Girard's accounts." Priscilla began rifling through Benoit's desk. Drawer after drawer, she came up empty. She picked up his day planner and flipped through the pages. Suddenly, she stopped. Her eyes widened. "Oh my God, I think I've found the codes." She held the small book out toward her lover.

He holstered his pistol and dashed around the desk, snatching the book from Priscilla. Arseneau carefully ran his finger down the page. A wide grin formed on his face. "That clever old bastard. Hide the keys to billions of dollars in plain sight where no one would ever think to look for them." Arseneau carefully ripped the page out of the day planner, folded it, and put it in his inside coat pocket.

"Now who's the idiot, Smith?" Priscilla cackled, as she jabbed her finger in Mark's direction.

Arseneau drew his pistol and aimed it at Mark. Suddenly, he swung the gun around and pointed it at Priscilla. "I'm afraid you are, mon amour. How incredibly stupid of you to tell me you'd found the passwords. You should have kept your big mouth shut, taken the book, and gone back to your wretched country a rich woman." He pulled the trigger, placing a bullet dead center in her forehead.

She crumpled to the ground.

Arseneau stood over his lover's body with a disdainful look on his face. Without the slightest hint of remorse, he said, "Vive la France, *bitch*."

During all this, Noelle had removed Mark's belt from his waist and cinched it tightly around his leg. The bleeding slowed to a trickle.

Arseneau came back around the desk and pressed the barrel of his gun into Mark's temple. "I won't ask again. What did you do with my cocaine?"

Mark raised his hands in surrender. "Okay, okay, I'll tell you. Don't shoot."

Noelle tilted her head. "Mark? What are you doing?"

He reached out for her hand. "It's over, Noelle. He's won. I'm all out of cards. I was never going to get away with stealing a million dollars of his cocaine. Only a fool would think no one would come looking for it."

"Tell me where it is," Arseneau demanded.

"I already told you, we threw it in the ocean," Noelle pleaded.

"He's seen my DEA file, Noelle. Hell, Arseneau put the dossier together. He knows about my past. He knows I would never throw a million dollars' worth of cocaine in the ocean. I hid it somewhere in New York City after we got back." Mark pulled himself upright and leaned back against the desk. "I'll tell you where your cocaine is."

Panicked, Noelle grabbed Mark by the shoulders. "Stop this! You don't have his cocaine. It's at the bottom of the ocean!"

Arseneau pushed Noelle aside. "Where is it?"

Mark looked into the killer's eyes. "I'll tell you, but not until you let Noelle go. She's no good to you. She has no idea where I hid it."

Noelle grabbed his arm. "Arseneau, you have to believe me. We threw the drugs into the ocean. Mark is lying." Eyes wet with tears, she turned to her ex-husband. "Mark, please don't do this. Tell him you're lying. Tell him you don't have his drugs."

Arseneau snickered. "I've got a better idea. I kill you both right now and be done with this game."

"You kill us, and you'll never get your coke back. And this 'cowboy' will die happy knowing I cheated you out of one million dollars." Mark growled, "Let Noelle go."

The wheels were turning in Arseneau's head. He shifted his weight between his feet while keeping his gun trained on Mark. Knowing full well Noelle could never get past the guards at the gate, he pushed her toward the door. "Go. You are free to leave."

Noelle cried out. "He's lying! Don't you see that?" She reached out toward Mark. "I won't leave you."

With misty eyes, Mark said, "You have to. There's no other choice." He pointed back and forth between them. "This. Us. It was never going to work. The cook on the ship was right: I'm cursed. I'm sorry, Noelle. You deserved better." His voice hardened. "Please, go."

Arseneau turned and aimed his gun at Noelle.

Then he pulled the trigger.

The bullet from the warning shot whizzed by her head, inches from her right ear. He snarled, "Leave now or die. Your choice."

Suddenly, a loud crash came from inside the study.

Startled, Arseneau's special forces training automatically kicked in. Unable to immediately identify the source of the sound, he labeled it as a threat in his mind. Instinctively, he turned and focused his gun on the door to the study.

Noelle rushed toward the study and cried out, "Mary?"

Mark lunged for the spear he had dropped. He seized it, pointed it upward, and thrust the tip of the spear deep into Arseneau's abdomen. With a look of total astonishment, the killer stood immobilized. Mark jammed the spear in deeper.

His gun fell to the floor as Arseneau stumbled back into the wall. He dropped to his knees, clutching the long wooden shaft protruding out of his body.

Mark grabbed the pistol, pulled himself to his feet, and staggered over to Arseneau. He propped the injured man up in a sitting position against the wall. Then he pressed the gun against the assassin's forehead.

Struggling to speak, Arseneau begged, "Wait! Think, Smith. This can still…work." Blood foamed from his mouth as he forced out the words. "We tell…we tell the police Priscilla kidnapped your daughter and killed Benoit. I scuffled with her and shot her in self-defense. I'll give you half the money, and you'll never see me again. It's perfect."

"Perfect? Not in my world, you psycho. Nobody hurts my daughter and gets away with it. Say goodbye, asshole." He pressed the barrel harder against Arseneau's forehead.

Noelle grabbed his arm. "Mark, no. Don't kill him. Give me the gun. Don't do this, Mark. Please, give me the gun."

Mark looked up at Noelle. Her pleading eyes and the look on her face said it all. He pulled the gun back, took his finger off the trigger, and handed it to Noelle. She took the pistol and lowered it to her side.

With a malevolent smirk on his face, Arseneau looked up at Noelle. "Merci, Mademoiselle Parker, merci."

Noelle lifted the gun, pulled the trigger, and fired a bullet dead center into Arseneau's forehead. His head jerked back as he collapsed against the blood-splattered wall.

She tossed the gun into his lap. "It's Mrs. *Smith*."

CHAPTER 68

NO LONGER FUELED BY ADRENALIN coursing through his body, and weakened from blood loss, Mark slumped down to the floor next to Arseneau. The altercation had caused the wound in Mark's leg to reopen.

Noelle took his hand and pressed it down over the bullet hole to slow down the renewed bleeding. Mark waved toward the study with his free hand. "I'm okay. Go help Mary."

Noelle ran to the open doorway behind Benoit's desk. Looking in, she saw pieces of a suit of armor scattered across the floor. Among them, Mary Smith lay blindfolded, bound, and gagged. She was flailing around on the floor to the extent her bindings allowed. Her feet connected with a lamp, sending it crashing to the ground.

Overcome with relief, Noelle cried out, "Mary! Thank God you're alive."

Mary lifted her head off the floor and searched blindly for the familiar sound of her mother's voice. Muffled screams for help came from behind her gag.

Noelle rushed to her side. "Mom and Dad are here, sweetie. It's okay. You're safe." She removed the blindfold and gag. Bruises and cuts on Mary's pretty face indicated she hadn't gone willingly when abducted by Arseneau. Despite being battered, her Smith family fighting spirit was alive and well. After removing the ropes binding Mary's hands and feet, Noelle helped her up to a sitting position.

Mother and daughter embraced, finally safe from the

horrors they'd endured. Minutes passed as tears of relief gushed out. Neither woman wanted to end the protective, comforting hold they had on each other.

Noelle pulled back to examine her daughter more thoroughly. It was obvious the ordeal Mary went through had taken a toll on her. "Can you walk?" Noelle asked.

She nodded. "I think so."

Noelle hooked Mary's arm around her shoulder and lifted her up to a standing position. Mary had trouble supporting her own weight. Circulation in her legs had been restricted by the ropes, making them feel numb yet heavy at the same time. Noelle supported her daughter until she could take a few steps.

Slowly, Mary dragged one foot across the floor, then the other, until some of the strength in her legs returned. They emerged from the study into the Grand Hall.

When she saw Mark, Mary stumbled across the room to him, arms outstretched. "Dad!"

Despite the pain, Mark willed himself to stand and reached out for his daughter.

She wrapped her arms around his broad shoulders then burst into tears. "It was so horrible. This man broke into our apartment. He killed Mr. Simpson. Then he…"

Mark drew her close and calmly said, "Shhh…it's okay. You're safe. I'm here. I'll protect you. No one is going to hurt you anymore. We need to go."

With Noelle shielding her view, they directed Mary away from Arseneau's dead body before she realized who he was. They walked out of the Grand Hall and sat down on the steps of the wide, sweeping staircase in the foyer. Noelle held her daughter tight, stroking her hair.

Mark snapped his head around at sounds coming from outside. Gunfire echoed in the distance. The thumping sound of a helicopter grew louder. Vehicles could be heard rushing toward the house. Mark quickly moved Noelle and Mary into the parlor, locked the door behind him, and hid everyone in a dark corner.

Heavily armed men in black SWAT gear burst through the front door, shouting commands. "*Police Nationale!* National police! Lay your weapons down and show yourself!" Guns raised, they fanned out in all directions. Finding the door to the parlor locked, a policeman reared back with his size-fourteen combat boot and kicked it open.

From the dark corner, Noelle raised her hands and screamed in French, "*Ne tirez pas, ne tirez pas!*" In English, she repeated, "Don't shoot, don't shoot! We are unarmed!"

Alarmed by the sounds coming from the darkness, the policeman crouched down on one knee and aimed his rifle at her voice. He squinted as his eyes adjusted to the dark and swept his aim side to side, shouting, "On the floor! Facedown! Now!" His comrades flooded into the room and turned on the lights. The Smith family lay prone on the floor, arms outstretched. The policemen rushed over and quickly bound Mark, Noelle, and Mary's hands behind their backs with plastic restraints. One of the men reached up to his left shoulder and keyed his microphone. "Parlor is secure." Similar reports from other locations crackled over the radio.

The policeman who initially broke down the parlor door barked, "Who else is in the house? Where are they?"

In French, Noelle directed the police to go to the room across the foyer. Three SWAT members hurried into the Grand Hall, yelling commands. The shouting stopped when they came upon the gruesome scene. There was no one alive to threaten their safety. "Grand Hall is secure. Target is dead," was calmly announced over the radio.

After the house was verified secure, a short, unarmed policeman with a wiry build and harsh demeanor marched into the parlor. The deferential way the hulking men in the room parted as he entered indicated he was of high rank. With a scowl on his face, he growled, "Benoit! Where is he?"

A man pointed toward the Grand Hall. "In there, sir. He's dead."

"Dead? *Merde!*" When he saw the Smith family bound on the floor, the official angrily asked, "Who are these people?"

"Americans, sir."

That information only seemed to increase his anger. "Take them to the helicopter," he ordered.

Mark, Noelle, and Mary were lifted to their feet and brusquely escorted out of the room. Before Mark could make it to the front door, he passed out on the floor. Medics rushed to his side and attended to his leg wound. After stopping the bleeding, they loaded him onto a stretcher and carried him to the waiting helicopter.

Sitting on the grounds, next to the police helicopter, was a menacing looking green VBMR Griffon armored personnel carrier with fragments of the front gate clinging to it.

With everyone on board the helicopter, the side door slid closed. Its engines roared to full speed, creating a tornado of wind. The helicopter lifted off the lawn and flew off into the night toward Paris.

CHAPTER 69

MARK OPENED HIS EYES TO a bright, pure light. Disoriented and confused by his surroundings, he struggled to sit up. A kindly looking man with a full gray beard and wearing a white coat hovered over him wielding a stethoscope.

"Where am I?" Mark asked.

"You're in a hospital, Monsieur. Please, lie back so I can complete my examination."

He rested his head back down on the pillow then looked over to his left. Two empty beds sat next to his. "Where are my wife and daughter? Are they okay?" he asked anxiously.

The doctor tried to calm Mark down. "They are fine, Monsieur. They went down to the cafeteria. I expect they will be back soon."

Unable to focus on the hands of the clock on the far wall, Mark asked, "What time is it?"

"It is three in the afternoon," the doctor replied.

"What? Three in the…" He tried unsuccessfully to recall the events of the past twelve hours. "What happened?"

"You were flown here last night with a gunshot wound to your leg and critically low on blood. I operated on you immediately after the police wheeled you in. Everything went well. You should be up and walking on crutches soon."

Mark lifted his left arm and saw a jumble of tubes and wires attached to him. An unflattering hospital gown was draped over him. In a panic, he asked, "Where are my clothes? What did you do with my clothes?"

"Not to worry. They have been sealed in a bag to prevent contamination from the blood and will be sent to the incinerator shortly."

Mark bolted upright. "The bag! Where is the bag?"

Mark's irrational behavior concerned the doctor. "It is in the closet." He pointed to a tall, narrow closet in the corner of the room.

"No, I don't want my clothes burned. I want to keep them as a souvenir of what happened."

"Okay, I will see that they won't be burned." He shook his head and muttered, "Crazy American."

"How long am I going to be here?" Mark asked, calmer now.

"If the wound heals properly, you should be able to go home within a few days." The doctor pointed toward the hallway. "The police have been demanding to interview you since you came out of surgery. Do you feel up to speaking to them now?"

"Um...no, not yet. Maybe tomorrow. I'm still too groggy from the anesthesia."

The doctor nodded. "I understand. It should be out of your system by then. I will tell the police they are not to bother you."

"Perfect. Thanks, Doc."

The doctor scribbled some notes in Mark's chart, hung it on the end of his bed, then turned and left. Shortly after, Noelle and Mary returned.

Mary had a small bandage on each cheek and bruises on her face. Out of curiosity, she picked up the clipboard containing Mark's medical records and tried to assess his condition. Her medical school training did little good since the notes were written in French.

Noelle smiled and said, "Hey there, sleepyhead. You're finally awake."

They went to opposite sides of Mark's bed and maneuvered around the tubes and IV stands to give each other much-needed hugs. The three spent the next hour talking about the frightening events of the past few days. After the difficult conversations had ended, the mood in the room seemed to lighten.

Mark and Noelle felt April deserved to learn the truth about her real parents before others did and left those details out of the discussion.

Mark grabbed the controller for the bed and raised the back up to a sitting position. He patted Mary's hand and asked, "Would you please go down to the cafeteria and get me anything that resembles American food? I'm starving."

"Sure, Dad. I'll be right back. Don't go anywhere." Mary's attempt at humor was an encouraging sign.

Noelle sat on the edge of Mark's bed. "She's been through a lot. It's going to take some time of course, but I think she's going to be okay." Mark nodded in agreement.

Once Mary was out of earshot, Mark said, "Grab my clothes. They're in the closet."

"You want to put on those blood-stained rags? They should be tossed in the trash. Relax, I've heard there are a few clothing stores here in Paris. I'll go buy you some new ones."

"I need to show you something. Trust me, you'll want to see this."

Noelle wrinkled her brow. "What is going on?"

"Hurry, before Mary gets back."

She walked over and pulled the plastic bag out of the closet, depositing it on Mark's lap.

He frantically tossed each article of clothing on the floor as he dug through the bag. With only one item remaining, Mark carefully lifted out his pants. Below the bullet hole, dried blood stained the left pant leg. Mark fished around in the pockets until he found what he was searching for. He pulled out a folded piece of paper splattered with blood.

Noelle's eyes widened. "Is that what I think it is?"

Mark nodded, wide-eyed as well. "Yep. It's the list of account numbers and passwords for Benoit's offshore accounts. I relieved Arseneau of it while you were in the study helping Mary." He unfolded it. "This piece of paper is worth two *billion* dollars. They were going to incinerate it any minute now."

"Jesus…" Noelle whispered.

An American speaking English could be heard approaching in the hallway. Mark quickly folded the piece of paper and handed it to Noelle.

Mary popped back in the room. "All they had were French fries, Dad."

Mark smiled. "That's perfect, just what I wanted. Can I pay you back later? I don't have any money on me."

CHAPTER 70

THE NEXT MORNING, THE SMITH family choked down a bland hospital breakfast while sitting up in bed. Bored with being bedridden for so long, Mark aimlessly pecked away at his smartphone screen. Finding nothing worth wasting his time on, he flipped through channels on the wall-mounted TV.

He stopped at CNN. A graphic photo of the bloody scene in the Grand Hall at Château Paradis flashed on to the screen. Benoit's vast fortune and what would become of it made the story irresistible to the media.

The reporter breathlessly read the scrolling teleprompter. "We are learning more about the shocking death of French billionaire Girard Benoit. Sources confirm that French National Police raided his estate two nights ago, killing Benoit, his personal bodyguard, and an unidentified woman. Reporters spoke to National Police Director-General Victor Arnoult yesterday."

On the screen, the high-ranking police official who had marched into the parlor that night now stood confidently behind a podium bristling with microphones. What couldn't be seen was the step stool he stood on. Clearly enjoying the spotlight, he briefed the media. "After years of dedicated police work on my part, I have put an end to years of lawless activity by one of France's wealthiest citizens. In addition, the brave men under my command rescued an American family kidnapped by Monsieur Benoit. No effort will be spared to see that others involved in illegal activity will be held accountable."

Back on the set, the reporter continued. "True to his word, Director-General Arnoult has issued arrest warrants for numerous high-ranking government officials suspected of being on Benoit's payroll."

A video rolled of the director of French customs being dragged away from his office in handcuffs by a gaggle of policemen. Spittle flew as the red-faced Brassard yelled something about his innocence at the cameras.

Furious at Arnoult for taking all the credit, Mary whined, "That jerk. He didn't rescue me; you guys did. That's not fair."

A hand reached up and pulled the plug on the TV. Accompanied by an entourage of minions, Director-General Victor Arnoult strode into the hospital room. He glared at Mary. "Mademoiselle, fairness is not my concern. Justice is. I've spent decades trying to prove Benoit has been diverting his fortune to avoid paying billions in taxes. His army of lawyers and corrupt officials were able to frustrate my investigations at every turn. Now, because of you reckless Americans, I'll never get a chance to look Benoit in the face when I locked him away for his crimes."

Not quite as idealistic as her twenty-four-year-old daughter, Noelle spoke up. "It's all right, Mary. As long as you're okay, that's all that matters." She looked back at Arnoult with a confused expression. "Director Arnoult, how is it that you just happened to show up at Benoit's estate in the middle of the night with an armored personnel carrier and a squad of heavily armed men?"

"When your plane disappeared from the radar screen, it was naturally assumed that you crashed. Minutes later, we got a call from a butler working at the estate reporting suspicious activity and a jet parked on the grounds." With a prideful air, he said, "Finally, after all those years of failure, I had probable cause to enter Benoit's estate. I wasn't about to knock politely, Madame."

He approached the foot of Mark's bed. "That brings me to the reason for my visit." Arnoult snapped his finger. A minion pulled a sheet of paper from a file and handed it to him. "My staff has put together a list of French laws you broke when you flew your plane into our airspace using a false tail number then landed it on private property. Justice demands that I—"

Mark interrupted him. "Director, you seem to speak English very well. By any chance are you familiar with the American phrase 'You scratch my back, I'll scratch yours'?"

Arnoult cocked his head. "What is this strange American phrase? I do not know it."

"If you would please ask your staff to leave, I'd be happy to explain it to you. In private."

Arnoult narrowed his gaze at Mark, sizing up his opponent. He turned, snapped his fingers, and shooed his staff away.

After the door clicked shut, Mark continued. "There are going to be a couple of US government agencies that will be very unhappy to see me when I get back. I was hoping you would contact them and put in a good word for me. Ask the DEA and FAA if they would let bygones be bygones and forget any current problems they might have with me as well."

"You are in no position to bargain with me, Monsieur. Laws have been broken. You must be held accountable."

"I know, I know. But it's not like they were really important ones, were they? Certainly not important enough for the French government to miss out on billions of dollars it was cheated out of."

Arnoult stepped back. "Monsieur, are you trying to bribe an official of the French government?"

"No, of course not. I would never think of doing such a vulgar thing. Just offering you a once-in-a-lifetime opportunity, that's all. I'm sure your superiors would be most impressed if all of your diligent efforts led to the discovery of Benoit's secret offshore accounts. Of course, no one would mention how you came about this information. It would be our little secret. Is my strange American phrase becoming more clear to you now?"

Arnoult checked the door to make sure no members of his staff were nearby. "No, Monsieur, it is not." He hurried to the side of Mark's bed. "Not until I am able to verify that the information I uncovered is indeed what you say it is. Only then will I consider the scratching of one's back." He folded his arms tightly and waited for Mark's next move.

Mark looked over at Noelle and nodded. She pulled the folded piece of paper from the nightstand drawer and extended it toward Arnoult. He had to yank the valuable piece of paper out of her hand.

After examining the information on the page, he tucked it safely away. "I shall return tomorrow morning with my decision." Arnoult spun on his heels and left.

Mary threw up her hands. "What the heck just happened? And what was on that piece of paper?"

Mark and Noelle held hands. They turned to her and explained in detail how they ended up with the codes to access the illicit money that Benoit had stashed away.

She was flabbergasted. "Two billion dollars? And you just handed it over to that guy? You know you can't trust him! What if he keeps it for himself and never tells the French government?"

Mark fished his phone out from under his covers. With one tap on the screen, the entire conversation with Arnoult started playing back over the phone's speaker.

Mary nodded and laughed. "Way to go, Dad. You rock."

CHAPTER 71

TRUE TO HIS WORD, DIRECTOR-GENERAL Arnoult returned to the hospital the next morning—with a pack of reporters and cameramen trailing behind him.

With the lights on and the cameras rolling, he announced, "Welcome to the representatives of the foreign press. Thank you for coming on such short notice. I have very important news. My extensive investigation has uncovered illegal bank accounts held by the late Girard Benoit in the amount of"—he glared at Mary—"two billion dollars. The French government is in the process of seizing the money as I speak. Then there is the matter of decades of deceit concerning his true net worth. Our accountants estimate another three billion dollars in back taxes, interest, penalties, and fines will be confiscated from Benoit's four-billion-dollar estate. America's president has telephoned me personally to thank me for saving the lives of the three American citizens you see before you."

Noelle gave Mary a stern look to keep her from speaking up and exposing the grandstanding going on.

Arnoult continued. "The Smith family has expressed their profound gratitude to the people of France as well." He looked directly at Mark. "Your president has assured me that America is looking forward to welcoming you and your family back home with open arms."

Mark nodded gratefully.

Arnoult ushered the reporters toward the door. "Thank

you for coming. You will be notified immediately if I have any new information on this case."

Before the door even clicked shut, Mary hopped out of bed and threw on her robe. "Real nice show you put on there, pal." Disgusted with the realities of the political world, she said, "I'm outta here. I'll be in the cafeteria." She brushed by Arnoult and left the room.

"Director, what happens to the remainder of Benoit's estate after the French government gets their pound of flesh?" Noelle asked.

He sniffed, "Unfortunately, I can't prove the remaining money is tainted. French law requires that it be dispersed to any heirs. Due to the large amount of money involved, DNA testing will be the only proof of lineage accepted."

Noelle looked over at Mark with complete astonishment. He shot her a cautionary look to silence any thoughts she might vocalize. His trust in Arnoult only went so far.

"If no heirs come forward, the French treasury will confiscate the balance." Arnoult pulled open the door to leave then looked back at Mark. "I checked with your doctor. He says you are healthy enough to leave today. I highly recommend you do so. Your plane is waiting for you at the airport, fully fueled. Two of our best Air Force pilots will fly you and your family back to New York. I suspect it will be some time before you ever think about coming back to my country. Au revoir." He stomped away down the hall.

Noelle couldn't hold it in any longer. "A billion dollars! April just inherited a billion dollars!"

CHAPTER 72

LUXURY JET CHARTERS' GULFSTREAM 500 cruised peacefully across the Atlantic Ocean. The divan had been folded down into a comfy bed. Mary lay sound asleep after an exhausting past few days.

Mark and Noelle sat in the back of the cabin, holding hands across the aisle. Mark's crutches were propped up in the corner.

He kept looking nervously up the aisle toward the cockpit. "Maybe I should go up and see if the pilots need any help."

Noelle reached out to stop him. "Easy, flyboy. You're in no shape to be flying an airplane. Relax, they are doing just fine without you." With a mock frown, she scolded, "You're not going to be one of those problem passengers, are you? Don't make me get out the fire extinguisher."

Mark put up his hands in surrender. "Okay, I'll stay out of the cockpit. For now." A devilish grin appeared on his face. "You know…I could be flying my very own Gulfstream jet right now if it wasn't for you."

Noelle rolled her eyes. " Great. You're not planning on holding that over my head from now on, are you?"

His grin widened. "No, of course not. I would never dream of reminding you of that every single day for the rest of our lives."

"No, of course you wouldn't. Besides, you're better off without one of these dumb planes anyway. You'd probably expect me to be your flight attendant, bossing me around the whole flight. That would never work. I should be up front in the cockpit with you."

"Really? So, you're a pilot now?"

"I did fly one of these planes all the way to France. Without running out of gas, I might add."

Ouch.

Their annoyingly playful banter continued for the rest of the flight—long enough to give Mary an excuse to go up to the cockpit and introduce herself to the handsome French pilots.

Hours later, the jet touched down at Teterboro Airport and taxied up to its hangar. Noelle and Mary helped Mark safely navigate the stairs down to the ramp.

Marty Dawson was waiting.

Noelle rushed up to him and smothered Marty with a hug. "We can't begin to thank you enough for what you did." She turned with tears in her eyes. "Marty, this is our daughter, Mary."

She walked over and gave him a heartfelt hug as well. "My parents told me what you did. You helped save my life. Thank you."

Unaccustomed to being treated affectionately, he clumsily responded, "Okay." In a more serious tone he added, "Young lady, you remember to take good care of your parents when they get older. They're good people. Don't forget that."

She noticed his eyes tearing up. "Not a chance, Marty, not a chance." Her compassionate side kicked in. "Hey, maybe you could come by once in a while and join us for dinner."

He nodded and smiled. "I think I'd like that."

When Mark walked up, Marty switched back to his tough guy persona. He pointed at the plane. "How's my jet? Hopefully better than you look, Air Farce."

Mark chuckled. "You might notice a little mud on the tires, but I brought it back in one piece. Which is more than I can say for myself." He pointed down at his leg. "I'm going to need a little time off for this bullet wound to heal. You think this lame operation of yours can get by without me for a couple of weeks?"

"Normally, I'd fire a slacker asking for time off just because of a little scratch like you've got there. But, since the FAA called and said everything is forgiven, I'll make an exception. I expect you back as soon as you're cleared to fly."

Mark nodded. "Thanks, Marty. For everything."

Noelle wrapped her arms around her family. "Let's go home."

When they arrived at Mark's car in the Luxury Jet Charters parking lot, he tapped his key fob, unlocking the doors. Noelle jumped in the driver's seat before he could object. She stuck out her hand for his keys. "Hand them over, flyboy. Until you get rid of those crutches, you are *my* copilot."

Mary rolled her eyes and groaned at the prospect of being stuck listening to her parents playful bickering during the long ride home.

As the car emerged from the Lincoln Tunnel into Manhattan, Mark said, "I'll never be able to enjoy my retirement without tying up a loose end first. Drop me off at Fifty-Second and Park Avenue."

Noelle narrowed her eyes. "Why?"

"I need to reel in a bull shark."

"Ben Meyer!" Mark bellowed out the lawyer's name as he burst through the door on his crutches and hobbled up to Meyer's desk.

The lawyer's panicked secretary trailed behind Mark, saying, "I'm sorry, sir, I tried to stop him, but…"

"Call security," Meyer barked.

"Right away, sir." His secretary scurried out of the office.

Meyer glared at Mark. "Have you lost your mind? Get out of my office!"

Mark planted himself in a chair in front of the desk. "Meyer, I'm here to straighten a few things out. First, you are going to remove me from the lawsuit."

He scoffed. "You *have* lost your mind. Your case is a slam dunk. I'd be a fool to let you out of it."

Mark leaned forward. "You'd be a fool if you didn't. I'm talking about a potential fortune in fees for your firm."

Two muscular security guards burst into the office and grabbed Mark by the arms.

Greed easily overcame Meyer's fear of Mark. "Let go of him." He waved off the guards. "Go away; everything is fine."

Confused, they turned around and stomped out.

Meyer crossed his arms. "I'm listening, Smith. You've got two minutes before I call the guards back."

Mark sneered at the shark in a suit. "Second, your firm is going to hold a news conference today announcing that after examining all the facts it has determined that not only am I not at fault in the Tech-Liner accident, my actions that day saved the lives of everyone on board. You are going to say that Meyer, Simpkins, and White has decided it will irrevocably remove me as a defendant in the lawsuit."

"And miss out on 40 percent of ten million dollars? Like hell I will."

Mark laughed. "Come on, you know you'll never see a dime from me."

"I might not get all of it, but I'll take every dollar you make for the rest of your life."

Mark leaned forward and rested his elbows on Meyer's desk. "How would you like to make 40 percent of one hundred million dollars instead?"

"Did you say one hundred million?" Now he had Meyer's attention. "Go on."

"The first officer on the *Lynda Ray* told us some very

interesting information while we were on the lifeboat. Noelle and I have firsthand knowledge of negligent actions by a huge company that will net your firm a hell of a lot more money than you'd ever get from me. Do the news conference, and Noelle and I will be happy to tell you everything we know." Mark stuck out his hand. "Deal?"

Meyer snickered. "You might be a good pilot, Smith, but you are a lousy lawyer. I can subpoena both of you and force you to testify on what you know. I don't need any crappy deal with you."

Mark leaned back in the chair. "You know, Ben, the memory can be a tricky thing. Especially after going through the traumatic events Noelle and I have just gone through. I believe the docs call it PTSD. I'd hate to see you embarrass yourself by hauling us into court and coming away empty-handed." He smirked. "Trust me, I have your best interests at heart when I say this." Mark looked down at his wristwatch. "Oh, look at that. My two minutes are up. Nice talking to you, Ben. See you in court." He stood to leave.

Meyer jumped up. "Wait, wait. I think we might have gotten off on the wrong foot. Funny that you should bring it up. We plugged the data from the Tech-Liner flight recorder into the simulator yesterday. It showed you weren't at fault for the accident after all. The negligent design of the computer software on the new plane was the problem. Of course, I planned on telling you all this. I think a news conference is in order to announce our findings in this matter." Meyer nervously reached out his right hand. "Deal?"

Mark propped himself up on his crutches and firmly shook the lawyer's hand. "Not that I don't trust you, Ben, but I'm going to need all this in writing before I leave your office."

Meyer punched the button on his intercom. "Ms. Simms, get in here."

"Oh, and one more thing," Mark said. "To show what a caring and compassionate place you run here, at the news conference today you are going to announce the firm has started a scholarship fund for deserving medical school students."

Meyer warily eyed Mark. "I don't suppose you happen to know of a deserving student, do you?"

With a big grin on his face, Mark opened the car door and maneuvered his body and crutches back in to the right seat.

Noelle playfully whacked him on the arm. "Well? Don't make us wait. Tell us what happened."

CHAPTER 73

THE SMITH FAMILY ROLLED UP in front of their apartment building with big smiles on their faces. Life had cut them a well-deserved break.

The joy they were feeling changed as they approached the concrete steps leading up to the building. Looking up at the third-floor window to their apartment, their mood turned somber. The thought of going back to the place where such a tragic murder had happened gave them pause. Memories of the sacrifice Ralph Simpson made for them weighed heavily on their minds.

When they pulled open the door to the building a surprise awaited them. A welcoming committee stood in the foyer. Tommy and Stephanie Parker were there. April held a homemade WELCOME HOME sign. Charlotte waited with open arms. Even Mark's old crash pad roommate, Andy Wilson, was there. Mary noticed him first.

The mob of family and friends surrounded the Smiths as they walked in. Charlotte spoke first. "Marty called to let us know you were on your way. We thought seeing some smiling faces when you got here would help."

Tommy teased his little sister. "Remind me not to go on vacation with you anytime soon. Too much drama." Noelle punched him in the stomach.

Andy went over to Mary. "I heard what happened. It's got to be tough going through something like that. How are you doing?"

She forced a smile and shrugged. "Okay, I guess. It's

going to be hard living in my apartment after what happened there. It will never feel like home again."

Andy's eyes lit up. "You don't know?"

"Know what?"

"The owner of the building felt terrible about what happened, so he agreed to let your family have a different apartment in the building for the same price. And it's bigger than your old one." He pointed at the welcoming committee. "We've been hard at work getting it ready for the last few days. I picked out all the furniture myself. Come on, I'll show you." Andy took Mary's hand and led her up one flight of stairs. He opened the door to the new apartment, shepherding the entire group in.

The place looked like an airline crash pad. An assortment of mismatched furniture of every type and color filled the space. Pictures and memorabilia that could be salvaged from the old apartment gave the place a hint of home. Their clothes and other belongings were neatly tucked away in closets and dressers. A new phone hung on the wall in the kitchen.

Andy beamed with pride. "Well, what do you think?"

"It looks…um…interesting. You have a real knack for… decorating." Mary gave Andy a kiss on the cheek. "Thank you."

Mark came over and slapped Andy on the back—hard. "Thanks, man." He steered him away from his daughter, then turned to the others. "Thank you for all that you've done here. We really appreciate everything—"

The telephone rang, jarring the celebration. Being closest to it, Charlotte walked into the kitchen and answered. After listening for a few seconds, she held out the receiver. "It's for you, Noelle. It's your oncologist."

"Oh my gosh, I completely forgot about the mammogram." Noelle walked over and warily put the phone to her ear. "Hello, this is Noelle." Her face turned serious as she listened. Mark went to her side. A moment later, a look of complete relief washed over her. "That's great news," Noelle said, as she gave a thumbs-up to the apprehensive crowd. "Thanks for calling, Doc." Noelle let out a deep sigh as she hung up, then embraced Mark.

Mark held her in his arms as he took up where he left off. "Charlotte, Andy, thanks again for everything you've done. We"—he drew a wide circle with his finger, indicating the Parkers and Smiths—"need to have a private family meeting, so I'm going to have to kick you guys out." He pointed a crutch at the door.

April and Mary turned and looked at each other with apprehensive expressions.

Charlotte nodded knowingly. She went over and wrangled Andy around the neck. "Come on, kid; time to go. This is a perfect opportunity for you and me to go have a little talk. Have I ever told you how protective I am of Mary?"

Mary wagged a finger at her. "Auntie Charlotte…be nice now."

Andy looked back with fear in his eyes as he was led away by Charlotte.

Mark, Noelle, Tommy, and Stephanie gathered next to each other in the center of the apartment.

Noelle stepped forward and reached out her left hand for her daughter. "April, there are some very important things I need to tell you." With her right hand, she reached for her other daughter. "Mary, you need to hear this as well. You girls should probably sit down." She led them over to the couch and released their hands.

With trepidation on their pretty faces, Mary and April clutched each other in a protective hold and sat nervously on the edge of the cushions.

Noelle took a step back, eyes cast downward. Hands trembling, she drew in a deep, shuddering breath and began.

AUTHOR'S NOTE

I hope you enjoyed reading *HURRICANE* as much as I enjoyed writing it.

Dan

P.S. Knowing everything that led up to the story in *HURRICANE* will make the experience even better. I recommend reading the previous book in the series, *MAYDAY*, to get the whole story.

Please consider leaving a review. Honest reviews are immensely helpful for self-published authors.

WANT MORE? Be the first to know about upcoming book releases, events Dan will be at, and more. Sign up for his email list at: *www.danstratmanauthor.com*

Follow the Dan Stratman Facebook page: facebook.com/DanStratmanAuthor

NOVELS IN THE CAPT. MARK SMITH SERIES BY DAN STRATMAN

MAYDAY (#1 Best Seller)

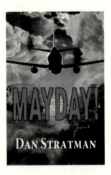

BETRAYAL (June 2020)

ABOUT THE AUTHOR

Dan Stratman is a retired major airline Captain with over 26 years of experience in the industry. Before flying for the airlines, he was a decorated Air Force pilot. In addition, Captain Stratman is a highly sought-after aviation consultant, media aviation spokesperson, and NASA Astronaut applicant. He is a World traveler, having been to 38 countries so far.

Dan has an entrepreneurial side that stretches back many years. He developed the popular air travel app, Airport Life. The app did something that was sorely needed, it made flying easier and less stressful for passengers. In addition, he created a specialty photo printing eCommerce website, ran a multi-expert aviation consulting company he founded, and has filed numerous patents. In his spare time Dan enjoys mentoring budding entrepreneurs and volunteering weekly with Habitat for Humanity.

The two things he is most proud of are his long marriage to his lovely wife and his three wonderful kids.

Made in United States
North Haven, CT
22 September 2024